W9-COG-728

ASIMOV LAUGHS AGAIN

ALSO BY ISAAC ASIMOV

ASIMOV LAUGHS AGAIN

More than 700 Favorite Jokes, Limericks, and Anecdotes

ISAAC ASIMOV

HarperPerennial

A Division of HarperCollinsPublishers

A hardcover edition of this book was published in 1992 by Harper-
Collins Publishers.

ASIMOV LAUGHS AGAIN. Copyright © 1992 by Isaac Asimov. All rights
reserved. Printed in the United States of America. No part of this
book may be used or reproduced in any manner whatsoever without
written permission except in the case of brief quotations embodied in
critical articles and reviews. For information address HarperCollins
Publishers, Inc., 10 East 53rd Street, New York, NY 10022.

HarperCollins books may be purchased for educational, business, or
sales promotional use. For information please write: HarperCollins
Publishers, Inc., 10 East 53rd Street, New York, NY 10022.

First HarperPerennial edition published 1993.

Designed by Alma Hochhauser Orenstein

The Library of Congress has catalogued the hardcover edition
as follows:

Asimov, Isaac, 1920–
    Asimov laughs again : more than 700 favorite jokes, limericks, and
anecdotes / Isaac Asimov.
        p.   cm.
    ISBN 0-06-016826-9 (cloth)
    1. Jewish wit and humor.   2. American wit and humor.   3. Jews—
United States—Social life and customs—Humor.   I. Title.
PN6231.J5A84   1992
808.82—dc20   91-58353

ISBN 0-06-092448-9 (pbk.)

99   RRD - H   10   9   8

ASIMOV LAUGHS AGAIN

In 1971, I had a book published entitled *Isaac Asimov's Treasury of Humor*. It is still selling—not in quantities designed to make me wealthy, but in amounts that satisfy my sense of pride.

In that book, I told 641 jokes, anecdotes, and amusing incidents taken both from history and from my personal life. Between these jokes, I discussed the matter of how to tell jokes.

Just the other day, I reread the book (which I had not opened since the day it was published) and enjoyed it immensely—for I am one of those authors who (a) likes his own books and (b) has no qualms about saying so.

Nevertheless, I was left with a vague feeling of disquiet.

First, I now know a great many funny stories that I didn't know then and there is more that I want to say about telling jokes and about the philosophy of jokes.

Second, and even more important, I had written the book as though it were a long joke session, with one joke reminding me of another in no particular order. This made it, to my way of thinking, a rather rollicking work.

However, I was harassed by the editor of that book into dividing the stories into eleven categories, and this bothered me for two reasons. In the first place, I couldn't always tell in which category a particular story fell, and that created an irritating uncertainty as I prepared the book. In the second place, it gave the volume a vague textbooky feeling I found unsatisfactory.

So in this second book of jokes, I don't intend to allow my editor to interfere. It is going to appear exactly as I wrote it. And, as in the first book, I will have words to say on how to tell jokes effectively.

Follow my reasoning here. It gives one great pleasure to hear a funny story, or to read one. There is almost universal enjoyment here, if we omit those few unfortunates who don't have a sense of humor and whom, far from despising, we should pity with all our hearts.

But take my word for it, there is infinitely more pleasure in telling a funny story than in either hearing or reading one—that is, provided you tell it right. If you tell the story and the audience breaks into wild and prolonged laughter (and if you laugh, too, for there is nothing wrong with laughing at your own joke after you have told it), the wonderful feeling you have is like nothing else.

While everyone can hear and read funny stories equally well, the ability to tell a funny story varies enormously from individual to individual, and those who just happen to have the knack of being funny represent only a tiny fraction of the population.

I won't pretend that I can teach you to tell funny stories at the professional level. I'm not sure I can do it myself. After all, there is such a thing as an innate talent. A person may spend his whole life studying music and never attain the abilities that Mozart had at the age of eight.

Who says, however, that we all have to be Mozarts? To learn how to play the piano sufficiently well to amuse yourself and your friends, for instance, is surely something; and in the same way, to learn to tell jokes that will amuse your friends, even if you don't attain a professional level, will certainly add to your enjoyment of life.

In order to educate, I will occasionally have to analyze a joke. This may strike you as a dreary business. We've all gone through it at school. We are asked to read William Shakespeare's *Julius Caesar* and then, instead of being allowed to enjoy the play, we are plagued by line-by-line analyses that turn the whole thing into dust and ashes and convince many students that they must never read Shakespeare again.

However, a funny story is short and quickly read. You will have a chance to read it undisturbed and, perhaps, if I am lucky (and if you are a jovial and good-natured person), you will laugh. Having had your pleasure, you can then turn to the analysis, which will not ruin the pleasure you have already had and which may enlighten you as to how to tell that particular joke, and others, with greater effectiveness.

I'll start with a joke I heard only five days ago, one I had never heard before. (You can well imagine that by the time I have reached my present stage of life, there are few jokes I have never heard before.)

The joke, I must explain, was told very poorly and I listened with a fixed smile on my face. It is very important, as a matter of politeness, to laugh at someone else's joke, even if it is only a small chuckle, no matter how badly it is told or how unfunny the joke is. (Only if the joke is disgusting or cruel would I refuse to laugh, but if I may say so, the people I know rarely sink to that level.)

This is not only politeness. Sometimes even a bad joke can be salvaged, if told properly. And even if you have heard the joke before, there is always the small chance that the jokester will make a point or put in a twist you haven't heard before.

What you are doing, then, is watching carefully to see if some joke that you hear, however bad, can, with the proper changes, be added to your own repertoire.

You may interrupt at this point to ask: If it is jokester etiquette to laugh at all jokes you hear, without exception, what is the importance of the laugh? How can you tell a genuine laugh from a merely polite one?

Believe me, you can tell. There can be no mistake about it.

So now we are back to the gentleman telling me a joke

poorly while I maintain a fixed smile on my face. He comes to the end of the joke and, heaven help me, I burst into a belly laugh. The joke was so good that it could not be ruined even by his own miserable performance.

I promptly added it to my own repertoire, and here it is, told as I would tell it:

•1

Michael Moriarty's great cross in life was his golf game. On this beautiful summer day he was in the rough, where he usually was, sweating and swearing. And then, suddenly, he looked up as a golf ball went shooting past him toward the hole, straight and true.

He looked about and there were three little men, each one dressed in a long, black coat, with homburg hats crushed down on their heads, with beards and with earlocks. They were obviously Chasidim—that is, ultra-Orthodox Jews. The first one had already driven, then the second, then the third. All the balls landed on the green, within spitting distance of the hole.

In amazement, Moriarty accosted them. "Hey," he said, "how come you guys play golf like that?"

One of the Chasidim looked at him and raised an admonitory finger. "It's because we go to the shul—the synagogue. Every day, we go there. We pray. We read the holy books. We listen to the wise elders. We interpret the Law. And, as we do so, a golden glow falls upon us from the Holy One and we can play golf like champions."

Moriarty said, "How long does it take?"

"It takes about a year."

Moriarty had to decide between his faith and his golf, and his golf won out. The next day, he joined a synagogue and announced he wished to be converted to Judaism. He went there every day. He learned to pray. He read the holy books in translation. He listened to the wise elders interpret the Law and, after a year, he went back to the golf links full of confidence.

And there he was, back in the rough. And once again, the three Chasidim were passing him.

Again he accosted them. "Listen," he said, "I adopted your religion. I went to the synagogue. I did everything you told me to do for a whole year. And nothing has happened."

The Chasidim frowned in astonishment and one of them said, "What synagogue did you go to?"

Moriarty said, "Beth-hakodesh!"

Whereupon the Chasid clapped his hand to his forehead and said, "You should have asked. Beth-hakodesh is for tennis."

Why is this joke funny?

In the first place, it is a tissue of absurdities. To begin with, it is instantly funny as soon as you bring up the notion of Jews playing golf.

Why? Why can't Jews play golf? They can. Jews have so assimilated themselves to the American way of life of the end of the twentieth century that they not only play golf, but some of them are even alcoholics, addicts, and/or gangsters.

However, we are not talking about Jews of the real world, but the stereotypcial Jews of the world of jokedom, which is a generation or two behind reality. In jokes, Jews are still Eastern European immigrants, totally unsuited to things American, and with a way of life to which the aura of the Eastern European shtetl, or village, still clings—in short, exactly what I was as a small child sixty years ago.

The stereotypical Jew does not play golf, and the thought of his doing so is in itself funny. Golf is a game for WASPs.

Worse yet, even if one could conceive of the stereotypical Jew playing golf, one could not imagine the Chasidim doing so. They would probably be scandalized, in reality as well as in jokes, by merely holding a golf club.

The second incongruity is the suggestion that going to the synagogue can possibly improve your golf game.

The third incongruity is that Moriarty would sacrifice his religion for golf. That, in fact, is the reason for choosing Michael Moriarty as the name of the poor golfer. The stereotypical Irishman is no more likely to play golf than the stereotypical Jew, but we must have an Irishman here, for in the world of jokes, no person is as staunchly Catholic as a good Irish Catholic. To have him change his religion for golf is totally incongruous.

These incongruities, however, should not be played for laughs. You should tell the entire joke with a straight face as though it were completely realistic. You don't want any more than a smile or a soft snicker at any of these intermediate points.

Why? Because if, for any reason, a loud laugh comes anywhere in the middle of the joke, that is almost sure to ruin the laugh that should come at the end. The listener is laughed out, so to speak, and the end comes as an anticlimax.

What is the purpose of the incongruities, then? Why, even if you manage not to make the listener laugh, you put him in a good humor. He's aware that he is living, for a brief time, in a fantasy world, and he's ready for the crowning bit of fantasy with his laugh on a hair trigger.

Are there any ways in which the joke can be improved and made even funnier? Yes. Tell it rather than write it, and it is at once funnier. After all, in telling a joke, you have the advantage of voice intonation, of facial expression, of gestures, and so on. In writing, all you have is cold print.

This, however, only works if you tell it well. Not everyone can handle the intonations, expressions, and gestures well, and if you cannot do so, then the told joke is much worse than the written one. But how do you learn the proper body language if you're not born knowing it? You must watch someone who does have it and observe what it is he does. (It's the same principle as learning how to write by studying the great writers.)

How else can you make a joke funnier? By using an appropriate accent. Accents are funny—whether it is the upper-class accent of an Oxford graduate, or the lower-class accent of an immigrant Italian shoemaker.

There's a warning that goes with this, however. We live in

times when there is nothing funny about racism. For that reason, an accent should not be used to disgrace or demean someone. Even more important, it should not be used if you cannot handle it perfectly. A false accent is not only not funny, but is taken as offensive by those people whom the accent is supposed to represent.

The only accent I can handle perfectly is the Yiddish accent. I come by that honestly, for I was brought up among people to whom that was the only form of English that existed. I grew up, as a matter of fact, as a trilingual person, speaking Yiddish, Yiddish-English, and English. My accent, being authentic, offends no one, especially since everyone knows that I myself am Jewish.

In a way, as a jokester, I believe I am fortunate, since it is my belief that of all accents, the Yiddish accent is the funniest.

Why? I would suggest it is because over the past fifty years, most of America's comedians and comic writers have been Jewish and that Jewish humor has therefore been grafted onto the American psyche.

In telling Joke #1, therefore, I must be aware of the nature of the audience. Even if gentile, they would laugh at the joke, but I would have to translate *Chasidim* into *Ultra-Orthodox Jews* and *shul* into *synagogue* or even *temple*. Something like this should be done quickly and without pause, for it would otherwise introduce a glitch that would damage the joke.

Of course, if you're telling the story to Jews or to New Yorkers—who, even if not Jewish, know something about Jewish ways—you can skip the translation. You can also have the Chasidim speak with a strong Yiddish accent. That is guaranteed to make the joke funnier.

Why, then, do I not write the joke with a Yiddish accent by misspelling the words and say, "Ve leesten to de vise elders?"

I don't do that because that's offensive. I'm not sure why, but though I can listen to a good Yiddish accent and enjoy it, to see the accent as distorted in print upsets me. Besides, no amount of orthographic distortion gets across the change in the vowel sounds.

Let's look at the joke again. Are there any simple changes that would make it less funny? Changing the Irishman into a Frenchman, or the Chasidim into three Lutheran ministers, would reduce the fun even if the joke were otherwise still told word for word.

More subtle is the choice of *tennis* as the last word. What if you had said *polo,* or *handball?* The humor would have been more subdued. Polo is too highbrow for belief, while handball is too lowbrow for consideration. Only tennis matches golf at a level.

You may, at this point, feel disheartened. How on earth can you tell a good joke if you have to take all such points into consideration?

It's the same as learning to play golf and having to hold every part of your body just so before you can make a useful swing. It's the same as learning to play poker and having to follow the fall of the cards. Eventually it all becomes second nature and you don't have to do it consciously.

But let's go on. Obviously, if I'm going to talk this much about every joke, I won't have room for many, but what I've said won't have to be repeated, so we can move along more rapidly.

Sometimes a funny story does not have to be told for a laugh. A wry smile may be all that is wanted or expected. This happens where there is a philosophical or psychological edge to a story. The story can still have its funny aspect, but it has to be short. You can't maunder on without losing the point. An example:

•2

An elderly man is sitting on a park bench reading a newspaper. A bird flying overhead lets go and a copious drop of excrement splashes onto the paper. The reader looks up in fury, shakes his fist, and cries out, "For others, you sing."

The humor, which may elicit a chuckle, lies, of course, in the man's belief that the universe is run for the sole purpose of spiting him. The wry smile must arise from the realization that what is described here is a universal phenomenon. There are times when every one of us is convinced that the universe has no purpose but to get in our way and infuriate us.

It is easier to see the folly of false or useless attitudes in a funny story than in a long and tedious sermon, sometimes. Abraham Lincoln knew it and was always telling funny stories to make very serious points. Aesop knew it, too, and his fables are sometimes short and funny for that very reason.

Since I have mentioned the stereotypical Jews of jokedom, I will have to admit to you that there is much in me that is stereotypical in this sense. I don't drink, or smoke, or take drugs. Nor can I dance, ride a bicycle, or play any game that requires physical dexterity. ("What the devil do you do?" you may well ask. The answer is that I write, and do so with such fiendish assiduity that I have published, at this time of writing, 466 books.)

Sometimes my naïveté sticks out uncomfortably because I lack the ability to wear a mask. What you see of me is what you get.

•3

Some two years ago, when I was already an elderly man who had spent a long lifetime surrounded by the American way of life, I was taken to a very posh country club in Connecticut so that I could give an hour's talk for the generous sum of fifteen thousand dollars.

I got there and found that I was going to be talking to a group of yuppies who were working for some prosperous firm. They were all young, all thin, all handsome, all American upper class to the core.

What's more, they were there in order to spend the afternoon playing golf and tennis, with those who did best winning prizes that would be valuable to people interested in these games.

I felt terribly out of place, but I was there to do a job and earn some money, so I made myself as much at home as possible. For one thing, I studied the prizes that were to be handed out and that were displayed on a long table. One prize in particular fascinated me, for I didn't know what it was. It was a tall cylindrical object that seemed complex but also seemed (to me) to have no conceivable use.

I studied it gravely and finally said to one of the yuppies who happened to be near, "Pardon me, but what is this?"

He looked at me as though I had asked that a baked potato be identified. He said, "It's a golf bag."

"Oh," said I, innocently, "I've never seen one before."

You can well imagine that that episode sent a little earthquake through the group that was waiting to hear me. Were they going to spend fifteen thousand dollars to listen to some idiot who didn't know a golf bag when he saw one?

Fortunately, I proceeded to give the talk and prove that I was worth the money.

That brings up a point about funny stories that I have never seen emphasized. Telling a funny story well to an audience is an exercise in public speaking. A person who is a skillful jokester is sure to be able to get up and address a much larger gathering for a much longer period of time on a much graver subject. I have been doing it for forty-two years now, and I speak without notes and for large sums.

So if you are eager to learn how to tell a funny story and succeed, you will have simultaneously learned how to be a public speaker, and will have done so much more effectively (and pleasantly, perhaps) than if you had attended any number of courses on elocution and allied subjects.

I wish I could say that my ignorance of the nature of a golf bag was my only example of ineptitude. A much more humiliating experience of the same sort occurred thirty years ago, when my son, David, was about ten years old.

You'll have to understand David. He's a nice kid, but he seems to have inherited my naïveté in spades and I just never expect him to show any deep understanding of the world about him. Here's the story:

•4

I once spent a few years writing articles for the *World Book Encyclopedia*, and they would occasionally send out presents to some of their writers. One year, I received such a present, unwrapped it, and stared at it with utter puzzlement. It was an aluminum cylinder about a foot high or so and I hadn't any idea at all as to what it could possibly be used for.

I showed it to my (first) wife, Gertrude, and she stared at it and found herself at an equal loss. We speculated, but nothing we thought of seemed to make any sense.

At this point, there walked in my ten-year-old David, the original know-nothing. He took one look at the object and said, "Who sent you a champagne bucket?"

Gertrude and I stared at each other. How on earth could David possibly recognize a champagne bucket? Never in his life had he drunk champagne (nor had we).

I said to him, "How do you know it's a champagne bucket, David?"

And he said, "I've seen them on the 'Three Stooges' show."

From this you can see that Gertrude and I learned that, by not watching the Three Stooges on television, we failed to learn an important aspect of the American way of life.

The height and peak of a storyteller's art, however, is the ability to tell a long story, hold the listener's attention throughout, and manage to send him into hysterics at the end. It is not easy to do and it wears one out. I have several long stories of this nature in my repertoire and I do not like to tell them more often than once a year. It reduces me to a shambles if I try to do them more often.

Now, once a year over a period of about eighteen years, I would travel to a little town in upstate New York, to the Rensselaerville Institute, and there I would conduct a four-day seminar on some imaginative topic or other. Evenings, after the labors of the day, we would gather in a recreation room to drink beer or soft drinks, to nibble at crackers and cheese, and to tell jokes.

I was, of course, the star performer, and each year they would ask me to tell my "Moishe Ginsberg the Salesman" stories. Since a great many of the people in the audience come to the seminars year after year, I invariably point out that they have already heard the stories. Each time, they insist they want to hear them again, and there are always a few newcomers who (say the old-timers) must be told the story.

So I have to gird my loins, take a deep breath, and begin. Now, mind you, I cannot possibly write the stories in such a way as to get across the full flavor of the stories as told. For one thing, Moishe Ginsberg must speak with a Yiddish accent, and I can't do that in writing. For another, I improvise each time so that the joke is never told in exactly the same way twice—the improvisations are chosen to fit the audience. The more good-humored the audience seems, and the readier to laugh, the more I spin it out. So here goes a shortened, written version:

•5

Moishe Ginsberg managed to achieve an interview with Alexander Chumley-Smythe of Abercrombie and Fitch of sainted memory, and he said:

"Mr. Chumley-Smythe, my name is Moishe Ginsberg and I am a ribbon salesman. I am the best ribbon salesman in the world. I have sold ribbons to every important department store in all fifty states, including Alaska and Hawaii. The only exception, the only flaw, is that I have never sold anything to Abercrombie and Fitch.

"Next month, Mr. Chumley-Smythe, I retire and go to the land of my people—Miami Beach. I would like to retire with a perfect record and I hope you will help me do so. I would like to sell you some ribbons. I don't ask you to give me a large order; give me a small one, as small as you wish. I merely want to end up with a perfect record."

Alexander Chumley-Smythe listened to Ginsberg with a visible sneer on his face and said, "Very well, if that's what you want. You may sell me a piece of ribbon, equal in length to the distance from the tip of your nose to the tip of your pecker."

For a moment, Ginsberg seemed taken aback, but he recovered and said, "All right, Mr. Chumley-Smythe. As you say. What color ribbon do you wish and what style?"

And Chumley-Smythe said wearily, "Mr. Ginsberg, I don't care a continental what color and what style. Just sell me a strip of ribbon equal in length to the distance from the tip of your nose to the tip of your pecker."

And Ginsberg nodded his head and said again, "As you say. But please, Mr. Chumley-Smythe, can you put it in writing? I need some written proof that my record is perfect."

Chumley-Smythe pulled down an order blank and wrote, "Ordered, from Moishe Ginsberg, ribbon salesman, a strip of ribbon, any color, any style, equal in length to the distance from the tip of said Ginsberg's nose to the tip of his pecker."

Ginsberg left with his copy of the order, and Chumley-Smythe also left for a well-earned vacation in Newport, Rhode Island.

Chumley-Smythe had not been in Newport for more than a few days when he received a furious phone call from his boss at Abercrombie and Fitch.

"Chumley-Smythe," shouted the boss, "what the hell is going on here? A truck arrives every hour on the hour with ribbon. Our storage bins are filled with ribbon all the way up to the fifteenth floor, and more keeps arriving. The story is that you have ordered it."

Chumley-Smythe choked. "I'll be right back, boss, and get to the bottom of this."

Back in his office, he called in Moishe Ginsberg and, waving his fists, shouted, "Listen, you bastard, what the hell do you mean sending in all these ribbons? Are you crazy?"

Ginsberg's eyebrows lifted. He said, "I beg your pardon, but I have your order blank right here. I'll show it to you, but don't try to snatch it and tear it up because it is only a Xerox. I have the original in a safe-deposit box. You see it says you want a length of ribbon equal to the distance from the tip of my nose to the tip of my pecker?"

"Yes, and that's all I wanted."

"And that's all you're getting. The tip of my nose is right here, but the tip of my pecker is in Poland."

I was told this joke in a synagogue when I was attending the bar mitzvah of a young man, and it was told me by the young man's father. He led me carefully from one room in the synagogue to another in order to tell me the joke. It was my notion he had taken me from a more holy room to a less holy room where God might not overhear this story—which was most unsuitable for a synagogue.

Now for the other Moishe Ginsberg joke. He is still a salesman, but there is otherwise no connection with the previous story.

•6

Moishe Ginsberg appeared at the desk of the general manager of Abercrombie and Fitch and asked for a job as a salesman in the store.

The general manager shook his head. "We're very sorry, Mr. Ginsberg, but you would not suit the general aura of the store."

"Why?" said Ginsberg. "Because I speak with a Yiddish accent? That doesn't matter. I'm the best salesman in the world. I can sell anyone anything."

"Nevertheless," said the general manager firmly, "we cannot use you."

Whereupon Ginsberg said, "I tell you what. Is there a department in the store that is currently losing money? If there is, put me in charge for two weeks. You need not pay me any salary, nor any commission. I will work for nothing. At the end of the two weeks, if you want to throw me out, I will go quietly."

The general manager thought quickly. As it happened, the fishing department was losing money, and had been for quite a while. Why not try the gamble?

"Very well," he said. "You may have the fishing department for exactly two weeks without pay, Mr. Ginsberg."

The general manager then forgot the matter until a week later when he was going over the reports from the various departments. He then found himself staring with a wild surprise at the report of the fishing department. The sales figures had gone up steeply. He had seen nothing like it in years. What on earth could have happened?

The next morning, he went quietly down to the fishing department and stood behind a pillar to listen. Ginsberg was leaning over the counter with two hooks in his hand and was speaking earnestly to a customer. This is what the general manager heard:

"These two hooks, Mr. Anderson, are a marvelous advance of modern science. They are each covered with a monomolecular film of a chemical that is absolutely attractive to any fish. If you hang these hooks over the water, even without bait, the fish will jump out of the water to snatch at them. Naturally, don't do that, but use bait so that the other fishermen won't realize your advantage.... You'll take them? Good!

"I'm telling you, Mr. Anderson, with these hooks and your lines—what kind of lines do you use, by the way? Nylon? Nylon! That's useless. They will break like a piece of rotten thread if you get a really big fish. Now, listen to me. We have here lines containing a thin metallic thread that gives them enough strength to hold up a ton. Nothing could possibly break them. You could catch whales. They are the lines of the scientific future.... You'll take them? Good!

"With these hooks, Mr. Anderson, and these lines, and with your rods—what kind of rods do you use, Mr. Anderson? Bamboo? Bamboo! Mr. Anderson, I am anxious to make a sale; sales are my bread and butter. But I will absolutely refuse to sell you these hooks and these lines if you are going to use them with bamboo rods. Bamboo is worthless. Now, what we have are special rods designed for the astronauts. They work in outer space because they are made of a new kind of plastic that is stronger than steel and yet as flexible as rubber. Take my advice.... You'll take them? Good!

"Mr. Anderson, I wish you joy with your new kind of fishing with these hooks, these lines, and these rods. Where are you going fishing, by the way? Lake Oohoochiwaba. I know it well. Very good place for fishing. How do you do it? You stand on the shore? Oh, Mr. Anderson, what's the use of standing on the shore? What fish will come out by the shore? Minnows, Mr. Anderson, minnows!

"If you want real fish, you've got to go out five or six miles into the middle of the lake. That's where you'll find them. You'll need a boat. And not just a regular motorboat either, or a rowboat. A motorboat makes noise and scares the fish. A rowboat is too slow and riles the water.

"We have a boat that works by a reaction jet underneath. It is as silent as a whisper and it races along. You get into that and you're in the middle of the lake immediately and you start pulling in the fish till the boat is full.... You'll take it? Good! Sign here, Mr. Anderson. Everything will be delivered today."

The customer left and the general manager staggered over. He said, "Ginsberg, how much was that sale?"

Ginsberg looked at the sales slip and said, "Sixteen thousand, two hundred and fifty dollars."

"Good heavens," said the general manager, "you're hired permanently. Imagine, making that sale when you started with two hooks!"

Ginsberg said, "Started with two hooks? For goodness' sake, you came in the middle."

"In the middle? What was the beginning, then?"

"Well, I was standing here this morning and Mr. Anderson came in and walked over to the drug department across the way and asked for two boxes of super-Kotex for his wife. So I called him over. 'Hey, mister,' I said, 'as long as for the next few days you're not going to be doing anything—'"

And that's when the explosion comes.

You can't tell a joke this long with the utmost gravity. You'll wear out the audience. Their attention will wander, they will begin to resent you, and nothing will move them at the end.

How, then, do I keep them at the edge of laughter? In my case, I raise my voice half an octave, introduce the slight singsong Jews have developed from years of praying in the synagogue, and make full use of the Yiddish accent.

If you can do this perfectly, as I can, and if you can remember all the details and improvise further if the audience seems receptive, then the joke will work. As it happens, virtually no one who hears the joke can ever possibly repeat it with any hope of success; nor can anyone expect to hear it from someone other than me. That is why each year I am asked to repeat it.

At one time, I couldn't help but notice that the loudest laughter in the audience was coming from George.

"George," I said, "why are you laughing?"

"Because the joke is funny."

"But George, you're the one who told me the joke in the first place."

"Yes, but not the way you tell it."

Joke #5, as I pointed out, was told me in the synagogue by the father of a bar mitzvah boy. A bar mitzvah comes when the boy is thirteen, but I had met the kid the year before at the Rensselaerville Institute, when he was twelve.

Twelve-year-olds are dangerous for any speaker. They are bright enough to ask embarrassing questions, but not old enough to know they shouldn't do that. So when a young boy, with bright and snapping eyes, asks me a question designed to make me look foolish, I say to him, "You're twelve years old, aren't you?"

Invariably he answers, "Yes, how did you know?"

"Never mind," I say dangerously. "Just watch yourself."

•7

After my talk was over, I met the young man in the recreation room and was determined to get even.

I said, "When will you be thirteen, Alex?"

He told me, and I said, "Gee, that will be too bad. Suddenly you will stop being a bright twelve-year-old and become a stupid thirteen-year-old."

And he said, calmly, "Is that what happened to you when you turned thirteen?"

•8

It is wise not to call on any boy who looks twelve, but once when I was addressing a junior high school class, I forgot and called on one.

The boy said, "Dr. Asimov, what is the second closest star?"

I smiled benignly. Everyone knows the name of the closest star but the youngster obviously thought he would catch me with the second closest.

I said, "The second closest star is Barnard's star, a single star that is 5.9 light-years from us."

The boy looked puzzled. He said, "Then what is the closest star?"

I grinned even more broadly, "The closest star is Alpha Centauri, a triple star system that is 4.3 light-years from us."

"That's funny," said the vile brat, "I thought our Sun was the closest star."

Which it is, and people had to hold me back to keep me from killing the kid.

Incidentally, in Joke #5 I use the word *pecker* several times for the male generative organ. Behind that lies a tale.

Many of the best jokes ever told are off-color. They either make use of vulgar expressions that are not entirely acceptable in polite society, or deal with human actions that most people pretend to believe do not exist.

In my first book of humor, the *Treasury*, I made the point over and over that vulgar words should be avoided if possible and that unacceptable actions of excretion or reproduction should not be described in detail. The reason was simple. The use of vulgar words and actions might embarrass some in the audience, and that is undesirable.

My joke book included no vulgarisms, therefore, and it was enormously moral.

There were two exceptions, and these were the last two jokes in the book. In the penultimate joke, I gave an example (one example in the entire book) of a joke that simply could not exist without the use of a vulgar term. In the final joke, I gave an example where the overuse of a vulgarism deprived it of its true meaning, with the clear moral that such terms should not be used gratuitously.

Would you believe, then, that the reptiles of the religious right pounced upon the book in a few places, calling it immoral and directing everyone to read the last joke, totally ignoring the intentions of the book as a whole?

They didn't win out, I am glad to say, but it did rather embitter me. Why should they have engaged in such an unfair and vicious distortion—aside, of course, from their being pernicious slime?

In any case, I have decided that in this second volume, I shall avoid vulgarisms as much as possible, but if a good joke requires it, I am going to use it. I might as well be hung for a sheep as for a lamb.

Therefore, when it was important to deal with the male generative organ in Joke #5, because the entire point rested on the fact of circumcision, I had to choose my word. It was not so many years ago that any word for the male organ was beyond the pale, but with a general loosening of hypocritical rigor, it has become possible for the word *penis* to appear even in the pages of the *New York Times*.

Nevertheless, I didn't want to use *penis* because it was simply too formal to carry conviction in the context of the joke. *Pecker* was much better, though *prick* and *cock* would have done as well.

• • •

Having explained all this, I will now tell you a joke that is the most tasteless that will be appearing in this book. I must include it because of the effect it had on me. I was told the joke by a fellow member of the Dutch Treat Club (a Tuesday luncheon club of which I am currently the president) just as I was stepping into a taxi.

I just had enough strength to give the taxi driver my destination and then I went into hysterics and remained in hysterics for the entire length of the trip. What the taxi driver must have thought of me, sitting in his backseat and howling, I don't know. I can only imagine he must have been greatly relieved to have gotten rid of me at last.

Here is the joke:

•9

A man, crossing a bridge one evening, saw another man teetering at its edge. He rushed over, pulled him back, and said, "What are you doing?"

The other said, "Let me go. I want to jump. I want to drown. I want to die."

"Are you mad? You seem reasonably young and healthy. Why should you want to die?"

The other said, "Why not? I designed this bridge you're standing on and it's a beautiful bridge, but does anyone point at me and say, 'There goes Edwin, the bridge builder'? No!

"I helped draw up the blueprints for half the skyscrapers you can see from here, but does anyone point at me and say, 'There goes Edwin, the great architect'? No!

"I am the publisher of the largest daily in the city, but does anyone say, 'There goes Edwin, the great newspaperman'? No!

"But I suck one little cock, and everyone says—"

You can't get past that point without the explosion. I certainly didn't get past it and, as I said, I laughed for fifteen minutes.

20

Here's an example, by the way, where my judgment is not absolute. In telling the story to Neil Felshman, another member of the Dutch Treat Club, he laughed gently and said, "It's funnier if you say 'one little cock.'"

Of course it is. I had left out the adjective, but its presence is a feckless attempt to mitigate the grossness of the action, and I accepted the correction with gratitude.

This reminds me that occasionally, very occasionally, you can hoodwink a listener into cooperating, unwittingly, in the development of a punch line. For instance:

•10

Moses, one day, looking down from heaven, seemed struck by what he had seen and, turning to the Lord, he said, "It seems to me, Lord, that the people of earth, whom thou hast created, have utterly corrupted themselves. At least half of them engage routinely in oral sex."

The Lord look down and said, "You are right, Moses, but the percentage is 89.6 percent."

Moses said, "Nine-tenths of all people do this? It is against all laws, human and divine. Lord, let all the sinners perish in fire from heaven."

The Lord shook his head. "No, Moses, I tried that with the Flood and it didn't work. Nowadays, it would be more suitable to treat the matter positively in accordance with the tenets of modern psychopathology. I will give each human being who has kept his mouth and mind pure of this abomination a solid gold watch, suitably inscribed."

[You then turn to someone in the audience, preferably a young and attractive woman, and say, "And do you know what the inscription read?"

She is bound to say, "No, I don't."

Whereupon you say, "You mean you didn't get one, either?"]

Not once have I received any objection from the people I've victimized in this fashion. In fact, one young woman, when I said she hadn't got one, replied, "No, I didn't, thank goodness."

• • •

One time I told this joke to a Dutch Treater and did so in much more painstaking detail than I have written it here. The Dutch Treater was the well-known band leader Emory Davis, a dear, sweet man. This time, however, it fell into his head to beat me to the punch line, since he happened to know the joke. This is an absolutely unforgivable offense in the world of jokedom.

I turned red with fury and I said to him, "Listen, Emory, I may someday forget what women are for, but I will never forget what you have just done, and I will get even."

And the very next week, I managed. The story goes as follows:

•11

We used to take our lunch in those days, at least during the summer hiatus, at a restaurant that offered us a prix fixe meal for $19. There wasn't much choice permitted, but it was very cheap compared to à la carte. The only catch was that no substitutions were permitted.

The week after my punch line had been stomped, Emory, who was sitting next to me, said, "I don't feel like a salad today."

The proper procedure in that case was to order the prix fixe of your choice and then simply ignore the salad.

However, I said to him, "Well, just tell the waiter you don't want the salad."

He did so, and that counted as a substitution, as I knew very well it would be, and his lunch was thrown into the à la carte column and he received a bill for $35. When Emory (always a close fellow with a dollar) found out the price was nearly doubled when he omitted an item, he turned the most charming shade of magenta you ever saw, and I laughed like a fiend.

It was a terribly vicious act on my part, but no punishment is too great for a punch line stomper.

•12

Sometimes, of course, it is I who get it in the neck at a Dutch Treat meeting. One of our members had missed several luncheons on the specious excuse that his wife was hospitalized.

Whereupon I raised my nose haughtily into the air and said, "The only reason I would miss a Tuesday lunch is if the woman in bed with me simply wouldn't let me go."

"Which accounts," said Joe Coggins at once, "for Isaac's perfect attendance record."

I saw that coming the instant I had made my unfortunate remark, but it was too late to cram it back into my mouth.

One of the prominent members of the Dutch Treat Club is Herb Graff. He is a jokester of formidable talents and he has a couple of great advantages over me. He lectures on movies of the thirties and forties (and is one of the great experts on motion picture history), which involves him with show business people, who always have a fund of new jokes. He also travels over the country giving his talks. In the process, he picks up funny stories that stay-at-homes would not hear until after a time.

Fortunately, he tells me the jokes he hears and I can frequently add them to my repertoire. Of the jokes he's told me, this is the one I think is the funniest:

•13

Mr. Ginsberg, age eighty-three, went to the doctor for a complete examination, head to toe.

About halfway through, the doctor was called to the telephone.

He said, "Mr. Ginsberg, this will not take more than a few minutes. Here is a jar. While I am gone, go to the bathroom and place a semen sample in it for examination. Then we'll continue."

A few minutes later, the doctor indeed returned, and there stood Mr. Ginsberg with the jar—totally empty.

"Doctor," said Mr. Ginsberg. "I did my best. I tried with my right hand; I tried with my left hand. I even tried with both hands, but nothing happened."

The doctor said soothingly, "Now, Mr. Ginsberg, don't feel embarrassed. At the age of eighty-three, it is quite common to be impotent."

Whereupon Ginsberg said, with towering indignation, "What do you mean, impotent? I couldn't open the jar."

More recently, Herb told me the following joke, which I include here as an example of the geographical sensitivity of funny stories.

•14

A young Chinese couple, having made love one evening, were lying in bed in comfortable relaxation and the young man said, "What I would like now is some sixty-nine."

Whereupon the young woman said, "Are you crazy? Do you want me, at this point, to get out of bed, get dressed, and make you some broccoli and rice?"

This joke depends for its effectiveness entirely upon the fact that in New York, at least, the cheaper Chinese restaurants number their dishes so that the patron can order quickly. In New York, therefore, the joke gets a hearty laugh. Outside New York, it may merely elicit a confused, what's-so-funny look.

•15

Herb tells me he once told Joke #14 to a New Yorker who listened stolidly. This annoyed Herb, who resents anyone who doesn't laugh at his jokes. He said angrily, "Why don't you laugh?"

And the man answered, "Because in my neighborhood, sixty-nine is pepper steak."

24

As Herb very justly remarked, "That was funnier than the joke."

Some professions attract jokes. Lawyers, for instance, are the butt of many jokes and I will scatter a few through the book. I told my favorite lawyer joke in Evansville, Indiana, where I attended an enormous banquet that lasted six hours. (I traveled somewhat in those days—I don't anymore.)

At that banquet, the featured speaker was the lawyer Louis Nizer, who gave a terrific speech (that he had clearly memorized) on the world of seventy-five years in the future. It was an excellent bit of science fiction, but it made me uneasy. I somehow thought that no one ought to do so well in science fiction when he was not a science fiction writer, and when I, one of the best known of the species, was in the audience.

He spoke for forty-five minutes, but I (along with others) was given only five minutes. Here is how I spent my five minutes.

•16

Mr. Nizer [I said] told us of a glowing future, but the nature of the future depends on our politicians, who are almost all lawyers. We must ask, then, what we ought to expect of lawyers and, in that connection, let me tell you the following story.

A physician, an architect, and a lawyer were once sitting about a convivial dinner table and the conversation fell upon which of the three labored at the oldest profession.

The physician said, "Clearly, medicine is the oldest profession, for when Adam was formed, God realized it was not good for man to be alone. He therefore caused a deep sleep to fall upon Adam, and while he slept, he withdrew a rib from one side, fashioned it into a woman, and when Adam awoke, presented her to him. Since that was obviously an operation, with anesthesia, and took place at the very beginning of human history, medicine is the oldest profession."

To which the architect said, "Hold on, there. Adam was created on the sixth day, so the medical procedure you speak of could not possibly have taken place earlier than that. On the first day, however, God created heaven and earth out of primeval chaos and that, I submit, was the greatest conceivable architectural achievement. Architecture is, therefore, the oldest profession."

To which the lawyer said, "Hold on, there. And who do you think created the primeval chaos?"

This got the greatest laugh of the evening, and I was tremendously relieved to notice that Nizer was laughing as hard as anyone.

Joke #16, by the way, is an example of a joke that does not require an accent to be funny—as will be true of a large number of jokes I will tell you in this book. In fact, the humor is advanced if the English is absolutely standard. Make the physician's and the architect's speech as pompous as is convenient and then slide in the lawyer's relatively short comment quickly, catching the audience completely off guard.

Here is another lawyer joke.

•17

Nathan Birnbaum, a lawyer, died and went to heaven. He had no sooner gotten inside the Pearly Gates when a tremendous chorus of angels began to sing gorgeously in his honor. The air was filled with a golden aura, delicious perfumes wafted everywhere, and approaching Birnbaum was the tall and magnificent form of the Recording Angel, smiling at him graciously.

"Birnbaum," said the Recording Angel in mellow and musical tones, "we have long been awaiting you. You are the first human being ever to break Methuselah's mark for longevity. You have lived one thousand and twenty-eight years."

"What are you talking about?" said Birnbaum, astonished. "I died at the age of fifty-six."

"At the age of fifty-six?" said the Recording Angel, astonished in his turn. "Aren't you Nathan Birnbaum?"

"Yes."

"A lawyer?"

"Yes."

"From Brooklyn?"

"Yes."

"But the Record Book has you down for one thousand and twenty-eight years."

"Sorry. Only fifty-six."

"Something must be wrong," said the Recording Angel. "Let me study the book."

He did so and suddenly clapped his hand to his forehead. "Ah, I see where we made our mistake. We added up the hours you charged your clients."

•18

My own lawyer, Robert Zicklin, is a close friend of mine, whom I trust implicitly, and who is one of the nicest and sweetest guys I know. (I may weary you by telling you of all the "nicest and sweetest guys" I know, but I am very fortunate in that so many of the people I know are wonderful individuals.)

When I first heard Joke #17, I phoned Bob at once on the off chance that he had never heard it. Ordinarily, he laughs himself silly at my jokes, but this time he was dreadfully silent.

Then he said, "It's an old joke, and I'm placing this call on your bill."

I think he was kidding about charging me, however, for he never did.

And here's one more lawyer joke, a fantasy, that I got from my good friend the science fiction writer Ben Bova (one of the nicest and sweetest guys I know):

•19

Since there must be communication between heaven and hell, the Trans-Paradisiac Bridge was built eons ago under the co-sponsorship of the two regions, each supplying half the money required for its upkeep.

One day, the Archangel Gabriel came to God and said, "Lord, the

Trans-Paradisiac Bridge is in pretty bad shape. I've looked up the records and I'm afraid Satan hasn't contributed one cent to its upkeep in the last two thousand years."

"Really?" said God. "It must be an oversight."

He waved his hand and a beautiful scroll appeared, along with a graceful feather pen, which moved of its own accord, and wrote in Spencerian handwriting:

Dear Satan Baby,
　　It has come to my attention that you are somewhat remiss in your payments for the upkeep of this bridge of ours. Will you check your records and make up the missing sum at your earliest convenience? And by the way, let's do lunch together one of these days.
　　Yours, God

The scroll disappeared and, in a very short order of time, an asbestos sheet appeared with charred letters on it that still exhaled sulfurous fumes. It read:

God:
　　Nuts to you and nuts to the bridge. I don't intend to pay a cent.
　　Satan

When God read that, he swelled with fury and said to Gabriel, "How do you like that for insolence? After all I did for him, too. I gave him hell for his own, and a vast coterie of demons to rule over, and see how he treats me. If he thinks he's getting away with this, he's greatly mistaken."

Again a scroll appeared. Again the feather pen wrote.

Satan:
　　If you don't pay up instantly, I am going to sue you till your eyes bubble.
　　God

And at once another asbestos sheet came back, reading:

God:
>Where will you find a lawyer?
>Satan

Why lawyer jokes? Obviously, most people distrust lawyers. If you are forced to go to law, then even if you have a lawyer you find satisfactory (aside from the very high fees that professional ethics seems to force him to charge), there is always the lawyer on the other side who can only be an absolute demon in your eyes. Everyone experiences this phenomenon, and the only relief (and a rather ineffective one, I must admit) is to tell lawyer jokes.

Naturally, there are other professions that are equally unpopular. To writers, at least, agents and critics are often the personification of demons—greedy and unscrupulous demons.

Here is a very short agent joke that Herb Graff told me.

•20

An agent's child rushed to him and said, "Pop, can I have a dollar?"

The agent's eyes narrowed and he said, "What do you want ninety cents for?"

Would you believe that I missed on that joke? I don't have an agent, so I just stared at Herb blankly till he said impatiently, "An agent takes ten percent of everything, you yutz."

A much more intensely antagonistic joke is the following, which was told to me by the drama critic Doug Watt, who is also a Dutch Treater.

•21

An agent woke up one night and found his bedroom dusky with red light and foul with a sulfurous stench, and there at the foot of the bed was someone he recognized instantly as Satan.

Satan smiled and said, "Mr. Jones, if you wish, I will give you untold wealth, all the women you want, together with fame and long life. How about it?"

The agent's eyes narrowed. "What's the catch?"

Satan said, "The catch is that in exchange for all this, I will eventually have your immortal soul."

And the agent said, "Come on. What's the real catch?"

•22

The great vaudeville and radio comic Fred Allen once said, "You can take all the sincerity in Hollywood and stuff it into a flea's navel and still have room for three caraway seeds and an agent's heart."

Of course, since I don't have an agent, I don't particularly dislike them. Critics, though—well, I have critics. As far as I know, every writer who ever lived loathed critics. I loathe them, too. Why should I be different?

I'll give you two remarks about critics. The first is not mine, and I don't know whose it is. The second is mine.

•23

A critic is like a eunuch in a harem. He sees what is done; he knows why it is done; but he cannot do it himself.

•24

No man can qualify as a critic till he presents written and notarized evidence to the effect that he beats his mother.

Incidentally, you will have noticed in Joke #19 that God is a character and gets the worst of it. That is not unusual. There is no fun in God being almighty and slashing around with fire and flood. It may be very moral, but it's nothing to laugh at. It's only funny when God loses, and what's bad about that? It makes God more human and sympathetic.

I often hesitate to tell God-jokes unless they are clearly in a Jewish setting. We Jews are more comfortable with God than Christians are. After all, God is one of us, for no Jew doubts but that God is himself Jewish. Let me explain the feeling with a story:

•25

Rabbi Feldman had been having trouble with his congregation. It seemed they could agree upon nothing, and controversy filled the air until the Sabbath itself became an area of conflict and unhappiness filled the synagogue.

The president of the congregation said, "Rabbi, this cannot be allowed to continue. Come, there must be a conference, and we must settle all areas of dispute once and for all."

"Agreed," said the rabbi.

At the appointed time, therefore, the rabbi, the president, and ten elders met in the conference room of the synagogue, sitting about a magnificent mahogany table.

One by one the issues were dealt with and on each issue, it became more and more apparent that the rabbi was a lonely voice in the wilderness.

The president said, "Come, Rabbi, enough of this. Let us vote and allow the majority to rule."

He passed out the slips of paper and each man made his mark. The slips were collected and the president said, "You may examine them, Rabbi. It is eleven to one against you. We have the majority."

Whereupon the rabbi rose to his feet in offended majesty. "So," he said, "you now think because of the vote that you are right and I am wrong. Well, that is not so. I stand here"—and he raised his arms impressively—"and call upon the Holy One of Israel to give us a sign that I am right and you are wrong."

And as he said so, there came a frightful crack of thunder and a brilliant flash of lightning that struck the mahogany table and cracked it in two. The room was filled with smoke and fumes and the president and the elders were hurled to the floor.

Through the carnage, the rabbi remained erect and untouched, his eyes flashing and a grim smile on his face.

Slowly, the president lifted himself above what was left of the table. His hair was singed, his glasses were hanging from one ear, his clothing was in disarray.

He said, "All right, eleven to two. We still have the majority."

My personal belief is that God himself would laugh at that joke.

However, you must not get me wrong. I am the president of the American Humanist Association, a thoroughgoing materialist and rationalist organization. If anyone asks me, I will admit to being an atheist. However, in the world of joke-dom, God, Satan, angels, demons, Adam and Eve, and all the paraphernalia of mythology exist, and I accept them gladly. Anything for a laugh.

Authority figures are a natural target for jokes. (That is, if you dare. In a really thoroughgoing despotism, such as Hitler's Germany or Stalin's Russia, you wouldn't dare.) That includes spiritual leaders, of course. My Irish friends are full of stories about priests, monks, and nuns, and Protestants joke about ministers. (The religious right doesn't joke, having long since broken their sense of humor, assuming they ever had one.)

I'm careful about telling such jokes, for I do not wish to be offensive, but here's one I'll take a chance on:

•26

When Neil Armstrong and Buzz Aldrin walked on the moon in 1969, President Nixon, in a moment of jubilant hyperbole, said, "This is the greatest day in the history of mankind."

Whereupon the TV evangelist Billy Graham, in his usual sanctimonious and humorless fashion, pointed out that there were at least three greater days in human history: "the first Christmas, the first Good Friday, and the first Easter."

To which I responded (though, alas, no one paid any attention), "What Nixon meant was that the landing on the moon was the greatest day in the history of mankind that involved gentiles."

It always amuses me, in a very bitter sort of way, that the evangelists and other primitives of the religious right adore Jews so thoroughly, provided they have been dead for anywhere from two thousand to four thousand years.

•27

The British-Jewish novelist Israel Zangwill was told by someone that Jews were suspicious of gentiles, clannish, and unfriendly.

"Yes," said Zangwill, "two thousand years of Christian love has made us very nervous."

I think it's time for another rabbi joke, one that I call my eighty-eight-year-old rabbi joke. My dear wife was once sitting at some party where I was located in another room engaged in a joke-telling session. She told me afterward that she heard someone speaking in a high, cracked voice, and couldn't imagine who it might be till there was a burst of laughter and she realized I was telling my eighty-eight-year-old rabbi joke.

Here's the way it goes:

•28

The madam of a bawdy-house answered the ring of the bell and, on opening the door, she found standing there on the threshold an ancient, bearded gentleman dressed in rabbi's garb.

"May I come in?" asked the rabbi gently in an aged, quavering voice.

Feeling a little confused, the madam said, "But Rabbi, surely you must be in the wrong place. Here is where we—"

"I know what you do here," interrupted the rabbi. "You don't think I came for chopped liver, do you? Bring out the girls."

Still confused, but understanding her professional duty, the madam had several girls line up. The rabbi tottered from one to another until he reached Rosie, a large redhead with enormous breasts. He looked at her with appreciation and pointed. "Good! I'll take those."

The rabbi paid out the necessary sum, and Rosie led him upstairs. She helped him off with his coat and hung it up carefully on the nail on the door. Then she helped him off with the rest of the clothes and got into bed.

There, to Rosie's astonishment, the rabbi performed with an address and a skill that was unbelievable. In fact, Rosie, a hardened professional, found herself surprised into an orgasm.

As they lay in bed a few minutes afterward, relaxing, Rosie said, "How old are you, Rabbi?"

The rabbi said, "God has been good to me. I am eighty-eight years old."

"That is certainly amazing. Listen, Rabbi, if you are ever in the neighborhood again and if you should feel in the mood, please ask for me—Rosie. I would be delighted to oblige you."

The rabbi said, with a certain hauteur, "What do you mean, if I should be in the mood again? Let me sleep for five minutes right now and, believe me, I will be in the mood again."

"Really, Rabbi? Then please take a little nap."

"Okay." The rabbi adjusted himself into a relaxed position, face-up, placed his arms across his chest, and then said, "Wait one minute. This is important. While I'm asleep, scoop up my balls with your right hand and hold them an inch above the sheet, without moving them. Keep them absolutely motionless."

"Of course, Rabbi," said Rosie, and did as she was told, holding the rabbi's testicles free of the sheet.

For five minutes the rabbi slept, then woke with a start and said, "I'm ready."

And so he was, for, to Rosie's delight, he was even better the second time than the first.

As she lay panting, Rosie said, "It was wonderful, Rabbi, but one thing I don't understand. Why was it so necessary to hold your testicles motionless above the sheet while you were sleeping?"

"Oh, that," said the rabbi. "Well, you are a very nice girl and I like you very much. Still, the truth is I don't really know you very well, and over there, in my coat, hanging on the hook on the door, is five hundred dollars."

There are two things to note about this joke.

First, the fact that the old man is a rabbi has nothing to do with the plot. He could have been any old man; in fact, he need not even have been Jewish (except that the fact that he is gives me the chance to use the Yiddish accent) and the joke would have proceeded the same way, word for word. Why, then, make him a rabbi?

Simply because it heightens the incongruity. Any ancient capable of impressing a professional lady is funny, but an ancient rabbi is funnier by far, and you have to play for the laugh. I've never tested this joke by omitting the rabbi, because I couldn't bear to take the chance of ruining it, but I'm sure the rabbi bit is essential.

The second thing to note is that although the joke is drenched in sex (but note that I gave no clinical descriptions—that is not necessary and would, in fact, perhaps kill the joke), the punch line is totally asexual.

A sudden alteration in point of view is essential for laughter, and the greater and more radical the alteration, the louder the laughter. The switch from sex to nonsex in the last three words of the joke is as radical a switch as one can easily imagine.

Here's another rabbi joke:

•29

Rabbi Feldman had served his congregation in Long Island for twenty years with great efficiency, and he was greatly loved as a result. The congregation got together and decided to celebrate the twentieth anniversary by sending him on a two-week vacation to Miami Beach—at congregation expense, of course.

The rabbi was suitably grateful and was even more so when he realized that no expense had been spared. He was in a gorgeous suite on the top floor of a posh hotel, with flowers everywhere, and a magnum of champagne as well. And there, lying on a beautiful sofa in an alcove, was the most delightful item of all—a naked woman.

The rabbi, enjoying his surroundings, finally turned in the right direction and beheld the woman, who smiled at him fetchingly.

The rabbi's face contorted in fury. Seizing the telephone, he dialed the number of the president of the congregation.

When he came on, the rabbi shouted into the phone, "Hymie, you send me here for a vacation and what do I find—naked flesh! For twenty years I have tried to lead my congregation into the realm of righteousness for His name's sake, and is this how you treat me, by tempting me with the sins of—"

By this time, the young lady had caught on to the mistake that had been made and, in the last extreme of embarrassment, wriggled off the sofa and reached for her clothes.

The rabbi caught the movement out of the corner of his eye, turned to her, covering the mouthpiece of the phone with his hand, smiled winningly at her, and said, "Young lady, get back on the sofa. I'm not hollering at *you*."

A rabbi joke can, of course, be very short and yet full of significance:

•30

A rabbi who was seriously ill in the hospital received a large vase of flowers, along with a message which read: "The congregation wishes you a speedy and complete recovery by a vote of two hundred and twelve to seventy-four."

The most unusual rabbi joke I ever heard was told to me in Florida by a CBS news commentator. We were both addressing a convocation of IBM employees. It brightened a rather grim time for me, for the IBM people wore the uniform—dark suits, white shirts, narrow ties, and so on. They all marched into the auditorium exactly on time, too.

I wore a bright red jacket just to establish the fact that I was an American, and I got away with it. The news commentator had come down without a tie (it was Florida, for goodness' sake) and was sent back to get one before he was allowed on the stage.

Anyway, here's the joke:

•31

The Jewish community of Boise, Idaho, had been left without a rabbi when their old one had died. For a while it seemed impossible to get a new one, since they could not find a rabbi willing to bury himself in Boise.

At last they wrote to the Jewish Theological Seminary in New York, and imagine their joy when they were told that a fully qualified rabbi was en route to them. He was to arrive on the three P.M. train and the president of the congregation was waiting at the station for it.

It came. It stopped. Four people got off: a little Japanese gentleman, a woman who was apparently his wife, and his two sons.

No one else.

The president looked after the departing train with incredible disappointment, when he felt a light tug on his jacket. He turned. It was the Japanese gentleman, who said, "Ah, so, my name is Yoshuko Yamakuru, and I am a rabbi. Can you direct me to the Beth Emeth Synagogue?"

The president started. "I am from the synagogue. Are you indeed the rabbi?"

The rabbi presented his identification card from the Jewish Theological Seminary. There was his name, his picture, the Star of David. Everything. The president, in a daze, could do nothing but take the rabbi to the synagogue.

And then, to everyone's amazement, he turned out to be the perfect rabbi. He spoke a clear and liquid Hebrew; he intoned all the prayers with an amazing purity; he preached sermons remarkable for their fire and interest; and it turned out he had visited Israel three times. What's more, he was truly learned. All the holy books were known to him by heart. No one could come to him with a liturgical or a theological question that he could not answer instantly and satisfactorily. And he was the soul of charity and mercy.

His wife, moreover, ran the Hadassah with an iron hand, and his children were top students at the Hebrew school.

At the end of the year, the president of the congregation came to Rabbi Yamakuru and said, "Rabbi, I am glad to be able to tell you that the congregation has decided to renew your contract for a year, and at a substantial increase in salary."

The rabbi said, "That is good to hear. In return, how may I improve my services to you?"

The president waved that to one side. "No need. You are perfect."

"No, my friend," said the rabbi. "You must not say that, for there you tempt me to the sin of pride. None is perfect save the Holy One of Israel. You must tell me how I may improve."

"Well," said the president, "in that case, there is a small point I can bring up. Nothing at all important, but the ladies of the Hadassah sometimes wonder if, in circumcising our male infants, you will not slash downward with the knife and cry out, '*Hai.*'"

The joke depends, of course, on one's experience of carvers in Japanese restaurants as they slice shrimp and so on, and the manner of sword fighting in Japanese movies.

When I first heard the joke, I laughed, of course, but the laugh was more subdued than it ought to have been because I also clutched my stomach at the thought of that flashing knife coming down on a penis.

Remember that an element of cruelty, even when it is part of a fantasy world, can dilute a laugh. Use it with the greatest of care, therefore.

Here, however, is a very short joke that is cruel in another sense, and is one which, out of principle, I should refuse to laugh at. However, I am not perfect, and when I first heard it, it caught me and sent me into gales, so I pass it on to you. It is based on chicken teriyaki, a Japanese dish, and a very tasty one, too.

•32

Q: What is chicken teriyaki?
A: The name of the only living Japanese kamikaze pilot.

The news commentator who told me the Japanese rabbi joke also told me one in a German accent, an accent I can't handle, but I can tell it in writing.

•33

The German sergeant called his paratroopers together and said,

"Men, you will be taken out to the plane at exactly 6:32 A.M. The plane will fly you to your destination, which you will reach at exactly 6:55 A.M. There you will jump, pulling the string of your parachute after you have counted ten. If the parachute does not open, pull the reserve string. On the ground, you will find motorcycles waiting for you, and you will proceed immediately to the town of St. Lumières."

The paratroopers filed into the plane on time and reached their destination on time. They jumped. One pulled his string and nothing happened. He pulled his reserve string and still nothing happened. And as he plummeted downward, he said to himself bitterly, "This is an example of real inefficiency. Now when I get to the ground, I bet the motorcycles are not waiting."

Nearly half a century has passed since Hitler's time, but it is hard to forget, certainly for someone like myself, who lived through that horrible time (albeit safe in America) as a Jewish teenager. Now that West Germany and East Germany have united into a single nation (though smaller than the one that Hitler took over in 1933), suspicion remains.

•34

Doug Watt told me once unification was a fact that Germany was looking for a capital for their united country. "They're thinking of Paris," he said.

Shall we switch to poetry now—or, I suppose I should say, to comic verse?

I was lecturing in San Jose, California, in December 1978, getting there by train in four days and nights of travel, and was addressing an audience that included both doctors and lawyers. Searching for a subject that would interest both, I talked on cloning, the ability to produce a new organism from a body cell. It hasn't been done with warm-blooded animals yet, but if it ever is done with human beings, it would raise all kinds of medical and legal problems. Of course, a clone retains the original chromosome set of the cell from which it is grown, so that a male produces a male, and a female a female. The female has two X-chromosomes, while the male has an X- and a Y-chromosome.

While I was giving the talk, my friend Randall Garrett, a very clever science fiction writer who was in the audience (and who is now dead, alas), came up and put a piece of paper on the podium. I cast an eye on it and read it to myself without stopping my talk (not very easy) and realized that it was a verse parody set to the tune of "Home on the Range." He had written a verse and a chorus.

Since the audience had been receiving my talk with great good humor, I thought I would take a chance and sing the parody. This I did, and it was the hit of the evening. I then wrote four more stanzas myself and have sung it at least a hundred times to various audiences. Here it is:

• 35

Oh, give me a clone
Of my own flesh and bone
    With its Y-chromosome changed to X
And when it is grown
Then my own little clone
    Will be of the opposite sex.

[Chorus]
Clone, clone of my own,
    With your Y-chromosome changed to X
And when I'm alone
With my own little clone
    We will both think of nothing but sex.

Oh, give me a clone
Is my sorrowful moan,
    A clone that is wholly my own.

And if she's an X
Of the feminine sex
    Oh, what fun we will have when we're prone.

My heart's not of stone,
As I've frequently shown,
    When alone with my own little X
And after we've dined
I am sure we will find
    Better incest than Oedipus Rex.

Why should such sex vex
Or disturb or perplex
    Or induce a disparaging tone.
After all, don't you see
Since we're both of us me
    When we're having sex, I'm alone.

And after I'm done,
She will still have her fun,
    For I'll clone myself twice ere I die.
And this time without fail,
They'll be both of them male,
    And they'll each ravage her by and by.

I have written a number of poetic parodies, most of which are not worth printing here because they are very specialized and are adapted to a narrow audience.

Once, however, as I lay awake at night, unable to sleep (a frequent occurrence for me, since I can rarely slow the wheels of my mind into unconsciousness), I thought of a piece that Dorothy Parker wrote about someone who gave her one perfect rose when what she wanted was one perfect Cadillac. I couldn't remember the poem exactly, so I thought I would write a version of my own just to pass the wakeful hours away, and I did.

Having worked out the poem in my head, I fell asleep, and the next morning I wrote it down. (This always annoys my dear wife, Janet, who says that it is well known that if you think of something during the night, you cannot remember it in the morning. The fact that this is not true of me, she says, is an affront to humanity.)

In any case, I will now include it here for all of you. Please notice that there is only one rhyme word, *rose,* and that the tune is "The Battle Hymn of the Republic."

• **36**

When my lover wants to tell me I look great without my clothes,
As I lie upon the sofa in a soft, erotic pose,
He races to the florist, that's precisely where he goes,
      To buy one perfect rose.

[Chorus]
Glory, glory, hallelujah
Glory, glory, hallelujah
Glory, glory, hallelujah,
She has one perfect rose.

I should be much more grateful for the present, I suppose,
But I'd rather drip with ermine from my head down to my toes,
Or feel the grand security an emerald bestows,
      Than have a perfect rose.

I'd like to have a bank account that grows and grows and grows.
I'd like to watch my assets as they steadily unfroze.
All I ask is something more substantial, heaven knows,
      Than a stupid perfect rose.

I've told him this whenever he's in his orgasmic throes;
I've whispered it in poetry, I've shouted it in prose.
Then through the door he runs as his ecstatic frenzy glows,
      To buy another perfect rose.

I think that I shall kill him when he drops into a doze;
I'll strangle him tomorrow with a pair of pantyhose.

Then on his coffin I will place the symbol that he chose.
His goddamned perfect rose.

I sang this to a highly approving audience in the summer of 1990 (have I said that I have a very passable voice, with a considerable range?) and a woman came up to me and, in a soft, reproachful voice, told me I had no business desecrating the "Battle Hymn of the Republic" with these verses.

I said to her, "It was just innocent fun, ma'am. However, a little earlier in my talk I sang a funny song to the tune of 'The Star-Spangled Banner.' Didn't that bother you?"

Apparently it hadn't. The mind of the censor is a weird and incomprehensible thing.

I have written a number of parodies to Gilbert & Sullivan tunes (I am a G & S devotee), but the one I think is by far my best is a parody I wrote of the song "If You're Anxious for to Shine" from *Patience*. I kept the exact rhythm of the original and put in all the necessary internal rhymes—which is the mark of a good parody.

To understand the poem, you must first know that I have written a series of *Foundation* stories, which some of you may have read (millions have) and which, to my own never-ending astonishment, made me rich and famous. The stories, which I began writing when I was twenty-one, were inspired by Edward Gibbon's *The Decline and Fall of the Roman Empire*. I wrote about the decline and fall of the Galactic Empire and of the invented science of psychohistory, which could be used to predict the future.

• **37**

If you're anxious for to shine in the science fiction line
as a pro of luster bright,
I say, practice up the lingo of the sciences, by jingo,
never mind if not quite right.

43

You must talk of space and galaxies, and tesseractic fallacies
        in slick and mystic style,
Though the fans won't understand it, they will all the same
        demand it with a softly hopeful smile.

        And all the fans will say,
        as you walk your spatial way,
If that young man indulges in flights through all the Galaxy,
Why what a most imaginative type of man that type of man
        must be.

So success is not a mystery, just brush up on your history,
        and borrow day by day.
Take an Empire that was Roman and you'll find it is at home in
        all the starry Milky Way.
With a drive that's hyperspatial, through the parsecs you will
        race, you'll find that plotting is a breeze.
With a tiny bit of cribbin' from the works of Edward Gibbon
        and that Greek, Thucydides.

        And all the fans will say,
        as you walk your thoughtful way,
If that young man involves himself in authentic history,
Why what a very learned kind of high IQ, his high IQ must be.

Then eschew all thoughts of passion of a man-and-woman fashion
        from your hero's thoughtful mind.
He must spend his time on politics, and thinking up his shady
        tricks, and outside that he's blind.
It's enough he's had a mother, other females are a bother,
        though they're jeweled and glistery.
They will just distract his dreaming and his necessary scheming
        with that psychohistory.

        And all the fans will say,
        as you walk your narrow way,
If all his tales restrict themselves to masculinity,
Why, what a most particularly pure young man that pure young
        man must be.

Occasionally, I write a poem without having a song in my mind. I am not then constrained in scansion and rhyme and can do as I please. The most successful example of this sort was written in 1957, when two hard blows struck me at the same time.

In the first place, I was having a terrible fight with my superiors at the medical school where I was teaching biochemistry, and it looked as though I would be fired. (I eventually was, but it did me no harm. It would do me a lot of good, in fact, for it made a full-time writer out of me—but I didn't know this at the time I was fighting.)

In the second place, Doubleday had just rejected a book of mine—the only book of mine they ever rejected. (I sold it afterward elsewhere and it did reasonably well. Doubleday was sorry, and it served them right.)

As I was drowning in despair over these two blows, it occurred to me that the only thing to do was to write a terribly funny poem. I locked the door of my office and got to work and here it is, the title being "I Just Make Them Up, See!"

•38

Oh, Dr. A—
Oh, Dr. A—
There is something (don't go 'way)
That I'd like to hear you say.
Though I'd rather die
Than try
To pry,
The fact, you'll find
Is that my mind
Has evolved the jackpot question for today.

I intend no cheap derision,
So please answer with decision,

45

And, discarding all your petty cautious fears,
Tell the secret of your vision!
How on earth
Do you give birth
To those crazy and impossible ideas?

Is it indigestion
And a question
Of the nightmare that results?
Of your eyeballs
Whirling,
Twirling,
Fingers curling
And unfurling
While your blood beats maddened chimes
As it keeps impassioned times
With your thick, uneven pulse?
Is it that, you think, or liquor
That brings on the wildness quicker?
For a teeny
Weeny
Dry martini
May be just your private genie;
Or perhaps those Tom and Jerries
You will find the very
Berries
For inducing
And unloosing
That weird gimmick or that kicker;
Or an awful
Combination
Of unlawful
Stimulation
Marijuana plus tequila
That will give you just that feel o'
Things a-clicking
And unsticking
As you start your cerebration

To the crazy syncopation
Of a brain a-tocking ticking.

Surely something, Dr. A
Makes you fey
And quite outré.

Since I read you with devotion
Won't you give me just a notion
Of that shrewdly pepped-up potion
Out of which emerge your plots?
That wild secret bubbly mixture
That has made you such a fixture
In most favored s.f. spots—

Now, Dr. A.
Don't go 'way
Oh, Dr. A—
Oh, Dr. A—

In addition to the Dutch Treat, which is a weekly luncheon meeting, I also belong to the Trap-Door Spiders, which is amonthly dinner meeting. (I have used the Trap-Door Spiders as a model for my series of short mysteries which I call the-*Black Widower* stories.) Recently, at one of our TDS meetings, one of the group, Charles King, said:

•39

There's an Arab saying that goes, "If you meet a blind man, kick him. Why should you be kinder than God?"

The reaction of the group was most peculiar. All of us started to laugh, assuming, rather automatically, that it was funny. The laughter all choked off, though, as it suddenly occurred to us that if it was humor, it was humor of the darkest, darkest kind.

One of the features of every TDS meeting is that I suddenly call out, "Joke of the Month."

Instantly a dead silence falls around the table, and I tell my joke and there follows, inevitably, a great deal of laughter.

My lawyer, Robert Zicklin, who's a TDS-er, said to me, "After we've laughed so much, I go home and try to tell the joke as you tell it, and it falls flat. No one laughs. I just can't do the Yiddish accent."

So I said, "Well, I'll tell you one without a Yiddish accent so that you can repeat it."

•40

Five vagrants were picked up and were standing before the judge. They insisted they were not vagrants, but were merely unemployed at the moment. The judge, obviously disbelieving, said to the first alleged vagrant, "What do you do when you're working?"

Said the first vagrant, "I'm a cork soaker, Your Honor."

"A what?" said the judge, a little scandalized.

"I work for a bottling concern and I'm in charge of seeing that the corks are properly soaked so they will fit tightly in the bottle."

The judge passed his hand over his face and, turning to the second, said, "And what do you do?"

"I'm a cook seeker, Your Honor. I work at an employment agency and my specialty is finding cooks for those who want them."

"And you?" said the judge, addressing the third.

"I'm a coke sacker, Your Honor," he said. "I put lumps of coke into sacks."

The judge, very red in the face, turned to the fourth, who said, "I'm a sock tucker, Your Honor. I put tucks in socks before they're put into the boxes."

Moaning softly to himself, the judge turned to the fifth and said, "And what do you do?"

And the fifth said proudly, "Your Honor, I'm the real thing."

The Trap-Door Spiders laughed very hard at this and one of them said it was the best joke he had ever heard. However, they complained that they still couldn't repeat the joke because it was too complicated. They would never remember the four jobs that were not the real thing.

I offered to write it down for them, but that did not satisfy them. They said they would lose the paper. So I told them a joke without an accent and without complications, one that made vicious fun of writers:

•41

Jim Anderson was a writer who was on the edge of disaster. He had written nothing in years that was any good and he had become an alcoholic. His apartment had nothing in it but a typewriter, a table on which it rested, a chair, and, in a second room, a bed.

One night, as he lay on his bed in an alcoholic daze and was thinking he would have to hock his typewriter, he heard a steady tap-tapping from the other room, as though someone were using his typewriter. He was too far gone in his stupor to check—so he fell asleep.

The next morning he found, next to his typewriter, a beautifully typed movie script. He looked over it curiously and was galvanized by its extraordinary quality. It was much better than anything he could ever have written. He brought it to his agent, who, with the greatest reluctance, consented to glance at it. The agent was caught up at once.

"Jim," he said, "this is great. I don't know how you did it, but I'm sure I can sell it."

And sell it he did—for a large sum.

Thereafter, Anderson periodically heard the tap-tapping of the typewriter, periodically found another great script, periodically sold it for increasing sums of money. He grew rich and famous and lived in a wonderful mansion on the coast with everything his heart could possibly desire. In his new quarters, scripts continued to be turned out by his mysterious benefactor.

But by now his curiosity overwhelmed him. Who was writing these scripts for him?

One night when he heard the tap-tapping, he sneaked into his study, and there at the typewriter was an elf in the usual pointed hat.

Said Anderson, "Have you been writing these scripts?"

"That I have," said the elf.

"But why?" asked Anderson.

"Because I love to," said the elf.

Anderson said, "Do you realize what you have done for me? I was on the point of suicide and you have made me rich and famous and happy and I'll soon be married to the most wonderful woman in the world. Is there nothing I can do for you in exchange?"

"It's not necessary," said the elf. "I'm happy, too."

"But let me give you something: a house, special food, anything your heart desires. Anything. Anything."

"In that case," said the elf, "there *is* something. Can you put my name down as co-author to one of these scripts?"

And Anderson said, "Co-author! Fuck you!"

That satisfied the TDS-ers, though I don't know if any of them got any laughs out of telling the joke.

I must explain about the final two words, by the way. In accordance with my principles, I tried ending the joke with "Screw you" or "Go to hell" and all I got for my trouble was a greatly enfeebled laugh. Somehow, the proper attitude for the ungrateful writer is "Fuck you" and nothing else will do. So:

•42

A personal event took place that reminded me of Joke #41. I detest Hollywood and stay clear of it just as much as possible. However, when a very nice fellow who happened to be a Hollywood producer asked me to write up an idea for a new television series, I felt obliged to do so, after having warned him I would do no writing for it.

I did write a "treatment" and, in the end, a television program about a scientific detective, called *Probe,* appeared. It was delightful and I was very proud of it. Unfortunately, it only lasted six or seven episodes before being killed by a long-drawn-out writer's strike (in which, of course, I was not involved.)

The person who did write the scripts used my treatment as a starting point, but moved in his own direction with what I thought were brilliant results. The writer asked to have his name listed as co-originator of the program along with me, and the producer was willing. No one consulted me.

The first I learned of it was through a call from the Writer's Guild (or some association like that) which informed me of this use of two names as originator, and which offered to fight the matter out for me, since the contract stipulated that I was to be emblazoned on the screen as the sole originator.

Since I have no TV ambitions and since, in any case, I have a horror of being given credit that is not mine, I said carelessly, "That's all right. Let this other guy have his name on the screen along with mine."

There followed an extraordinary few minutes as the outraged people of the guild (or whatever) objected to my giving in like that. They wanted to fight it out and they clearly thought that I, like Jim Anderson, ought to prevent the possibility of co-authorship at any cost and regardless of the rights of the case.

But I simply and staunchly refused, and the writer's name appeared under mine on the TV screen.

Let me return to comic verse. The best known variety of comic verse, as far as the general public is concerned, is the limerick. It is a five-line poem with a rhyme scheme of *a, a, b, b, a,* and with the number of feet in each line equal to 3, 3, 2, 2, and 3.

I have amused myself now and then, in the course of my life, by writing limericks, but only now and then. In 1974, however, I was cruising with my dear wife, Janet, on the *Queen Elizabeth 2,* where I was slated to give talks. I was placed in the posh Queen's Grill for my meals and there I felt enormously out of place.

As I sat there, however, I could not resist startling the stuffed shirts who were eating there with a limerick. I had made one up while staring through a porthole at the gleaming sea and I recited it in an ordinary speaking voice one line at a time. Each line drew more effective attention, and when I squeezed out the last line, there was considerable laughter.

Well, if I could make *those* people laugh, I suddenly saw a future in limericks; maybe not in money, but certainly in fun. I proceeded to write others and before I got over the mood, I had written about 650 limericks, which were published in seven books—two of them clean.

The limerick with which I had delighted the stuffed shirts is this:

43

> There was a young lass from Decatur
> Who went off to sea on a freighter.
> > She was screwed by the master,
> > An utter disaster,
> But the crew all made up for it later.

As is well known, limericks are at their best when they are "dirty." However, as in all such things, discretion must rule the day. Many people, allured by the thought of writing a dirty limerick, write something that is dirty and nothing more; that is merely disgusting.

There's no value in that whatever. A limerick should be bawdy, yes, but my own rule in constructing limericks is simply this: A limerick should be wittier than it is bawdy.

I think that #43 illustrates this rule and that so do all the other limericks I have constructed (although it is always possible that in individual cases my judgment may be faulty.)

I won't try to give you all 650 of my limericks, but I shall give you what I consider the fifty or so best of them (in my opinion), scattering them through the book.

•44

> A certain hardworking young hooker
> Was such an enchanting good-looker,
> > There were fights 'mongst the fuzz
> > Over whose turn it was
> To pinch 'er and frisk 'er and book 'er.

•45

All was well with the Dowager Duchess
When trapped in the mad rapist's clutches.
          Till he turned on the light,
          Took one look, said, "Good night,"
So she hit him with one of her crutches.

•46

There was a young woman from Riga
With morals depressingly meager.
          She's seduced once a week
          By a lecherous Greek
If *seduced* is the word when she's eager.

I know a young woman whose last name rhymed with Riga. I recited the limerick to her, substituting her last name as the final word in the first line. She listened carefully, and did not laugh. Instead, she sighed and said, "I wish!"

•47

A young violinist named Biddle
Played exceedingly well on the fiddle.
          Yet 'twixt women and art
          'Twas the girls won his heart,
Hands down—and hands up—and hands middle.

•48

Said a woman with open delight,
"My pubic hair's perfectly white.
          I admit there's a glare,
          But the fellows don't care.
They locate it more quickly at night."

•49

> There was a young woman named Melanie
> Who was asked by a man, "Do you sell any?"
> > She replied, "No, siree,
> > I give it for free.
> To sell it, dear sir, is a felony."

Actually, I suspect that prostitution is a misdemeanor, but that doesn't rhyme.

•50

> There was an old Scotsman of Fife,
> Who had felt, in the course of his life,
> > Scores of well-rounded ends
> > Of the wives of his friends,
> And likewise of the friends of his wife.

•51

> At a bullfight, José made his bid.
> When his girlfriend agreed, he was rid
> > Of all inhibitions,
> > And despite the conditions,
> As the crowd yelled "Olé!" José did.

•52

> There was a young lady named Bates
> Who amused every one of her dates
> > By keeping one breast
> > In total arrest
> While the other described figure eights.

In connection with this limerick, I wrote that if it were recited, with earnest gestures, to a well-endowed young woman, then when you reached the part about keeping one breast in total arrest, you might try holding one of her breasts lightly, as though making sure it doesn't move—while your other hand describes figure eights in the air with the last line. Ideally, the young woman, thinking it is part of the limerick, would make no move to interfere.

I was joking when I said this, of course, but eventually I received a letter from a young man who quoted my advice and then added ecstatically, "It works! It works!"

•53

> There was a young woman named Vicki
> Who said, "I don't want to be picky.
> > If, in five hours or so,
> > As you say, you must go,
> At least we'll have time for a quickie."

Once my books on limericks began to appear, I gained a reputation as an expert in the field and people began to ask me to serve as a judge in limerick contests. These invitations I evaded assiduously, for I was in no mood to read thousands of awful efforts. However, the University of Connecticut trapped me into serving by swearing they would weed them out and send me only a few relatively bearable ones.

I agreed and it was a dreadful chore anyway. I did, however, come across an absolute gem by an elderly gentleman at Yale named Vail (since deceased) and I gave it the first prize at once.

•54

> The bustard's an elegant fowl
> With minimum reason to howl.
> > He escapes what would be
> > Illegitimacy
> By grace of a fortunate vowel.

I also listed a number of honorable mentions and, as it turned out, they were all by men. In writing to the person who was running the contest, I said casually that women seemed to produce limericks that were dirtier than those that men produced but less witty, and that I had to go for witty.

Time magazine reported on the contest and somehow managed to quote my letter about women and limericks. You can guess what happened. I got a blizzard of denunciations from women and I had to send in a limerick of apology to be printed in *Time*.

Here, though, is an interesting phenomenon. The myriad of letters I received all complained bitterly about my remark that women were less witty than men. Not one letter—not one—not one—objected to my having said they were dirtier than men.

There are some raconteurs who are so proud of the extensiveness of their repertoires and of their capacity for instant recall that they are willing to have someone in the audience call out a subject and they will tell an appropriate story at once. I have never quite had the nerve to do that, but if anyone ever shouted out "chastity belt" to me, the following is the story they would get:

•55

The Sieur de Tourneville had decided to go off crusading in order to fulfill a vow he had carelessly made, and this meant infinite preparations. Not the least of the problems was the matter of his fair lady, who was as true and as faithful to him as the day was long—provided he was around. If he were to depart and be gone for months or even years, who could tell in what fashion she might disport herself.

He therefore had her carefully fitted with a chastity belt, which made illegal sexual penetration impossible. Being a kindly man, however, who realized that it might sometimes be necessary for the sake of hygiene or other emergency to remove the belt temporarily, he decided to have the key to the chastity belt available.

This meant he would have to entrust it to a reliable person, and the obvious choice was his retainer, Rinaldo, who had proven himself true and faithful in many a fight with neighboring barons and in many a difficulty with serfs and vassals.

"Rinaldo," said the Sieur de Tourneville, "guard this with your life."

"I shall, my liege," said Rinaldo.

Off went the crusading party, but they had not progressed more than two miles when the sound of a galloping horse behind them was heard. The column halted and in among them raced Rinaldo.

"My liege," said the faithful Rinaldo. "You gave me the wrong key. It doesn't fit."

Talking about crusades reminds me of a cartoon I saw at the beginning of the Salman Rushdie affair. Rushdie, a Moslem, had written a book that seemed to insult Muhammad and Islam, and the Ayatollah Khomeini of Iran, then still alive, passed a death sentence on him. Rushdie had to go into hiding and will probably have to remain in hiding the rest of his life, since it would take only one fanatic to kill him. Naturally, the world, generally, froze in horror at the possibility of death sentences being handed out in this casual manner for offenses that might be minor, or even nonexistent.

•56

The cartoon I refer to shows a line of crusaders on their horses heading eastward to fight in the Holy Land. The horseman in the lead is talking to another horseman on his left, and the caption reads:

"I hope this won't offend the Muslims."

The trouble with Joke #56 is that it is topical. It is tied to a news event and such jokes grow quickly stale. Already the Rushdie affair is a thing of the past, and people are notorious for the shortness of their memories.

I remember when President Ford issued a pardon to Nixon

for his criminal actions. Ford's press secretary resigned, out of principle, because of his disapproval of the act. This astonished the American people, for officeholders never resign out of principle. This is not because they have *no* principles, but because they have one overriding principle, that of holding on to their jobs no matter what.

In any case, the press secretary was instantly in demand as a speaker, and he commanded high fees. I said to my lecture agent, regretfully, "Gee, Harry, he's getting higher fees than I get."

"Don't worry, Isaac," said the agent. "In six months, no one will know who he is, and you will keep right on going."

He was perfectly correct.

But wait, would you believe it is also possible to have a chastity belt joke set in contemporary times?

•57

Moskowitz entered the office of his partner, Finkelstein, just as the latter was carefully placing a little gold key in his private safe.

"What's this?" demanded Moskowitz, all curiosity. "What is that key?"

Finkelstein blushed. "Moskowitz," he said, "it's embarrassing to explain, but between partners there should be no secrets. This is the key to my wife's chastity belt."

Moskowitz was thunderstruck. "Finkelstein," he exclaimed. "Your wife wears a chastity belt?"

"Of my own design."

"But Finkelstein, with all due respect, why does your wife need a chastity belt? She's a fine woman and a good, loyal wife, but—how can I say it?—with her· looks, may good luck befall her, she doesn't need a chastity belt."

"I know. I know. With her looks, do you think *I* enjoy making love to her? So this way when I come home and she says, 'Tonight, darling, how about it?' I can always answer, 'I'm so sorry, darling, but I left the key at the office.'"

In the world of jokedom, it happens often that husbands are married to ugly wives at whom they shudder. The jokes don't usually say why the marriage took place to begin with. Did the man marry her for her money, or while blind drunk, or under the threat of a shotgun blast? We never find out.

Now, my dear wife, Janet, considers herself plain and, every once in a while, feels sad about that. To me, however, she is the most beautiful woman in the world, and my heart invariably leaps up when I see her unexpectedly, and she *knows* this. That means I can tell plain-wife jokes without hurting her feelings.

When we're in bed together, one of my innocent occupations is to pinch her rump, which she occasionally objects to when it is interfering with her desire to sleep. That gave me an idea.

•58

Janet [I said] I have thought up a brand-new frustrated-wish idea that no one has ever used.

A man with a very plain wife is offered one wish by a genie. The man wishes that he might be granted a different beautiful young woman to grace his bed each night. The wish is granted, provided that he never touches the woman's backside. If he does, she turns instantly into his wife.

Each night the man begins to make love to a beautiful woman. No way can he prevent himself from stroking her beautiful rear and so, each night, he finds himself making love to his wife.

I laughed heartily at this, but Janet said, "You have a sick mind, Isaac."

Here's another reluctant-husband joke.

•59

Over the dinner table, Mrs. Moskowitz said to her spouse, "You know how nervous and tense I've been lately, Jake? Well, I went to see a doctor."

"Yes?" murmured Moskowitz, never lifting his eyes from the soup he was eating. "And what did the doctor say, Becky?"

"He examined me thoroughly, Jake, and said that, physically, I was in fine shape. He said all I needed was some sex."

Moskowitz's attention was now caught. "Is that so?" he said. "And how often did he say you needed sex?"

"He suggested maybe eight times a week, Jake."

"Fine," said Moskowitz. "Put me down for two."

There are many stories of old men and their sexual prowess. Such jokes are always popular because I think that the people who tell them and those who hear them rather long to be reassured that their sexual abilities will continue into old age.

However, I have made a great discovery as I stumbled into old age. Here it is: As sexual powers decline, so does sexual desire, so that one is not left desolate and inconsolable. There's a story about Sophocles, the great Greek tragedian of the fifth century B.C.:

•60

In his extreme old age, Sophocles' children tried to gain control of the old man's property, on the grounds that he was no longer capable of making decisions.

Old Sophocles got up in court and read from the play he was writing at the time, *Oedipus in Colonus*. So clear was it that Sophocles' mind was in great shape that he was left in charge of his own affairs.

•61

On the other hand, Sophocles, as an old man, was asked if he regretted the loss of his sexual prowess.

"Not I," he responed. "Say rather that I feel grateful at having been released from a stern and relentless taskmaster."

But back to elderly Lotharios:

•62

Said old man Caruthers, "I have this young woman whom I screw every night even if I *am* ninety years old."

Said a listener incredulously, "Every single night?"

"Well, every night but Thursday."

"Why not Thursday?"

"That's my valet's day off."

"What has that to do with it?"

"He lifts me onto the woman and, later, lifts me off."

That reminds me of a true story, absolutely true, which I will now give to you:

•63

A few years ago, I was in Boston getting some sort of award or other, and also present and also getting an award was a distinguished scientist who was ninety-four years old. He was a lovely, good-humored old man with a mind as sharp as a well-honed knife. Janet and I were much taken with him, and we fell into conversation.

"Every month," he said, "I fly to Vienna, where I maintain another home."

This flabbergasted me. I don't travel. I won't even cross the Hudson River if I can avoid it. And here was a nonagenarian who crossed the Atlantic every month.

I said, "Who takes care of your home in Vienna?"

"Oh," said the old man, "I have a woman there who takes care of it and who takes care of me."

I was more impressed than ever. "And your home here in the United States—is there a woman who takes care of it and you here, also?"

"Oh, no," said the old man with a twinkle in his eye. "With two women, there's bound to be trouble."

My internist is Paul Esserman. His favorite joke (at least, he's told it to me on five separate occasions and, of course, I never let on that I've heard it before) is the following one:

•64

Johnson, ninety years old, said, "I satisfy my wife every night."

"You do?" came the standard incredulous response.

"Yes, indeed. Every night as I get into bed, I say, 'Martha, tonight I would just like to sleep.' And every night she says, 'All right. I'm satisfied.'"

•65

Moskowitz visited the doctor in a state of dejection. "Doctor," he said, "I can only manage to have sex maybe once a week."

"How old are you, Mr. Moskowitz?" asked the doctor.

"I'm seventy-three."

"In that case, there's no reason to be disturbed. At seventy-three, once a week is not at all bad."

"But my neighbor, Finkelstein, tells me he has sex twice a week and he is eighty-one years old."

"In that case," said the doctor, "all you have to do is tell your neighbor that you have sex three times a week."

My favorite elderly Lothario joke is the following:

•66

Mr. and Mrs. Moskowitz were celebrating their golden wedding. The children and grandchildren were determined to make the occasion a huge celebration and no expense was spared. A tent was set up; a long table was placed for the more important descendants; separate tables were set up for collaterals; an orchestra would entertain on one side, an open bar on the other.

And while everyone was jubilating, one of the grandchildren was recounting with great exuberance his successful adventure with a young woman. The aged partriarch, sitting in state at the head of the table, heard this and frowned.

Finally he could stand no more. He pointed his finger and said, "You, you snot-nosed kid, don't go around talking so much about what a big sexpot you are. I may be seventy-eight myself, but last night I slipped it to your grandmother fifteen times."

At this, a deathly hush fell on everyone in the tent. Even the orchestra stopped playing, and the barman stood openmouthed as he interrupted his pouring of a drink.

The grandson who had in this way been assailed said falteringly, "Grandpa, you really slipped it to her fifteen times?"

"That's exactly right," said old Mr. Moskowitz staunchly.

The grandson turned to Mrs. Moskowitz, who was sitting at her husband's side with her arms folded calmly over her chest.

He said, "Grandma! Is Grandpa right? Fifteen times?"

"Absolutely," said Mrs. Moskowitz. "I counted it myself. He slipped it in, it fell out; he slipped it in, it fell out; he slipped it in—"

Incidentally, one can never be entirely safe telling a joke. I was at a picnic once at a summer resort and a sudden and brief squall of rain sent Janet and me scurrying under one of the large umbrellas set up to take care of such an emergency. Seeking shelter with us was another couple, about three years older than ourselves, a couple we knew well and dearly loved.

They seemed a little downcast at the rain, so I cheered them up with a few jokes and eventually told them Joke #66.

The results paralyzed me. The wife went into prolonged and absolute hysterics, while her husband frowned more and more deeply. It didn't take a genius to see that I had accidentally touched on a very tender point as far as they were concerned.

Nor was there anything I could do. I couldn't take back the joke. I could only stand there awkwardly and wait for the rain to stop.

The next morning, the wife went to a lot of trouble to hint to me that she and her husband had had a veritable sex orgy the preceding night. Of course, I pretended to believe her.

In the world of jokedom, various nations are considered to be different in sexual prowess. Great Britain lags behind and France races ahead. Thus:

•67

An Englishman, making love to his wife, said, "Did I hurt you just then, darling?"

"Why, no, dear," she said. "Why do you ask?

"You moved."

•68

Eamon de Valera, the leader of post–World War I Ireland, had made a trip to France. On returning, he was asked what he had learned as a result of the trip.

"I have learned," said de Valera, "that sex, in Ireland, is in its infancy."

•69

Madame Dupin had ended her struggle on earth and was being buried before a somber audience of her friends and loved ones. Monsieur Dupin was behaving with a becoming gravity, but Jacques, who had been Madame Dupin's lover, could not contain himself. Weeping and sobbing bitterly, he rocked back and forth in the agony of his loss.

Finally Dupin could stand it no longer. Walking quietly to Jacques and placing his arm about the other's shoulder, he whispered, "Jacques! Jacques! Control yourself. After all, I fully intend to marry again."

•70

Alphonse and Gaston, longtime friends, were walking jauntily down the boulevard together when Alphonse, turning pale, said, "*Mon dieu*, Gaston, coming toward us are my wife and my mistress, arm-in-arm."

"What an enormous coincidence," said Gaston. "I was about to say the same thing."

Although unhappy marriages are a major component of the world of jokedom, divorces are surprisingly few. Perhaps the feeling is that you don't want to break up an unhappy marriage and spoil the fun. Still, that doesn't mean that divorce jokes are nonexistent.

•71

The judge was ready to give his decision on the alimony case pending before him. Fixing Mr. Jones with a cold eye, he said, "I am giving Mrs. Jones twelve thousand dollars a year as alimony."

"That's very nice of you, Your Honor," said Jones, gratified. "And to show you I'm a sport, I will voluntarily give her two thousand a year myself."

•72

Old Mr. Anderson and his equally aged wife were filing for divorce. The judge, eying them with astonishment, said, "How old are you, Mr. Anderson?"

"Ninety-three, Your Honor."

"And your wife?"

"Ninety-one, Your Honor."

"And how long have you been married?"

"Sixty-six years."

"Then why do you want to get a divorce now?"

"Well, you know how it is, Your Honor. We were waiting for the children to die."

This is an example of what used to be called "black humor," but nowadays that means something else—the humor of black comedians. A possible substitute is "dark humor," the laugh you get out of something that is not really funny at all.

Joke #72 is a takeoff on all the times children wait for their parents to die before, let us say, breaking away from a religious affiliation or marrying a mate outside their own ethnic circle.

For myself, I detest all these nonsensical old customs that interfere with the freedom of life.

•73

When I was twenty-two, I was getting married and a neighbor stopped me in the street and said, "I understand you're getting married."

"Yes," I said.

"That's wrong. What about your sister?" (I have a sister who is two and a half years younger than myself.)

"What about my sister?"

"A young man should not get married until after his sister is safely married."

This was an Old World custom to which I reacted with great outrage.

"Do you mean to say," I said hotly, "that you expect me to remain a lifelong bachelor?"

I had, you see, a brother's confidence that no one could ever possibly want to marry a sister. As it happened, I was wrong. A few years later, my sister did marry a fine young man and their marriage (ended only by his natural death) was extremely happy. In fact, my sister's marriage was happier than mine (though my second marriage is happier than anyone's).

Maybe it's time to have a nouveau riche joke.

Some of us are rich because we are born into rich families (rich-rich). Most of us are poor because we are born into poor families (poor-poor). A few of us are born into rich families who through various viscissitudes become poor (rich-poor), or are born into poor families who (like myself) become rich (poor-rich), either through hard work, good luck, or (as in my own case) both.

It is only natural that we don't very much dislike the rich-rich or the poor-poor; they're in the place where they were put. We're sorry for the rich-poor, but very often we bitterly resent the poor-rich, especially if they are ostentatious about it. The resentment takes the form of jokes in which we deride them for having all the financial appurtenances of wealth while lacking the necessary manners.

•74

Mr. Goldberg, having succeeded in business, bought a spacious house in the suburbs and was not reluctant to show it to his old friends who were still sweating away in the garment district.

Mr. Finkelstein visited him and was openmouthed at the rooms, the furnishings, the swimming pool, the latest electronic devices.

Mr. Goldberg said to him, "After a lifetime in the slums and the city with the noise and the dirt, it is such a pleasure, Finkelstein, to be here in the country, with the flowers, and trees, and birds, and fresh air. But the best thing of all is, whenever I am tired, I can just lie down on the veranda. To lie on the veranda is the best thing in the world. Such pleasure. Such delight." Here, Goldberg put his hands together and said, "Oh, my beautiful veranda."

Back at home, Finkelstein reported on what he had seen to his wife. "What's more," said Finkelstein when he had finished his glowing description, "I think something has happened to Goldberg's marriage."

"What happened? Something wrong with Sadie?" asked Mrs. Finkelstein.

"I never saw Sadie. She never showed up. I think maybe Goldberg got rid of her and now has a gentile woman named Veranda."

•75

Mr. Goldberg, having grown rich in the garment district and bought a house in the suburbs, as already described, was now prepared to throw open the mansion to all his friends and confreres at once.

He intended to throw a party which, for sheer luxury and ostentation, would put in the shade the worst excesses of Rome. He was therefore filled with chagrin when, at the last moment, with incredible display at every hand, it turned out that not one of the eight bathrooms had a single sheet of toilet paper.

Goldberg, however, was known for his ingenuity. The stores might be closed and the humiliation of asking the neighbors was unthinkable, but as it happened, in the attic he had stored a supply of dress patterns that he had intended to keep as a reminder of the happy old days when he was known as the Wolf of Thirty-Fourth Street.

Without hesitation, he sacrificed them, had them cut into squares, heaped them into tasteful stacks, and distributed them to the various bathrooms.

The party, as it happened, went swimmingly, and to Goldberg's friends, one and all, the proceedings could scarcely be distinguished from a hashish dream. Finally, in the small hours, when the party was dispersing, Mr. Abramowitz, one of the guests, said to his wife, "What a party! Elegant and refined to the last detail!"

"Elegant and refined!" said Mrs. Abramowitz. "You know nothing about elegant and refined! Let me tell you. In the lady's bathroom, the very sheets of toilet paper were labeled 'front' and 'back.'"

•76

A rich-poor case is that of Mrs. Magnolia Culpeper, who had lived a life of luxury while young, but whom financial disasters had reduced to absolute penury.

Eventually there was no other way out than to invest in a supply of shoelaces and stand on the corner and sell them. Naturally, Mrs. Culpeper shrank from this, since what would her friends say if they saw her in so menial a guise?

She stood on the corner, therefore, whispering, "Shoelaces for sale. Shoelaces for sale. Oh, I hope no one hears me."

The ideal jokester should know every aspect of life, so that he can tell jokes of all kinds with ease, while getting across an aura of competence and knowledge. Naturally, such an ideal does not exist and certainly I do not exemplify it.

For instance, I am not an outdoors man. I have never gone camping, hunting, or fishing. If I tell a joke that involves activities of that sort, I have to fake it, as with Moishe Ginsberg selling fishing equipment at Abercombie and Fitch.

So here is a hunting story:

•77

Anderson was worn out with business cares and his friend, Mitchell, was ready with his advice. "Anderson," he said, "go on a vacation."

"Where?" groaned Anderson. "I can't stand those resorts: crowded, noisy, everyone playing volleyball."

"Not that," said Mitchell earnestly. "Get off to the north woods. Kill a moose."

"Kill a moose? I wouldn't know how!"

"What is there to know, Anderson? You go to Abercrombie and Fitch and they will outfit you. They will give you a nice red jacket so other hunters won't shoot you, and a nice hat to keep your ears warm, and a canoe to paddle on the streams, and a compass to keep you from getting lost, and a rifle with a trigger and a supply of bullets, together with instructions on how to shoot. Most of all, they will sell you a moose horn."

"A what?"

"A moose horn. When you are out in the woods and you see a male moose in the distance, one with antlers, you blow on the horn. It makes a sound like a female moose and that male moose comes running and bellowing and snorting. Then you shoot him and you will never have had such relaxation in your life. The only thing is, be careful about the kind of moose horn you get."

"What kind should I get?"

"Get a Model-A Klaxon Wailer, no other kind. The Model-A Klaxon Wailer makes a sound so beautiful and feminine, from the moose's standpoint, that a male moose goes wild, completely out of his mind."

"Well," said Anderson, "maybe you're right. I'll do it."

A month later, the two friends met again. Anderson's leg was in a cast and he was heavily bandaged. Mitchell was shocked.

"Anderson," he said, "how do you come to be in this condition?"

"Moose hunting," said Anderson, aggrieved. "It's all your fault. I got outfitted, all the equipment, including a Model-A Klaxon Wailer moose horn."

"So what happened?"

"I'll tell you. The moose came running like a completely insane animal and I got excited and dropped my rifle. And when I bent down to pick it up, the moose got to me and I was laid."

Animals aren't the only things that are hunted. A fellow faculty member at Boston University Medical School, William C. Boyd (dead now, alas), had a primitive house deep in New Hampshire. While there, every summer, as he told me, he would go foraging for mushrooms. He described the delightful taste of mushrooms that you could not get at the supermarket and pointed out that the common mushroom was the least tasty.

He made my mouth water with his tales, but I am a cautious fellow. "Bill," I said, "I'd be afraid. As you well know, some mushrooms are deadly poisonous."

Bill therefore told me two things about mushroom hunting.

•78

Naturally, in searching out new varieties of edible mushrooms, you had best be an expert on the exact appearance of those that are poisonous. There's the story of the mushroom fancier who occasionally gathered a mess of mushrooms concerning which he was uncertain. The story is that he fed one to the dog and waited. If the dog showed no ill effect, he fed one to his wife and waited. If she showed no ill effect, he ate the rest.

•79

Bill also said, "There are old mushroom eaters and there are bold mushroom eaters, but there are no old, bold mushroom eaters."

Time for more limericks:

•80

There was an old maid of Peru
Who swore that she never would screw
      Except under stress
      Of forceful duress,
Like, "I'm ready, dear, how about you?"

I get the best results with this one by reciting the first four lines grimly and heavily, and then become suddenly bouncy with the fifth.

•81

There was a young couple from Florida
Whose passion grew steadily torrider.
>   They were planning to sin
>   In a room in an inn.
Who can wait? So they screwed in the corridor.

•82

There was a young girl named Lorraine
Whom no one could think of as plain.
>   The fellows pursue her
>   In order to screw her
Again and again and again.

I once made the mistake of reciting this limerick to a young lady named Lorraine. She enjoyed it, but her father, also present, did not. I should have known better.

•83

There once was an odious brute
Who made love in his Sunday-best suit.
>   The result, as you'd guess,
>   Was a wet, sticky mess,
And a very chafed maiden, to boot.

•84

There was an effete, lazy fop
Who preferred all his women on top.
>   He said, "I'm no jerk,

Let them do the work.
But if I get pregnant, I'll stop."

●85

There is a young woman named Connie,
Intelligent, gentle, and bonny.
        Were she willing to screw,
        Men would yell, "Whoop-te-do,
Hallelujah, and hey nonny-nonny."

●86

There was a young woman named Bunny.
Whose husband found life quite unfunny.
        He said, with a pout,
        "Why don't you put out?"
And she answered, "I do it for money."

●87

There was a young woman named Nancy,
Delightful and sweet and romancy.
        But your hopes are in vain
        If you want your sex plain
For her style of performance is fancy.

●88

There was a young fellow named Keith,
Who liked to be fondled beneath.
        It was fun, he decided,
        But only provided
The girl used her lips, not her teeth.

The *New York Times* once asked me for a limerick appropriate
for the Iranian crisis, when the Iranians were holding our
diplomatic corps as hostage in President Carter's time. I

promptly wrote one, but the *Times* refused to publish it on the grounds that it might start an international incident. So I published it elsewhere and here it is:

•89

There was a young woman named Janie
Whom no one could think of as brainy.
    In her search for a man
    She went out to Iran
To wed Ayatollah Khomeini.

I entitled this limerick "Scraping the Bottom of the Barrel," which, I presume, made it even less acceptable as far as the *Times* was concerned.

•90

Janet and I were in Washington once, where I was slated to give a talk, and the fellow in charge of me drove me around to show me the sights. "There," he said, "is the Washington Monument, an obelisk designed as a memorial to George. It is five hundred and fifty-five feet high."

Then he said slyly, "They're thinking of a memorial for Martha, too."

"Oh?" I said. "What kind?"

"They're planning to dig a hole five hundred and fifty-five feet deep."

•91

Actually, that visit to Washington was the occasion of something I found very funny. I had been asked to speak at the celebration of the twenty-fifth anniversary of Montgomery Community College and the only place big enough to hold the attending crowds was the Washington Cathedral. What's more, I stood in the high pulpit to give the talk. (Janet told me afterward that it was the only talk she ever heard me give in which my grammar and sentence structure were perfect, as though I were writing rather than speaking informally. I told her that, under the circumstances, I presumed God took a personal interest.)

Now, as it happens, one of the members of the Trap-Door Spiders is Roper Shamhart, an Episcopalian priest, and he was, at one of our meetings, speaking of the Washington cathedral, which, I gathered, is the Vatican of American Episcopalianism.

After a while, I asked him innocently, "Have you ever preached from the high pulpit of the Washington Cathedral?"

"Of course not," he said. (Clearly, he was far too humble a member of the hierarchy to achieve such a distinction.)

"Really?" said I. "I did."

I let it go at that, of course, and returned to my meal, eating quietly and pretending I didn't notice that Roper was swelling dangerously. Then, when I felt that at any moment he might seize me by the throat and attempt to choke me to death, I explained, and, very slowly, he relaxed.

My dear wife, Janet, is a psychiatrist and a psychoanalyst by profession (though she is now retired) and, early in our relationship, she made it clear that she looked upon psychiatrist jokes with a jaundiced eye. To put it as briefly as possible, I'm not allowed to tell them. However, I don't suppose even Janet will object to the following very harmless joke:

•92

One psychiatrist met another and greeted him with, "You're fine; how am I?"

I am frequently asked if I have visited Israel. Worse yet, it is simply assumed that I have.

Well, I don't travel; I really don't. And if I did, I probably wouldn't visit Israel. I remember how it was in 1948, when

Israel was being established and all my Jewish friends were ecstatic. I was not.

I said, "What are we doing? We are establishing ourselves in a ghetto, in a small corner of a vast Muslim sea. The Muslims will never forget nor forgive, and Israel, as long as it exists, will be embattled."

I was laughed at, but I was right.

I can't help but feel that the Jews didn't really have the right to appropriate a territory only because two thousand years ago people they considered their ancestors were living there. History moves on and you can't really turn it back.

In any case—an Israeli joke:

•93

In the exciting days of 1961, when President Kennedy was sworn into office and a thrill of hope ran through the nation, Moskowitz was trying to express the nature of the hope to a visitor from Israel.

"Aaron," he was saying, "here in the United States, we are beginning a new pathway. For the first time in our history, we have elected a Catholic as president. We are breaking through the shackles of bigotry. We will see a rebirth of idealism. I wouldn't be surprised, Aaron, if, in twenty years, for instance, we would find a Jew will become president of the United States."

Aaron shrugged and said, "Listen, Moskowitz, in Israel we have had a Jewish president now for thirteen years and, let me tell you, it doesn't help."

Actually, since Kennedy's time, we have had six presidents, every one of them a Protestant, and every one of them tracing back his ancestry to the British Isles.

Incidentally, an "Irish bull" is any statement that is self-contradictory, without the knowledge of the person making the statement. It is called "Irish" because the English considered the Irish a mass of dull peasantry who would be given to such statements. In actual fact, "bulls" are produced by people of every kind and here are examples of "Jewish bulls."

•94

An American was boasting to an Israeli of the great achievement of placing a man on the moon in 1969.

The Israeli listened with scarcely concealed impatience and finally said, "Actually, the American feat was not very much. We in Israel are preparing something much more spectacular. We intend to land an astronaut on the sun."

"On the sun," exploded the American. "Are you crazy? Do you understand the heat—the radiation—"

"Don't be a fool," said the Israeli contemptuously. "We know what we're doing. We're going at night."

•95

Finkelstein took the news that he had inoperable cancer, and might expect to live only six months, with heroic stoicism. Uttering not one word of complaint, he carefully settled his worldly affairs and made provision for the security of his family and the continuation of his business. His friends were unanimously lost in admiration of him, none more so than Moskowitz.

Imagine, then, Moskowitz's puzzlement when one day he came upon Finkelstein emerging from St. Patrick's Cathedral.

"Finkelstein," he said, astonished. "What were you doing in there?"

Calmly, Finkelstein said, "I'm taking instruction because I'm turning Catholic."

"Catholic!" said Moskowitz, eyes wide with stunned disbelief. "But how is that possible? All your life you have been the most pious Jew I ever knew. Nothing was dearer to your heart than the precepts of the Law. Every Sabbath you were in the synagogue and always you were devoted to the study of the holy books. And now, with death so close—"

"Exactly," interrupted Finkelstein. "Soon I will die and I figured—better one of them than one of us."

As a public speaker, I am at the edge of show business and I appreciate the insecurity of the actor's life (which is like the insecurity of a writer's life). Reward attends only success, and no amount of success guarantees continuing success. Every day is a new struggle for recognition or even for a simple livelihood, and one is always at the mercy of an audience:

•96

The cross-examining attorney (severely): What is your occupation?
DEFENDANT: I am an actor.
ATTORNEY: To be precise, are you not a comedian?
DEFENDANT: Only when they laugh.

•97

Morris Fishbein, actor, came home one evening to find his bedroom in disarray and his wife, panting, with her clothes torn, on the bed.

He said in horror, "What happened?"

She gasped out, "Your agent was just here in a state of absolute madness. He tore off my clothes and raped me."

"My agent? Listen, did he say anything about the Paramount deal?"

Being a jokester and having a large repertoire on instant call sharpens the wits. At least, it gives me the ability to find a quick way of skewering someone in friendly conversation. (I emphasize the word *friendly*. These skewers should not be meant to hurt, merely to elicit laughter.)

There are a number of occasions in which I have crossed verbal swords with editors and fellow writers. They are all articulate enough to take care of themselves so that I am not picking on unarmed individuals, and all of them (or most of them, anyway) have enough of a sense of humor to take no offense. For that matter, I take no offense when the game goes against me.

It may seem to you, in the personal accounts I scatter

through this book, that I am mostly the person who wins out. Well, I mostly am. In addition to that, however, I find it particularly easy to remember passages in which I end on top. Why that is so I will leave to psychologists to puzzle out. Still, I'll start with one in which I lose:

•98

I was once visiting Horace Gold, then editor of *Galaxy* magazine. Horace is just about completely bald, something which, of course, is not his fault.

I happen to have a complete head of hair even at my present advanced age, but it has the disadvantage of frequently needing to be combed. So I stood in front of his mirror and combed away.

And after a while, Horace said to me mildly, "Look, Isaac, do I stand in front of you and flex my muscles?"

Horace had the peculiar habit of rejecting stories with inordinate scorn. Writers are sensitive souls and any rejection hurts them badly. In order not to hurt them past recovery, editors usually lie a lot and tell them how nearly good the story was and how almost suitable for publication the editor found it.

Not Horace. If he didn't like a story, he pulled out all stops and knew no moderation. In fact, I wrote a bit of comic verse about him one time describing the sort of rejections he handed me. Here it is:

•99

Dear Ike, I was prepared
(And, boy, I really cared)
      To swallow almost anything you wrote.
But Ike, you're just plain shot,
Your writing's gone to pot.
      There's nothing left but hack and mental bloat.

Take back this piece of junk;
It smelled; it reeked; it stunk;
          Just glancing through it once was deadly rough.
But Ike, boy, by and by,
Just try another try.
          I need some yarns and, kid, I love your stuff.

•100

Once, however, Horace went too far. He rejected a story of mine which he called "meretricious." The word is from the Latin *meretrix*, meaning "prostitute," so that the implication was that I was prostituting my talent and was writing a bad story that would get by on my name alone because I was too lazy to write a good one. (This was not true, by the way. This particular story was sold elsewhere and received considerable acclaim.)

Swallowing my annoyance, I said mildly, "What was that word you used?"

Obviously proud at knowing a word he felt I didn't know, Horace enunciated carefully, "Meretricious!"

Whereupon I said, "And a Happy New Year to you."

Horace went up in flames at that, and he and I broke off our friendship. It's the only time I ever actually lost a friend with a wiseguy remark, but I didn't care. No one has any right to call any story of mine meretricious. Even if one of my stories is bad, I've done the best I can.

Actually, Horace offended virtually every author he dealt with and eventually had to cease being an editor because writers refused to send him stories.

There were other editors who were sweet as pie. Anthony Boucher of *Fantasy and Science Fiction* also rejected, but did so hurtlessly. I wrote a bit of comic verse to celebrate Tony and it goes as follows:

•101

Dear Isaac, friend of mine,
I thought your tale was fine,
Just frightful-
Ly delightful
And with merits all a-shine.
It meant a quite full
Night, full,
Friend, of tension
Then relief
And attended
With full measure
Of the pleasure
Of suspended
Disbelief.
It is triteful,
Scarcely rightful,
Almost spiteful,
To declare
That some tiny faults are there.
Nothing much,
Perhaps a touch
And over such
You shouldn't pine.
So let me say
Without delay,
My pal, my friend,
Your story's end
Has left me gay
And joyfully composed.
P.S.
Oh, yes,
I must confess
(With some distress)
Your story is regretfully enclosed.

As it happens, though I don't know if it points out a moral or anything, the good editor died young and the harsh editor is still alive at this time of writing.

Most of my set-tos are with fellow writers. One such is Lester del Rey, a short, feisty fellow, a self-proclaimed curmudgeon who is nevertheless as straight as an arrow and is someone who can be thoroughly depended on.

•102

I was once telling a group of fellow writers about my father's Talmudic homilies to me when I was little and how they perverted my life. I said, "My father used to say to me, 'Never hang around bums, Isaac. You may think you will make a decent person out of a bum, but you won't. Instead, he will make a bum out of you.'"

Whereupon Lester couldn't resist saying, "So how come you still hang around bums, Isaac?"

And I couldn't resist replying immediately, "Because I love you, Lester."

Even Lester had to laugh.

•103

Lester and I went at it hammer and tongs whenever we met and did so to the point where our respective wives gave us severe instructions to stop. They were constantly afraid we would destroy the friendship and no amount of our assuring them that it was just a game helped.

Anyway, Lester and I were once to be interviewed on television together and we were sternly warned to behave ourselves. The only risk, of course, is that I am so self-centered that when I am on television, I invariably forget there is a camera trained on me and it becomes very hard for me to behave myself.

Toward the end of the interview, the interviewer said, "Why is it, Dr. Asimov, that you don't fly?"

To which I answered, "Well, I'm acrophobic, have a horror of heights, and hate to travel."

Lester then said, quite gratuitously, "It's because Isaac is a coward. Now, I fly freely whenever I wish."

And, in a dudgeon, I said, "That's because your life, Lester, is worth nothing." And then I realized I had said it on television.

You can imagine what Janet said to me when she found out. In fact, I don't want to talk about it.

Another science fiction writer with whom I trade comic insults is Arthur C. Clarke, perhaps the most successful (financially) of the entire fraternity. The game has to be played by letter, unfortunately, since he lives in Sri Lanka and I live right here in Manhattan.

•104

A couple of years ago, a plane crash-landed in Iowa and about half the passengers survived. One of the survivors told the newspaper reporters that he had been reading a novel by Arthur C. Clarke all through the attempted landing in order to keep his mind off the potential disaster.

The story was printed, of course, and Arthur was kind enough to send me a clipping of the story. (I claim he sent it to everyone he knew, but he claims he sent it only to me.) In any case, at the bottom of the clipping, Arthur wrote in longhand, "If he had only tried to read one of your novels, Isaac, he could have slept through the whole sorry mess."

To which I sent back the following letter: "On the contrary. He was reading one of your novels so that if there was a completely fatal crash, his death would come as a blessed release."

I recited this exchange of friendly remarks at a science fiction convention and to my amazement the tale was printed up in a science fiction news magazine and I was berated for insulting a great writer like Arthur Clarke. No matter how well I know that some people have no sense of humor, I am always astonished when I meet one.

Here's another one, which is quite recent:

•105

I got a letter from Arthur which gave me the glad tidings that he had heard that my novels were to be found in all the paperback stands in Asia. "My own books," he added, "are not. They disappear from the racks as soon as they arrive."

To which I responded, "That is because the rack owners throw your books away as fast as they arrive."

However, the most delightful Arthur story does not involve him directly at all. In order to tell it to you I must first explain two things. First, Arthur and I have similar writing styles, so that it is quite common for someone to attribute one of his books to me and vice versa. Second, Arthur's most famous and successful early novel is *Childhood's End*. Now for the story:

•106

At a science fiction convention, a woman said to me, "Dr. Asimov, I have just finished your book *Childhood's End*. I liked it, but I didn't think it was as good as your other books.

Maintaining a straight and solemn face (with an enormous effort), I said, "Yes, ma'am. I was frightfully disappointed in that book, which I thought was quite inferior. I therefore insisted it appear under the pseudonym of Arthur C. Clarke, Jr."

What I wouldn't have given to have had Arthur on the spot so that he could have heard that little exchange.

I must tell you about another wiseguy remark that back-fired on me, though this time it didn't break up a friendship.

It involves Judith Merrill, a large and determined science fiction writer, with whom one doesn't (or shouldn't) trifle.

•107

At a science fiction convention in 1959, I met my future dear wife, Janet, who was also a science fiction fan, and I was much attracted to her. We attended meetings together and I invited her to come have dinner with me and some other choice spirits from among the science fiction writing fraternity. Janet, delighted at a chance to meet some of the writers she admired, accepted gladly, and through the dinner, it was clear that all my attention was pinned on her.

After the dinner, Judy, who had been there, said to me rather severely, "You seem to be rushing this woman, Isaac."

"I like her," I said.

"Yes, but I don't think you know how to deal with women." (Where she could have picked up that notion, I don't know.)

"Sure I do."

"Did you invite her to dinner?"

"Yes, I did."

"And did you pay for her?"

(Of course I did, but at this point I decided to have some fun.)

Opening my eyes wide in surprise, I said, "Was I supposed to?"

"Of course you were supposed to," said she in disgust.

"All right," I said. "Let's see. I think her dinner came to about thirteen dollars, including tip." I began to fumble with my wallet.

Judy said, outraged, "What are you going to do?"

"I'm going to take out thirteen dollars and walk over to her and give it to her."

At which Judy could stand no more. "It's too late for that, you idiot," and leaning back, she slapped my cheek with a wallop that set my head to ringing for ten minutes. It was the only time in my whole life that a woman had slapped my face, and it was enough.

Actually, some years earlier I had done something, quite inadvertently, that should have earned me dismemberment at Judy's hands. She had had a love affair with another science fiction writer and it had broken up, but not of her volition. In any case, at this convention the lover had won an award and he was not there to accept it.

•108

The master of ceremonies called on Judy to accept the award on the ground that the winner had been "so often anthologized" by her.

I was sitting at the head table, because I was guest of honor on this occasion, and I turned to the person next to me and said, "Anthologized? Anthologized? Always euphemisms."

What I didn't know was that the microphone right in front of me was live and my remark rang out over the entire large room. Poor Judy, advancing to get the award, had to walk through a gale of laughter.

After that, you can bet I hid from her over the next few days. She would kill me, I was sure. And then she approached me when I wasn't looking in her direction and said, "Hello, Isaac."

I promptly threw myself into a posture of defense and she said, "Oh, stop it. I'm not mad. As I went up to get the award, I said to myself, 'Everyone is laughing. Everyone is thinking it's funny. So why should I carry the torch for the guy?' I feel much better about it now. Thank you."

By far the most colorful science fiction writer is Harlan Ellison. He is shorter than Napoleon and just as decisive. He is supremely articulate and is the only person I know who can keep up with me—more than keep up, very often. Fortunately, although he is short-tempered and capable of tearing up the place in anger, he and I are close friends and have never exchanged a harsh word.

I met him first at a convention in the 1950s, when he was scarcely more than a boy and so small and thin you had to use a magnifying glass to see him. But he was like quicksilver and had eyes that simply overflowed with intelligence.

I had never met him, knew nothing about him. Everyone

else there knew about him, but somehow didn't think there was any purpose to warning me. So I approached in all innocence and placidity and here is what happened. (I must tell you that Harlan violently denies this story—but he's wrong. I'll back my memory against anyone's in the world.)

•109

He said to me, with a great air of wonderment, "Are you Isaac Asimov, sir?"

"Yes, young man," I said.

"Really? The great Isaac Asimov?"

"Yes," I said, much gratified. "I am."

"Gee. No kidding. You're Isaac Asimov?"

"Yes."

"Well, I think you're a"—and his voice suddenly changed from wonder to contempt—"*nothing.*"

It was like falling off a cliff, and with everyone laughing heartily, I realized I had been set up.

I set about getting even, of course, and after that, it was back and forth, back and forth, but nothing in ill nature (at least to us).

I'll give you an example of the sort of thing that went on:

•110

At a convention one time, the people who were to run the first activity were late and the audience was getting restless. Whereupon, Randall Garrett said to me, "I tell you what, Isaac, let's you and I get on stage and entertain them with snappy patter till things get started."

"All right," said I, nothing loath. In those days I was quite chubby and Randall was even fatter. As we were having fun, Harlan appeared in the door in the back of the room.

"There they are," he called out. "Tweedledum and Tweedledee."

And I called back, "Come up here, Harlan. Stand between us and be the hyphen."

However, the best chance I ever had at Harlan is the following:

•111

Harlan was master of ceremonies at an awards banquet once and indulged in his specialty of insulting every person there. He could do it better than Don Rickles, in my opinion, and, of course, all the insultees enjoyed it. They would have been hurt if he had omitted them. I was the featured speaker of the occasion and, of course, I knew that I would get it when it came time to introduce me.

However, Harlan was held up when one insultee decided to take umbrage. Harlan had referred to her as an editress and her feminism was insulted. "I'm an editor," she shouted.

Harlan is not sexist. He is, in fact, a violent feminist himself, but he cannot give up a chance at a fight. In no time at all the air was thick with *poetess* and *actress* and *princess* and *aviatrix* and all the other special words for women. They were supported by Harlan and denounced by the editor.

By the time the dust settled and I was introduced with the usual quota of insults, I was ready. I said, "Though there are a great many special words for a feminine version of a masculine function, few people know that the reverse is also occasionally true. For instance, we all know that a 'yente' in Yiddish is a female scold. Well, Harlan Ellison is a 'yentor.'"

A delightful laugh followed and all hard feelings were washed away.

•112

I met a young man once at a convention—young, extremely quick, and intelligent. In fact, except that he was considerably taller, he seemed to me to be another Harlan Ellison.

I pointed this out enthusiastically to Robert Silverberg, a grave, almost dour science fiction writer, who is a great wit just the same. I said, "There's a fellow who's a new Harlan Ellison."

And Bob said, "Shall we kill him now?"

Knowing that my father had no sense of humor and being uncertain as to how genetic inheritance would affect my children, I brought up my daughter very carefully to feel free to laugh. Indeed, my beautiful, blond, blue-eyed daughter, Robyn Joan, has said, "I've spent my whole life laughing."

She was quoted in print to this effect in my dear wife's charming book, *How to Enjoy Writing.* (Since Janet's retirement from psychoanalysis, she has been busily writing science fiction herself and has published fourteen books.)

Recently, Robyn did something I strongly disapproved of and did so in my presence. Here's the story:

•113

As soon as she did it, Robyn knew I was displeased.

She said, "Do you mind, Daddy?" and I said, "No, of course not," because I make it a practice never to scold her, but it didn't help. I do not have a poker face and it was clear that I was furious.

Robyn, a practical girl, thought I might be furious enough to cut her out of my will and leave her to face a life of starvation and penury, so she quickly undid what she had done and looked at my face again. And there she was, back in my will.

Later that day, still trying to recover from her narrow escape from starvation and penury, she said to me coaxingly, "You wouldn't ever leave me out of your will, would you, Dad?"

And I put my arm around her and said, "Of course not, Robyn darling. You're like a daughter to me."

She crowed with laughter for quite a while, and I was so pleased. The worst thing she could have done would have been to look at me, puzzled, and say, "But I *am* your daughter, Dad."

If she had, then maybe I would indeed have cut her out of my will.

Of course, my training of my dear daughter took time. When she was quite young, she had not yet reached a level where she could understand my twisted sense of what was funny.

In order to appreciate the following story, you'll have to understand something about my first wife, Gertrude. We didn't get along very well, but that didn't alter the fact that she was an extraordinarily good-looking woman. At her peak, she looked precisely like Olivia de Havilland at her peak. I happened to be in love with Miss de Havilland (platonically) back in 1942, when I met Gertrude on a blind date. My eyes bugged at the vision and I was a doomed man from that moment.

Now for the story:

•114

Robyn was eight years old at the time. She was blond (there's blondness in my family even though my own hair was a dull brown until it became a dull gray) instead of brunette as Gertrude was.

Robyn and I walked into our town pharmacy one time, and the pharmacist, who had never seen Robyn with me, reacted in a kind of stunned way.

He said, "Is this beautiful little girl your daughter, Dr. Asimov?"

"Yes," I said, "and the odd thing about it is that my wife is even uglier than I am."

The pharmacist, who knew Gertrude, chuckled, but little Robyn, with eyes like saucers, set off homeward at a run.

I realized perfectly well what she was going to do and I started running after her to stop her.

I had no chance. She was eight and in perfect shape. I was forty-three and flabby. The whole neighborhood watched the pursuit over a track of three-fourths of a mile, and she got home first.

"Mommy, Mommy, guess what Daddy said," said the little stinker. Gertrude did not find it funny.

Thinking about Gertrude reminds me:

•115

Q: What is Jewish foreplay?
A: An hour and a half of begging.

•116

Q: What is Italian foreplay?
A: "Hey, Maria, I'm home."

•117

Sometimes my rejoinders contain the slightly off-color, but I won't bother you with those except to give you just one mild example.

Quite recently, I was talking to two beautiful women who happen to be editors of mine. (I've had more beautiful editors than you can imagine and I have never complained about it, either.)

In the course of our conversation, I mentioned the name of a character in one of my books and I got it wrong and one of the editors corrected me. Very embarrassing.

When, a few moments later, the editor made a trivial mistake, using a slightly wrong word, I promptly corrected her. Then I said, "I wouldn't have bothered correcting you, dear, but you had just corrected me."

"I understand," she said gravely. "It was just a case of tit for tat."

And I said, "If it's a case of tit for tat, wow, do you have the advantage over me."

The two young women looked at each other haughtily and said, "Listen to him laughing. He thinks it's funny."

You bet I thought it was funny. I laughed for quite a while.

•118

A certain aspiring young comic, back in Depression days, found himself in a bad way. New bookings had vanished, his wife was pregnant, and his funds stood perilously close to the zero point. Pocketing his pride, he made the rounds of the older and better established comedians whom he had come to know.

Bob Hope listened to his tale sympathetically and said, "Kid, things are a little tight with me, too, right now, and I can't help you just at present, but I'm amazed you're having trouble. I caught your act a couple of months ago and you're terrific. Once you get over this bad spot, you should have no trouble at all getting established."

George Burns was equally sympathetic. He said, "I wish I could help you, buddy, but I've had a streak of bad luck myself lately. However, don't be discouraged. I've heard you deliver and I want to tell you that as far as I'm concerned, there's the making of a major talent in you. Keep it up, fella."

Jack Benny listened and said, "Well, I'll write you out a check for what you need and if you need more, let me know. I've got to tell you, though, that I don't think you'll make it in this tough business of ours. You just don't have the spark."

Our young comic arrived home at last and said to his wife, "Well, I've got some money and it will see us through, maybe, till things turn better." Then he added bitterly, "But once you're down, you sure find out quick which so-called friends turn their back on you. That rotten, lousy Jack Benny—"

•119

A veteran actor had finally been offered a part, but it was only a single line. At one point in a Civil War play, he was to come on stage and say, "Hark! Is that not the distant sound of artillery?"

Scornfully, he told his agent he would not dream of taking it, but his agent felt otherwise.

"Monty, baby," he said, "you haven't been on the boards in a long time and you've got to keep your name before the public. I admit that this is only a single line, but it comes at a crucial point in the play and, properly delivered, it can do a lot for you. Besides, you're filling in for someone else, so you're coming through in an emergency. The producers will remember that, and they'll owe you one."

Grudgingly, the veteran conceded the point; it meant a little income, after all. He hastened out to Baltimore, where the play was getting its tryout, and all the way there he kept practicing the line with a variety of readings, trying to determine which one would be most effective.

Our actor arrived shortly before curtain time. While the play proceeded, he was put into uniform and makeup, and this was barely completed when his cue sounded. He rushed out onto the stage just as the sound effects man let loose a horrible clatter that sounded like twenty-seven anvils falling in rapid succession—this signifying the distant sound of artillery.

At which the actor jumped, turned, and cried out, "What the hell was that?"

•120

Mr. Moskowitz had invested a sizable bit of money in a play but had set up a single condition: He had to appear on the stage. He didn't specify a large part, for he was no actor and he knew it, but he wanted an appearance and a single line.

The producer and director did not want to offend him and lose the money he was giving them, so they went over the play and managed to adjust it in such a fashion that Moskowitz would appear at a certain point, say, "The king is dead," and with that, leave.

He was placed in an appropriate spot and, when the time came for the delivery of that one line during rehearsal, he dashed out and said, "The King is dead" in a level monotone.

They called him back. The director, straining not to sound nasty, said, "Mr. Moskowitz, you don't understand. The king was much beloved. His death may be a catastrophe for the country. You must announce the death as though you were very moved and upset. Got it?"

"I got it," said Moskowitz, and they tried again.

Out he came and said, "The king is dead," in the same level monotone.

The director, gritting his teeth, said, "Do you have a brother, Mr. Moskowitz?"

"Yes. My brother Mendel."

"Do you love him?"

"What a question! Of course!"

"All right, when you come out and say 'The king is dead' I want you to say it as though you were saying, 'My brother, Mendel, is dead.'"

"I get it," said Moskowitz, and they tried again.

Out he came and said, "The king is dead," in the same level monotone, but this time he immediately clapped both hands to his cheeks and said, "Oy, vay."

You can say "Oy, vay" even to a gentile audience without fear of being misunderstood. As it happens, the high incidence of Jewish comedians has spread some Yiddish words and phrases throughout the television audience.

Thus, we all know that to *shlep* means "to drag," that to *nosh* means to "eat enthusiastically," and so on.

I remember once when John Barrymore was in the twilight of his career on a radio show hosted (I believe) by Rudy Vallee. In it, he frequently spoke of "Camp Paskudnyak," the syllables rolling in his resonant voice.

That invariably broke me up. *Paskudnyak* is a Russian word that is extremely pejorative and is used with deep contempt. I never found out what it meant, but it must have been a very pejorative term indeed, because my mother used it on me frequently, and there was no twinkle in her eyes when she did so, either. (The feminine form of the word sounds even more insulting.)

•121

Peter O'Toole, in the motion picture *My Favorite Year*, discovered to his horror that, by participating in a television program live in the 1950s, he was going to have to either memorize or improvise lines. He said in agony, "I can't act! I'm a movie star!"

Once people have established themselves as well-known wits, they have a great many witticisms attributed to them that they have never said. If Dorothy Parker, or Robert Benchley, or Franklin P. Adams had said all the funny things they are supposed to have said, they would scarcely have had time to eat or sleep.

You can imagine my feelings, then, when I found funny things attributed to me that I have never said. On the one hand, I'm very pleased that people will believe I had said all sorts of funny things, but on the other, I don't like credit I don't deserve.

For instance, a friend of mine swears he once heard me invent a pun that I simply know I never did. Someone else must have done this and my friend remembered it as mine because he knows I'm a punster. Here it is:

•122

Someone who did not own an auto is supposed to have discussed with me his plan for buying one. He said, "With a car, travel becomes a great deal easier. You just throw your clothes into the backseat and take off."

And I am supposed to have said, "But what if you have clothes-throw-phobia?"

There are some towns that have intrinsically funny names and that therefore appear in the world of jokedom oftener than they deserve. It has been pointed out that the letter *k* seems to lend humor to a town's name—Kankakee, Kalamazoo, Shamokin, Hoboken, Podunk, Brooklyn, Yonkers, Cripple Creek, and so on.

A special case is Green Bay, Wisconsin. It is the curious anomaly of being a small town with a first-class football team that competes with the big boys.

•123

At the bar, the conversation had turned to the town of Green Bay, Wisconsin.

Jones snorted. "Green Bay!" he said. "I was once in Green Bay and it's nothing. There are only two things Green Bay produces. A pretty low grade of prostitute and that professional football team of theirs, the Green Bay Packers."

At this, a large man from the other end of the room rose to his feet, approached Jones, and in a voice full of menace said, "Sir, it may be news to you, but my wife comes from Green Bay, Wisconsin."

"Indeed?" said Jones, not batting an eyelash. "And what position does she play?"

Actually, my very good friend and co-anthologist Martin Harry Greenberg lives in Green Bay, Wisconsin, and his wife is a beautiful and charming lady who fits into neither of Jones's categories. But then, she was born in Lancaster, Pennsylvania.

•124

Jones noted an advertisement in the newspaper offering a current-model Cadillac in prime condition for $50 cash. Certain it was a typographical error, he called the advertiser out of curiosity.

To his astonishment, he found that the advertisement was legitimate. The Cadillac was indeed brand-new and it was indeed in spit-and-polish condition. The title of ownership was clear and the price asked was indeed $50. The woman who was selling it calmly accepted the five ten-dollar bills he handed her, wrote him out a receipt, and handed him the keys.

With the deal successfully concluded, Jones was driven by curiosity to ask, "But why is it, madam, you have done this? This is a car worth many thousands of dollars. How can you accept fifty?"

"It's quite simple," said the woman, placing the bill of sale and the money in her purse. "My husband died shortly after buying this car, and in his will he directed that I sell it and that the proceeds go to his mistress."

•125

Mrs. Finkelstein was having her portrait done.

She said to the artist, "Now, listen, make my face so that everyone will know it's me. Never mind pretty, just lifelike. My husband is going to hang it up in the living room and his solemn oath is that it will stay there even if I die and he marries again.

"But the thing is, I want jewelry on me. A real beautiful pearl necklace around my neck, an elaborate tiara in my hair, diamond bracelets on both arms, a ruby pendant on my chest. Squeeze in all you can."

The painter said, "Do you mind wearing the jewelry so that I can paint it realistically?"

"Are you crazy? I don't have any jewelry like that. Make it up out of your head."

"But Mrs. Finkelstein, if you don't have the jewelry, why do you want to be painted with it?"

"Because if I do die first, and if my husband, that rat, does marry again—probably some baby-faced floozie—I want her to go crazy trying to find the jewels."

Norman Cousins was of the firm belief that laughter helped the body cure disease and lengthen life. I certainly hope he is right, for I have always laughed a lot.

Certainly I discovered that laughter helps assuage what could be a very tragic experience.

Back in 1973, while I was still waiting for my divorce from Gertrude to be final, and therefore had not yet married my dear second wife, Janet, poor Janet was forced to undergo a mastectomy. It was tough, but I would rather have had a Janet who had been hacked up a little than no Janet at all.

The problem was how to make her see it at the time. Once Janet had fully emerged from the anesthetic and realized what had happened to her and that her condition was permanent, she was utterly woebegone. We don't use the expression *flat-chested* in my family, but Janet was dainty-breasted and the loss of one of those little things seemed the last straw to her. And since I was not yet married to her, she was convinced that I would tip my hat and say, "Well, baby, it's been fun!" and go out in search of someone else with two breasts.

I tried the only cure I know. Funny stuff.

•126

I said, "Look Janet, what's the big deal? If you were a Broadway showgirl, a mastectomy would really be a tragedy. Aside from losing your livelihood, you would be forever tipping over to one side. In your case, though, within a year, I'll be looking at you as you step into the shower, and I'll be saying, 'Which breast did he take off?'"

Janet laughed delightedly and, as the surgeon walked in just then, she proceeded to tell him what I had said. I was afraid the surgeon might kill me as a callous, sadistic brute, but instead he laughed also. It was good medical humor. (Of course, we must remember that Janet is also a physician.)

Janet was even capable of joking about the matter herself.

•127

Soon after she got out of the hospital, Lester del Rey and his wife, Judy-Lynn (now dead, to our great sorrow) visited and spoke cheerfully of everything under the sun but the operation.

After a while, the conversation veered toward the subject of "swinging singles" bars, where people who were unattached, or pretended they were unattached, could meet others of similar bent.

Judy-Lynn said to Janet, "Were you ever at a swinging singles?"

I interposed. "At a swinging single? She *has* a swinging single."

Judy-Lynn screamed and rushed at me to kill me, but Janet said, "Leave him alone, Judy-Lynn. He's just boasting. I don't have one big enough to be a swinging single."

Well, I married Janet a few months after the operation and I've hung on to her for almost eighteen years at the time of this writing, and have done so in unalloyed happiness, so you see it all had a happy ending.

• • •

I don't make much of a fuss about being intelligent—not so much because I don't enjoy being admired, but because I know that my intelligence is highly specialized and that outside the narrow limits of knowing everything about science and the humanities, and being able to write like a dream, I am pretty much an idiot.

Thus, my brother, Stanley, who is not considered as "brilliant" as I am, possesses something better—common sense—and I frequently turn to him when I find myself helpless.

•128

One time I was in Long Island of a Sunday morning and my car would not start. I was helpless. Then I remembered that Stan lived only a mile away and that, since he was the soul of accommodation (unlike me), he would cheerfully drive over to help me.

I called him, he came, and he couldn't start the car either.

I said blankly, "What do we do, Stan?"

He said, "We'll have to get a mechanic."

I said, "The gas stations are closed. It's Sunday."

He said, "We'll find one that's open. You read the numbers out of the telephone directory and feed me the coins, and I'll call."

It did no good. Even if a gas station was open, there was no mechanic in attendance.

Finally Stan quit, turned, and said to me, "It amazes me, Isaac, that a supposed genius like yourself should not be sensible enough to be a member of the AAA."

"Oh," I said, "I'm a member," and produced the card.

We had the AAA over in no time, and my car was started. When it was all over, Stan said to me, "Why didn't you call the AAA yourself to begin with?"

And I answered in all honesty, "I never thought of it."

•129

Once Stan asked me if I would give a talk under the auspices of

Newsday, the newspaper through whose ranks he has climbed for thirty years, and where he is now the "grand old man" of the paper.

I agreed, of course. I wouldn't refuse my brother anything within reason. He said they would pay me $4,000 and I agreed. Money was no object in this case and I wouldn't dream of insisting on my full fee.

So, months later, I gave the talk and it was a great success and I grinned and accepted the plaudits and went home.

Two months later I got a call from the *Newsday* people, and someone said, "What's your social security number, Dr. Asimov?"

Suspiciously, I said, "Why do you want to know it?"

"So we can send you a check."

"A check? For what?"

"For the talk you gave to us some time ago."

"Oh," I said, totally forgetting what Stan had told me. "Am I getting paid for that?"

"Yes," came the answer. "Four thousand dollars."

So I recited my social security number and then got to thinking. They were going to call Stan and say, "Your brother didn't know he was supposed to be paid. He thought he was speaking at no charge, so do we have to pay him?"

I called Stan at once, told him the story, and said, "So when they ask you if they have to pay me, tell them yes, they have to pay me."

There was a short pause and then Stan said, "Why do you call to tell me this on a Friday evening?"

I said, "What does it matter when I tell you?"

And he said angrily, "Because now I have to wait till Monday morning to tell everyone the latest 'my-stupid-brother-Isaac' story."

I am very grateful to Stan, though. He is forced to live in my shadow. Almost everyone he meets for the first time, on being introduced to someone with the name of Stan Asimov, seems impelled to ask, "Are you a relation of Isaac Asimov?" The girl he later married (very happily) asked him that question immediately upon meeting him.

He doesn't mind, and he has never let it spoil our relationship. I'm afraid I wouldn't be as pleasant about it if the situation were reversed.

•130

Of course, there are times when the situation does gall him a little. He was waiting in a surgeon's office for some sort of consultation and he had to wait for hours. He turned to his wife, Ruth, and said in an aggrieved tone, "They wouldn't treat me like this if I were *Isaac* Asimov."

He called me afterward to tell me this, and I said, "Yes, they would, Stan. I once waited in a surgeon's room for hours, got mad, and left, and never returned, and my name was *Isaac* Asimov."

•131

Stan and I are very alike in appearance. We are similar to the point where, if someone knows one of us and meets the other, he instantly inquires as to whether there is a relationship.

What's more, both Stan and I look very much like my father, especially now that we are the age my father was when he was old. I have frequently walked into a dim room and seen a mirror I didn't know was there and my heart jumps, for I think I see my father. When I told this to Stan he told me he had precisely the same experience.

I sighed and said, "And I was born in Russia and you were born in America. What a tribute to Mama's fidelity!"

•132

Robyn has always enjoyed our relationship, especially when she was younger and was going out with boys.

They'd meet her, find out her name, and say, with a certain awe, "Are you related to Isaac Asimov? Is he your uncle or something?"

And she would say, "Of course not."

She would wait for the boy to relax and then would say, "He's my father." It gave her a great deal of pleasure to do this.

And yet Robyn, who has just turned thirty-six and has always been beautiful, has never married. I have always blamed myself for this. She is under no economic push to get married, thanks to me, and I'm afraid that she admires me so greatly that other men seem a little pipsqueakish to her.

I have asked her what she would do once I died, if she were still unmarried. She said she would use the money I left her in order to buy a house in the country, with a garden and a lot of animals, and live as happily as the day was long. I hope so.

Probably the most stupid thing I ever did took place when I was seventeen. It was also the most successful witticism I ever uttered. Let me tell you the story. It is completely, word for word, true:

•133

In the 1930s, Fiorello La Guardia was mayor of New York, probably the most popular and successful mayor that city ever had. Not everything he did was popular, however. For instance, in a fit of morality, he closed down the burlesque houses, which by present-day standards were as mild as mother's milk.

I was taking English literature at the time as a Columbia University undergraduate, and the professor was a gentleman named Lyon. He had the precise appearance of a superannuated Shakespearian actor—clearly aged, with a lined face, but showing signs of theatrical good looks, and a perfect profile.

He lectured with delight. I have never had a lecturer like him. Every lecture was a masterpiece of preparation and he delivered it as though he were on the stage. No student was allowed to interrupt him or to ask questions. They must only listen as he performed, and I must admit he was compelling. I may have learned some of my own tricks of public speaking from him.

And one day, he felt it necessary to describe a theatrical production he had once seen, and he could not forbear to describe all its glories in the most purple prose, comparing it very much to its advantage to the pallid productions that graced Broadway at the time he was speaking and we were listening.

He described the sets of the old production he had seen, the luxurious appointments, and was most ecstatic over the leading lady, describing her grace, her beauty, her charm, the way she caught at the audience, the way she reclined on a sofa in a diaphanous costume, and on and on.

Finally he concluded by saying, "I'm sorry to say that you poor gentlemen will never see anything so delightful and fetching."

And from the ranks of the students listening, I heard my voice ring out, saying, "Of course not, now that La Guardia has shut them down."

There was, perhaps, a five-second silence while the class absorbed the enormity of my implication that Professor Lyon had been describing a cheap burlesque shtick, and then came the laughter. The entire class went into hysterics and would not—could not—stop. In vain Lyon tried to calm the class. The laughter would dwindle, then break out again. Lyon had to dismiss the class when it was only half over.

The class left, still laughing all the way down the corridor, but I sat in my seat, stricken. I had not laughed. All through school I had been in trouble with teachers for my wiseguy remarks, but never anything like this. I had never broken up a class before. I had never utterly humiliated a teacher who clearly held a sky-high opinion of himself.

It seemed to me that I would be expelled from college and that I would then have to explain to my humorless father that I had merely been making a joke, and that I would then be expelled from my family and that my whole life would be ruined.

No sleep for me that night. I crawled back to school the next day and made my frightened way back into the English lit class, hoping Lyon wouldn't notice me. He did. He gave me a big hello. Don't ask me to explain the psychology of it—I never understood it, never—but from that point on I was his fair-haired boy, his favorite.

Of course, I was careful never to cross him again. I felt that one wiseguy remark was my lifetime supply where he was concerned.

• 134

I had a variety of different ways, none of them lucrative, of making a little money while I was in college so that I could pay my tuition. For one thing, I would occasionally do odd (intellectual-type) jobs for some professor who would pay me $15 a month by way of the National Youth Administration. One such professor taught psychology, something I've never been interested in—at least as an academic subject.

One of his graduate students was designing a maze, one in which other students would touch a series of metal points at random, trying to hit only those which lit a green light and avoid those that lit a red light. The trick was to make the path of the green lights sufficiently intricate to make it necessary to have a sizable number of missed efforts before the maze was learned.

The graduate student worked out a maze and used me as an experimental subject. Since I solved it too quickly, he made it a little more difficult, then still more difficult, until he got to the point where I had a little trouble working it out.

"That's it," he said.

He showed it to the psychology professor, who stared at the plot of correct points and said, "Isn't that too difficult?"

"No," said the graduate student. "I checked it with an undergraduate."

"What undergraduate?"

And the student pointed at me, who was an interested listener, and said, "That one."

The professor knew me, however. He looked at the graduate student and said, "Start all over, and use someone else."

• 135

I remember that psychology professor without favor. I saw a slide rule on his desk, and I had never seen one before.

I said to him, "What's this, Professor?"

"Put it down, Asimov," he said. "I have no time to explain it."

All he had to do was show me how to multiply 3 by 2 on the slide rule to get 6. It would have taken him one second and then I would have been able to work out everything else by myself. But he didn't, and it wasn't till four years later that I taught myself how to use one. I have never forgiven him for this.

•136

As early as 1950, I predicted the use of pocket computers in my science fiction stories. In 1965, however, I had a book published on how to use a slide rule because I didn't want anyone to have to wait to learn how to use it without help, as I had done.

The only trouble was that a few years later, pocket computers—real pocket computers—came out and the book went right down the drain, and so did slide rules. How's that for being skewered by something I had myself predicted?

•137

Gertrude was well aware of my many bad points and never wearied of reciting them to me for fear I might forget a few. However, she was also perfectly aware of the fact that I had a very high IQ (something most people mistake for intelligence).

Indeed, when I was in the Army, I took an intelligence test of sorts, called, I believe, the AGCT. With a 100 being a normal score, I received 160. It was the highest score anyone on the base had seen, and they made a big fuss over me. It died down, however, and nothing changed. I was still a buck private, I still drew KP, and no one ever mentioned it again.

However, since in those early days of my marriage I was dying to impress Gertrude, I called her and told her of my triumph.

At my next furlough, she said to me with indignation, "I told my friend, so-and-so, that you had had an AGCT score of 160, and she said, 'A hundred and sixteen?'

"And I said, 'No, a hundred and sixty.'

"And she said, 'How do you know it's a hundred and sixty?'

"And I said, 'Isaac told me so.'

"And she said, 'Isaac is lying,' and I'm completely mad at her for saying that."

I was amused. I said, "But Gertrude, how do you know I'm not lying?"

And Gertrude said indignantly, "Because for you, a hundred and sixty is just normal. Why should you lie?"

•138

The previous anecdote took place in the early days of our marriage. Now I'll tell you one that took place as the marriage was breaking up a quarter of a century later.

A friend came to visit. In fact, it was the friend who had arranged the initial blind date with Gertrude, so that I viewed her with mixed feelings. It had been a difficult marriage, but after all, it had also given me my beautiful daughter, Robyn.

The friend said to Gertrude, "When you first married Isaac and he was just going to school, would you have believed he would turn out like this?"

"Sure," said Gertrude.

"How could you know that?"

"Because he *told* me it would happen."

•139

I was sitting in a restaurant, having lunch with friends, when a pleasant, gray-haired woman stopped at my table and said, "Dr. Asimov, I'm sure you don't remember me, but I knew you when your father and mother had the candy store on Windsor Place."

That was in the thirties and I was sure she did know me then, though, of course, I didn't remember her at all. I greeted her kindly.

She said, "You know, even in those days, so long ago, I was sure you would amount to something."

"Really?" I said. "I wish you had told me that at the time. I wasn't all that sure I would."

As you can see from my story about Professor Lyon, one of my problems is that I speak before thinking. Innate ability and long practice fill me to the brim with wiseguy remarks and they pop out before I can stop them. It sometimes gives unintended offense, and it sometimes convinces people that I am a monster of vanity and arrogance, which I'm not (even if, in places in this book, it seems that I am).

•140

I was stopped in the lobby of a theater by a nice woman who wanted me to autograph her playbill. I was glad to do so, and she said, "You're only the second person I've ever asked for an autograph."

Out of curiosity, I said, "Who was the other?"

She said, "Laurence Olivier."

And I heard myself say, "How proud Larry would be if he knew that he was the other one."

I wasn't serious, of course, but the woman left hurriedly, and I presume she thought I was.

•141

I gave a talk at George Washington University in Washington, D.C., once, in return for a nice round sum that was to be paid out by the Student Activities Department.

When the check arrived, it did not specify the nature of the occasion. It merely stated that I was being paid for one appearance. And under the department responsible for the payment they carefully typed out STUD ACTIVITIES.

There can be but few males in the United States with so warmhearted, generous, and official an endorsement of the remarkable worth of their talents in this direction.

Great are the mysteries, complexities, and wonders of the English language, which makes the same word have two widely different meanings.

•142

Mrs. Jones had never looked so good. She was, indeed, permeated with a renewed bloom of youth; her eyes sparkled and her step was light.

Said Mrs. Finkelstein, "How is it, Rosemary, that you seem to be in such good shape recently?"

Mrs. Jones looked rapidly about, drew Mrs. Finkelstein aside, and whispered, "Frankly, Bella, I'm having an affair."

"Really?" said Mrs. Finkelstein. "It's a secret, I see."

"Absolutely a secret."

"But surely not from me."

"From you? Of course not. You're my best friend."

"So how come," said Mrs. Finkelstein, "I'm not invited?"

It's time for limericks again:

•143

There was a young woman named Robbie
Who would wait in a theater lobby
      To catch all those guys
      Who had unzippered flies.
Oh, well, it's an int'resting hobby.

As you can guess, this has something to do with my beautiful daughter, Robyn. She has no shame and in college she would drag over her friends when I visited her and would insist that I write limericks for them.

"Dirty ones," she would specify.

Finally she said, "And how about one for me?"

"All right," I said, "a clean one."

"No," she said, "a dirty one."

Well, the previous limerick is as dirty as I could make it for her. Where are the sweet pure damsels of yesteryear? (Answer: They never existed.)

•144

There was a young woman named Lynne,
Who said, "Very well, let's begin."
      "My God," said her beau,
      "What a heartbreaking blow,
It's an hour since I put the thing in."

•145

The virginal nature of Donna
Had for many long years been a goner.
      When asked why she screwed,
      She replied, "Gratitude,
Politeness—and just cause I wanna."

There is another version of this one:

•146

There was a young woman named Donna
Who decided that she was a goner.
      She'd been screwing all day
      Every possible way,
Quite forgetting it was Rosh Hashanah.

I like the second one better because of the unusual rhyme. Rosh Hashanah is, of course, the Jewish New Year, one of the high holidays. To tell you the truth, I don't know if it is, or is not, permissible to have sex on Rosh Hashanah.

Talking about unusual rhymes, I once wanted to write a limerick on Veronica, but try as I might I could think of only one rhyme—harmonica—and I needed another. When I met a young woman named Veronica, I said to her gloomily, "There's only one rhyme for your name."

"I know," she said, and told me—and it was the third

rhyme. I almost fell off my chair with astonishment. Here is the limerick:

• 147

> A certain young woman, Veronica,
> Plays a hora upon her harmonica.
> > But spell the word right
> > Or you'll be in a fight,
> For she screws without charge during Hanukkah.

• 148

> A young whore who beguiles on the Nile,
> Brings out satisfied smiles with her style.
> > She has for her clients
> > Both pygmies and giants,
> In a line stretching miles double-file.

Note the internal rhymes in this last limerick. I'm very pleased with the construction effort that went into it.

• 149

> Said a certain young woman named Valerie
> When screwed in the National Gallery,
> > "Oh, well, call it Fate
> > But at least I lost weight.
> Now for lunch I can have one more calorie."

• 150

> There was a young man of Connecticut
> Who tore off a young woman's petticoat.
> > She said, with a grin,
> > "You will have to get in,
> To do nothing more isn't etiquette."

• 151

A stammering young woman named Kate
Got in trouble when out on a date.
> She refused to have fun,
> Saying, "nun-nun-nun-nun—"
And by then it was simply too late.

• 152

"In Boston," said Jane, "it makes sense
To go for the specialty; hence
> I've come to get scrod."
> And her friend said, "That's odd,
You've used the past pluperfect tense."

• 153

"Well, Sammy," said Mr. Moskowitz to his young hopeful, "how is it going in school?"

"Not so good, Papa," answered Sammy. "The teacher wanted to know the name of the highest mountain in the world and I couldn't tell her."

"The highest mountain in the world? That's what she was anxious to know?"

"That's right, Papa."

Whereupon Moskowitz sighed and said, "She should only have my troubles."

In the world of jokedom, Jewish mothers are after husbands for their single daughters, especially potential husbands who would shine with prestige. Maybe that's the way it is in real life, too.

• 154

The theater was crowded when a woman in the balcony rose suddenly and cried out, "Is there a doctor in the house? Is there a doctor in the house?"

At several points in the orchestra, gentlemen rose.

The woman cried out, "If one of you is single, would you like to meet a nice, well-brought-up young Jewish girl?"

Herb Graff told me the following:

•155

At a certain summer resort a Jewish woman noted the arrival of a man who was well along in middle age and who was very pale.

She said to him, "How is it you're so pale?"

He said, "I've been out of the sun for a long time."

"Oh, how is that?"

"I've been in prison for twenty years."

"Why?"

"I killed my wife."

The woman's eyes glittered. "Then you're single."

•156

"Well," said Mrs. Jones to her young daughter, "and what did you learn in Sunday School today?"

"We learned," said little Nancy, "about Moses."

"Ah," said her mother, "and what did you learn about Moses?"

Nancy said, "Well, he was a general leading an army on a retreat from Egypt. The Egyptians, in hot pursuit, had the weight of tanks on their side, and Moses, taking casualties, was forced back upon the Red Sea, where he faced annihilation. Calling for air cover, however, he proceeded to throw a pontoon bridge hastily across—"

By this time, Mrs. Jones had finally managed to catch her breath and said, "Nancy! Surely that is not what they taught you about Moses."

"Well, not exactly," said Nancy, "but if I told it to you the way the teacher told it to me, you'd never believe it."

Talking about modern warfare reminds me that there's one story that makes me laugh every single time I think of it. The only trouble is that to tell it properly requires a Swedish accent, something I can't handle. But here it is:

•157

It was during the war and Ole Johnson had come back on furlough to his little town in Minnesota. He was an air pilot and had done wonders, and the principal of the local high school thought it might be very nice if Johnson would give a small talk to the students and recount his air adventures.

Johnson was perfectly willing to do so, and there he was on the stage of the auditorium, with red, white, and blue bunting everywhere, and with the eager faces of the high school students listening eagerly.

The talk went swimmingly as Johnson spoke of training and preparation, and finally of air battle.

He said, "At this time I managed to fly far behind enemy lines, but didn't know it. I thought I was safe and I was even singing a little Swedish folk song, when all of a sudden, out of the clouds, came two Fokkers. I snapped to attention and sent my plane climbing in a wide circle and, descending, I got one of the Fokkers in my sights and shot him down. I then turned to the other Fokker, who was closing fast, when I noticed that three other Fokkers were approaching from the other direction—"

With each repetition of the word *Fokker* there was increasing hilarity from the students, and it was clear that they were getting out of control.

The principal was equal to the occasion. He rose to his feet, held his arms high for silence, and said, "Students, the Fokker is a German warplane that was first designed by an engineer named Anthony Fokker." And, turning to the speaker, he said, "Isn't that correct, Mr. Anderson?"

Anderson looked confused. He said, "Yah, you are right, Mr. Principal, but these Fokkers I was fighting were Messerschmidts."

My father had had a complete Jewish education in Russia and could therefore speak Hebrew fluently. Or at least he could quote from the Bible in Hebrew fluently. I went to

Hebrew school for six months in 1928 and learned the Hebrew alphabet and a number of other details, which, since all this was over sixty years ago, are beginning to fade from my memory.

Still, I disapprove of the fact that Israel has established Hebrew as its national language. It is so small and specialized a language that anyone speaking only Hebrew would cut himself off from the world community, with the result that all Israelis must speak English (or, in the case of recent immigrants, Russian). So I enjoy the following:

•158

Mrs. Yarmolinsky, a recent immigrant to Israel, persisted in having her son talk Yiddish around the house. A neighbor protested that Yiddish was a German dialect and, considering what had happened in Germany in the forties, it should be scorned. He should talk Hebrew.

But Mrs. Yarmolinsky said, "I don't care what you say. My son will speak Yiddish, so that he will never forget he is Jewish."

Speaking of Mrs. Yarmolinsky, as I did in the previous story, reminds me of that odd phenomenon, the Jewish mother. I won't bother trying to describe her, for all of America knows about her from the stories of the Jewish comedians and from motion pictures and theatrical productions by Jewish scriptwriters.

I had a Jewish mother who completely fit the type. She smothered me with love and banged at me with a heavy hand whenever that love wavered ever so slightly because of my high crimes and misdemeanors. I like to say that she walloped me whenever she passed me, and that was very nearly true.

But it was not so bad. When my father was saddened at my behavior, he never struck me (never, not once). Instead, he would lecture me interminably with saws from the Talmud and sayings from the great wise men of Jewish history, till I was dying to have him give me one good sock and get it over with.

I used my Jewish mother once to get me out of a terrible difficulty.

• 159

My brother, Stan, had asked me to show up at a book and author luncheon that *Newsday* was sponsoring and I said I would. I made one stipulation. My mother was spending her last years in Long Island, after the death of my father in 1969, and I wanted her brought to the luncheon.

"Sure," said Stan, "she's my mother, too." And he sent a limousine for her.

Unfortunately, the book-and-author luncheon had all the makings of a disaster. The speaker ahead of me was a gentile, but he had written a book about Jews and since the audience consisted of about ninety-eight percent Jewish women, he had them enthralled. It seemed absolutely unfair. I was going to have to follow him, and there I was, Jewish as the day was long, but I was going to have to speak on subjects that had nothing to do with Jews and I would end with an audience half indifferent and half hostile.

So when I rose to my feet, I said, "The previous speaker can talk about Jews all he wants, but I have something he doesn't have—a Jewish mother. What's more, she's right in the audience. And, goodness, is she a Jewish mother? She's only four feet ten inches tall and that's a good thing because she didn't stop hitting me till I got too tall for her to reach. But in between hocking me and hitting me, she loved me with unbelievable fervor. In fact, I was always her favorite.

"So today when I told her she was coming to the luncheon and would hear me talk, she said to me, 'Would it be all right if I sat with you at the same table, Isaac?'

"I said, 'You can't, Mama. I'll be on the dais. You will sit with Stan.'

"And my mother said, 'With Stan who?'"

That got a good laugh, and I got through my non-Jewish talk without trouble. The laugh came especially from a large number of *Newsday* people in the audience to whom Stan was a semi-divine creature, because of his long service and high office with the paper.

Of course, since the story was made up and was completely untrue, my mother was furious. She rose in her seat and shook her fist at me, which got another big laugh. If I had been closer, I think she would have given me a good hock. As for Stan, when he got back to his office, he found a sign on the door: STAN WHO, VICE PRESIDENT.

•160

A history was written recently about *Newsday* and I read it dutifully because I thought Stan would be mentioned. He was, but mostly in the form of quotes, and I was a little annoyed because I thought his service to the paper was slighted.

In one passage, however, it was mentioned that it was routine for politicians and other people looking for favorable treatment to slip a hundred dollars to reporters as a kind of Christmas bonus. It wasn't much money, but at the time it represented more than a week's wage to Stan.

According to the book, though, Stan was the only reporter to refuse the bribe.

I phoned him at once, told him what I had read, and said, "I'm proud of you, Stan. It's exactly what I would have done."

"Well," said Stan, "we had the same father."

A-ha, I have another psychiatrist joke which is not apt to be offensive to my dear wife, Janet.

•161

The young man said to the psychiatrist, "I had the oddest dream last night. I dreamed you were my mother. I woke and couldn't understand it. Why should I dream you were my mother?"

The psychiatrist said, "Well, let's see. What did you do after having the dream?"

"I had this appointment with you first thing in the morning, so I grabbed a cookie and a Coca-Cola for breakfast and rushed out here."

The psychiatrist frowned. "A cookie and a Coca-Cola? That you call a breakfast?"

I have a very good dentist, and dental techniques have advanced to the point where there is no pain, but I still remember the days of my childhood, when dentistry was torture, so I enjoy the following:

•162

The patient sat in the dentist's chair, head far back and mouth open. The dentist was about to insert his equipment when the patient's arm shot out toward the dentist's groin and the patient's hand seized the dentist's testicles in a firm grip.

Smiling beatifically, the patient said, "Now, Doctor, we're not going to hurt each other, are we?"

As long as people insist on believing that the world is run by supernatural agency and that the universe can be made to veer this way and that according to appeals made by human beings to such agencies, we're bound to have such appeals part of common speech, with sometimes ludicrous results.

•163

As Mr. Jones looked over the world and found it utterly dissatisfying, he felt himself sneering at those who felt it to be in the care of a Creator, one who obviously cared so little for his creation.

Whereupon he said loudly, "At least I'm not like that. Thank God I'm an atheist."

•164

The habit of asking God to prevent calamities is a hard one to break. Thus, it came about that one Jewish businessman, driven to distraction by the devious practices of another, finally shouted at him, "You should only drop dead—God forbid."

•165

My father, in line with his highly moralistic viewpoint, never used bad language (my mother did) and never swore. In fact, when chivied to the last extreme of human endurance, all he could say, in Yiddish, was "Eighteen black years." I presume that, by this, he was wishing someone or something eighteen years of unbroken bad luck and catastrophe.

I told him once that this was a highly efficient means of swearing because it allowed for quantitative discrimination. According to the extent of the offense, you could wish someone twelve or fourteen or six and a half or thirty-three black years.

My reward for pointing this out was that my father called me an idiot.

•166

Back in 1970, a veteran air pilot's position was shaken when a new type of commercial aircraft came on the market. It was necessary for all pilots, including our veteran, to undergo a complete physical examination in order to make sure he was equipped to handle the new plane.

The veteran passed with flying colors and the doctor said, "I must ask you one more question from the psychiatric standpoint. Tell me, sir, how long has it been since you have had a successful sexual experience with a young lady?"

The pilot's eyes narrowed and he said finally, "I should say it was about 1955."

The doctor looked startled. "That long ago. Isn't that unusual?"

The pilot looked at his wristwatch. "That's not so long ago. It's only 1105 now."

I heard the following told by the newspaper writer Bob Considine, who was a devout Catholic, so I'll take the chance of repeating it.

•167

Jesus was having dinner with his disciples one time and as they gathered reverentially about him, more or less in the attitudes since immortalized by Leonardo da Vinci, he looked about at them.

There, in one direction, he saw Judas Iscariot, who, he well knew, would betray him to the authorities before three hours had passed. On the other side was Peter, the prince of the disciples, who, as he well knew, would deny him thrice ere the cock crowed. And almost immediately opposite him was Thomas, who, on a crucial occasion, would express doubts.

There seemed only one thing to do. Jesus called over the headwaiter. "Max," he said, "separate checks."

•168

Talking about Irish Catholics reminds me of the time when I was laboring to get a divorce. It was a difficult process that took years and I was bewailing this once at lunch with a gentleman named Sullivan.

He listened sympathetically and told me he was having precisely the same trouble, and from the details he gave me, he certainly was! I listened to him with growing astonishment and finally said, "But, Sullivan, you are Catholic, aren't you?"

"Yes, I am."

"Then how can you be getting a divorce?"

"Don't you know there's a loophole?"

I thought carefully, then said, "No, I don't know of any loophole."

And Sullivan said, "I'm a *bad* Catholic."

•169

Once I was talking to a Pakistani man. His complexion was a beautiful dark gray and his face was entirely handsome by Caucasian standards and, somehow, he got on the subject of his mother.

His description of his mother was eloquent indeed and I listened with increasing surprise. Finally, it struck me that a Pakistani could be Pakistani and still be—

So I said, "Pardon me, but is your mother Jewish?"

And he looked down upon me from his aristocratic face and said gravely, "My friend, all mothers are Jewish."

•170

The huge ship was barreling through the waters one inky night (in the days before radar) and you can imagine the captain's indignation when he saw, up ahead, other lights coming closer.

Cholerically, he ordered the message sent ahead, "Veer off!"

The message come back, "You veer off."

The captain, beside himself, had the message sent off, "Veer off, you blasted idiot. This is a battleship coming toward you."

And almost at once a message came back, "Well, think it over. This is a lighthouse coming toward you."

•171

Although I am not a traveler, I have been on a number of cruises and have generally enjoyed them. The big liners move steadily and there is no feeling of the sort of swaying that is supposed to give rise to seasickness. Only one day was I ever on a ship when the sea was rough enough to discommode it, and then I found, to my extreme delight, that I was immune to the sensation of nausea.

My dear wife, Janet, spent some hours communing with her soul in our cabin, but she denied she was seasick and, of course, I believed her implicitly. Half the rest of the ship was likewise communing, but those I believe were seasick.

At any rate, I was walking down the mostly empty corridors, lurching right and left now and then, and singing. One of the ship's officers stopped and said to me, "Are you all right? You're not sea-sick?"

"I feel great," I said.

"What an inspiration you will prove to the other passengers."

Whereupon I said, "For God's sake, don't tell them. They'll kill me."

•172

I always enjoy the shows on board ship, too, especially the stand-up comedians. One comedian on our ship, the *Statendam*, had trans-ferred from the still larger, and posher, *Rotterdam*, and he was enter-taining us with jokes about the passengers on the other ship. "They were old," he said judiciously. "In fact," he added after a moment's thought, "I would say that their average age was deceased."

We "young" fellows laughed at that, but, of course, I am quite certain that on the *Rotterdam* he said exactly the same thing about the *Statendam*.

The master of ceremonies aboard the *Statendam* had a favorite joke he told several times. It goes as follows:

•173

At the captain's party, a rather elderly woman had overimbibed with the liquor that was being dealt out with a lavish hand, and a young officer was detailed to get her back to her stateroom.

He placed his arm about her waist, held her elbow firmly with his other hand, and began to march her down the corridor.

She said, with a faint hiccup, "You're passionate."

He said, "Ma'am, I'm just trying to get you to your room."

She repeated, "But you're passionate."

"Ma'am," he said, "I'm a married man and I'm only interested in getting you to your room."

"But my room is back there. You're pashin' it."

•174

Two violinists were sawing their way through their piece at Carnegie Hall before a most appreciative audience when one of the two, allowing his mind to wander for a moment, lost his place. Desperately, he tried to listen to his companion while continuing to play and finally he had no choice but to lean toward the other and say out of the corner of his mouth, "Where the hell are we?"

And his companion, continuing to saw calmly away, said, "In Carnegie Hall."

I am a teetotaler, not out of conviction or stern morality, but out of circumstance. My father, that moralist, would not allow me to drink as long as I was under his thumb, and when, having grown old enough to be independent, I tried to drink, I found, to my horror, that even a small drink got me drunk. I simply cannot carry my liquor and so I don't try. (The tragedy is that there are millions of people who can't carry liquor and who try constantly just the same.)

It is rather a bore, this nondrinking attitude of mine. At cocktail parties, I am forever having drinks pushed on me and my refusals are often taken in bad part. Either I'm considered to be unsociable, or I'm thought of as a member of Alcoholics Anonymous. Very few seem to get it through their heads that I simply don't drink. It's no wonder that I generally avoid cocktail parties whenever I can.

•175

Once I was stuck at a cocktail party and a woman approached me. She had a drink in one hand (obviously not her first one, either) and a cigarette in the other.

I leaned away from her to try to avoid the cigarette smoke and she said to me with a certain hostility, "What's the matter with you? Don't you smoke?"

"No, ma'am, I don't," I said civilly, in my fairly loud speaking voice.

"I'll bet you don't drink, either."

"No, ma'am, I don't."

"Then what the hell do you do?"

And I said, my voice not dropping one decibel, "I fuck an awful lot."

You'd be surprised how immediately that destroyed the conversation.

•176

Only once did I actually try to get drunk. I was having dinner with a bunch of people who were supporting the Hayden Planetarium and they asked me what I did. I told them that on that day I was writing an article on the planet Jupiter.

"Oh," they said ecstatically. "You're an astrologer."

"No, indeed," I said, "I'm writing on astronomy. Astrology is superstitious crap."

With that, they turned away from me haughtily (and they were supporting the planetarium, too) and there was nothing left for me to do but sample the various kinds of liquor on the table, since no one would speak to me.

I made an interesting discovery. As I got drunk, my speech became more careful and better enunciated, but the long muscles of my legs went kerblooey and when I stood up I found myself swaying from side to side.

Janet, who was sitting at another table, was disturbed at my flushed countenance, came over to me, and said, "What's the matter, Isaac?"

And I said, enunciating perfectly, "My dear, I am dead drunk."

Sure enough, she found she had to keep me steady, if I was to walk at all, and she dragged me home as quickly as she could.

•177

My first experience with liquor came when I was twenty and I was at the home of the great science fiction editor John W. Campbell, Jr., in order to meet the science fiction writer Robert A. Heinlein. Heinlein was already recognized as the greatest writer in the field, even though his first story had only appeared a year earlier (and half a year after my first story).

Everyone was drinking in the ordinary fashion, but I, of course, refused and simply continued to talk in my jolly, extraverted fashion, telling jokes, laughing, and in general having a good, loud time.

Finally Heinlein came to me and said, "Here's a Coca-Cola. Surely you can drink that."

"Of course," I said, but as I lifted it to my lips, I frowned and said, "It smells funny."

"Nonsense," said Heinlein. "That's your imagination. Drink up."

I didn't like to disoblige Heinlein, so I chug-a-lugged it the way I would if it were Coca-Cola. But it wasn't; it was a Cuba Libre, loaded with alcohol.

Within five minutes, I was drunk and the sensation frightened me to death. I had never before felt that swimmingness, that looseness of leg muscles, that shakiness of vision. I thought I had suddenly been taken sick, so I sat down in a chair in a corner and waited in dead silence for my body to overcome whatever it was and for me to feel better.

Whereupon Heinlein whooped, "No wonder Asimov doesn't drink. It sobers him up."

• 178

Heinlein and I worked at the Philadelphia Navy Yard during much of World War II and Heinlein was a thorn in my side. He always insisted on having his own way and, although I put up a fight, I almost always gave in.

One of the things he wanted to do was eat lunch at the Navy Yard cafeteria. To do so meant a half-mile walk over a frozen wasteland in winter and a sea of mud in the summer, and when you got there the food was simply awful. What I wanted to do was sit in the air-conditioned comfort of the lab and quietly eat the delightful sandwiches Gertrude prepared for me. I would also read a book till lunchtime was over and no one would bother me.

But I suffered myself to be dragged out. (Heinlein, that odd person, actually made it a matter of patriotism. He was always a gung-ho patriot in all the little useless things.) About the only thing I could do was complain about the food, and Heinlein thought such complaints were unpatriotic (so help me!). He took to fining me a dime every time I made such a complaint.

I said, "If I find a way to complain about the food, Bob, without complaining about it, would you stop all this nonsense?"

He said he would, but I simply couldn't think of a way of complaining by way of noncomplaint—until a stranger happened to sit down at our table and, after eating awhile, said, "Boy, this food is lousy."

Whereupon I jumped up from my seat, raised my hand high in the air, and declaimed, "I disagree with every word that this gentleman has said, but I will defend with my life his right to say it."

And Heinlein gave up.

•179

It was a huge cafeteria at the Navy Yard, so large that from one end you could not see the other, just a purple mist. We usually sat near one end and one day, from the other end, there came a blood-curdling woman's scream. (We never found out what caused it.) Naturally, the hubbub of the conversational confusion stopped at once, and an eerie silence fell upon the cafeteria.

And in that silence, a voice rang out (mine, of course) saying, "That's funny. I'm way over here."

That broke the tension at our end of the cafeteria anyway.

•180

Also with us at the Navy Yard was another first-rate science fiction writer, L. Sprague de Camp. I have known him for fifty-three years and in all that time, he has scarcely changed in appearance. He's a wonderful person, honest and decent. He has a touch of pedantry about him, but he's so lovable, one forgives him this.

In the early days at the Navy Yard he was doing his best to qualify as a naval officer. (He succeeded and was a lieutenant commander by the war's end.)

We used to go together to the Navy Yard in the morning and one morning, as we got to the gate, Sprague clapped his hand to his chest and said, "I forgot my badge." Without it, he couldn't get in and would have to go through a lot of trouble to get a temporary badge. It might be a black mark on his record.

So I took off my badge and said, "Use mine, Sprague. No one will look at it."

He said, "How will you get in?"

I shrugged. I'd had trouble with authority all my life. I said, "Sprague, I'm not bucking for officer. And as for getting jerked around a bit, I'm used to it."

Sprague gulped and said, "Kind hearts are more than coronets."

In later years, Sprague said he did not remember the incident, but year in, year out, he has done nothing but praise me for my warm heart and kindly nature, and that's a big return for a very small favor.

Since I'm talking about the Navy Yard, I can't help but repeat two stories that show what sort of villain I can be when it comes to hurting people's feelings. My only defense is that this happens only when I strike back at someone who, without provocation, struck at me. Still, that's no real excuse, where the other person can't really take care of himself. In the battle of wits, never fight an unarmed person, something I manage to forget now and then. Here are the tales:

•181

During my stay at the Navy Yard, I decided to grow a mustache. (It didn't stay long. It was a very ugly mustache—matched my face, I think.) During its very early stages, of course, a growing mustache just makes your upper lip look dirty.

A rather swarthy young woman stared at my upper lip at this time and then said, "Are *you* trying to grow a mustache?" in a tone that cast obvious doubt on my virility.

"Why not?" I said. "You've managed."

•182

I was carefully decanting liquid from one vessel into another in the Navy Yard, and in so doing, my abdomen (I never had one of your flat abdomens) protruded rather more than usual. A young, very thin woman in the lab lifted a long piece of glass tubing, pointed it at my abdomen as though it were a spear, and said, "I think I'll let the air out of your belly so that you'll look more like a man."

"Good idea," I said, still decanting. "Then you can take the air and use it to puff up your chest so that you'll look more like a woman."

In both cases, the young women concerned first burst into tears and then suddenly turned savage. In both cases, I had to leave the laboratory hurriedly and remain away for the rest of the day.

But it was they who thrusted. I merely riposted. As I said, that's no excuse.

•183

I was once kicked out of class for giving what I thought was a very intelligent answer to a question.

The class in high school had read *Abou ben Adhem*, in which good old Abou said he loved his fellow man and, as a result, he found his name first on the list of those whom love of God had blessed.

The teacher then pointed out that since the list was of those who loved God, why did Abou's name come first when he only loved his fellow men?

I raised my hand at once.

The teacher, who should have known better, said, "Asimov!"

I said, "Alphabetical order, sir"—and got kicked out of class.

•184

Despite the fact that I'm a teetotaler, I don't mind showing the other side of the coin. The stand-up comedian Joe E. Lewis, a massive non-teetotaler, said, "The trouble with being a teetotaler is that when you wake up in the morning, that's as good as you're going to feel all day."

•185

I don't have many happy memories of my courtship of Gertrude, but here is one. Gertrude and I were at Coney Island, stretched out on the sand and totally absorbed in each other.

So absorbed, in fact, that it was only when a vague notion penetrated that there was a crowd about us that we finally looked up.

Yes, indeed, there was a large crowd about us, and a police car, too, which was slowly driving away.

We never found out what had happened, but whatever happened, it had happened all about us and we never noticed.

I don't like medical humor. It is usually cruel, and here is an example, to show what I mean:

•186

Said the doctor, "I have some bad news and some good news for you. The bad news is that you have inoperable cancer and will die in agony in less than six months."

"Good heavens," said the patient. "With bad news like that, what's the good news?"

"See that pretty nurse over there?" said the doctor. "The good news is that I will be screwing her tonight."

•187

The Pope had called together a meeting of the cardinals and said, "I have some good news for you and some bad news. The good news is this. Our blessed Savior, the Lord Jesus Christ, has returned to earth for the long-awaited Second Coming, and the Day of Judgment is at hand."

There was an exalted silence for a few moments and then one cardinal said, "But Holy Father, with good news like that, what's the bad news?"

The Pope mopped his forehead with his handkerchief and said, "The information has reached us from Salt Lake City."

•188

Said the doctor, "I'm afraid you have inoperable cancer and have only six months to live."

"What shall I do, doctor?" said the patient, appalled.

The doctor said, "I would recommend that you marry a nice Jewish woman immediately and move to Montana."

"Will that help my condition?"

"No, of course not, but it will make the six months seem much longer."

•189

During the Civil War, when General U. S. Grant was about to start his drive against the army of General Robert E. Lee, a woman approached Grant and said, "What are your plans for the campaign against Lee, General?"

Grant said, "Can you keep a secret, madam?"

"Oh, yes. Absolutely."

"Good," said Grant. "So can I."

Joke #188, by the way, is another one of those jokes that traduce and insult Jewish women. For some reason, Jewish comedians are fond of such stories. Perhaps it is a way of getting back at their mothers, who ruled them with an iron hand during their youth (I remember!). Or perhaps it's a way of getting back at their wives, who have been carefully trained by their mothers to establish a matriarchy in the family.

The stereotypical Jewish married couple consists of a loud, domineering, unbearable wife and a shy, passive, quiet husband. An example:

•190

A largely unsuccessful actor was in a mood of triumph as he said to a friend, "Well, I've gotten a part in a Broadway show, and we get to work next week."

"Good," said his friend. "What kind of a part is it?"

"I'm going to be playing a Jewish husband."

"What a shame! Couldn't you get a speaking part?"

•191

When I was married to Gertrude, she had a mother and father who exactly matched the stereotype. Her father, Henry, was a quiet, passive fellow, who was a real angel and beloved by all. He was so quiet, however, and so passive, that I would go around telling the following story:

When Gertrude was fourteen, she could no longer suppress her curiosity. "Mom," she said, "who is this man who eats with us every evening?"

Naturally, I only told the story outside the family. Gertrude had no sense of humor whatever concerning her parents, particularly her mother.

•192

Gertrude's mother, Mary, was loud and unbearably domineering and it drove me mad to see how submissive the family was. I refused to be submissive and that probably helped make my marriage a failure, since my mother-in-law didn't like me, and that strongly influenced the submissive Gertrude.

I met my mother-in-law when she was forty-seven years old. She was in bad health at the time and in a state of rapid decline. The entire family was forever catering to that bad health (which was not really surprising, since she was very obese—something Gertrude never admitted.) Just the same, her ability to decline in health was amazing. She lived to be ninety-two, and poor Gertrude survived her by only four years. (However, credit where credit is due: My mother-in-law was a wonderful cook and, when eating at her table, I forgave her much.)

So you have to picture my wedding day. Gertrude was beautiful and I was not by any means pretty. I had very little money (only $400 in the bank) and held a wartime job that could end at any time. I felt very uncertain about the whole thing, feeling that Gertrude would not endure me, and privation, for long. And since I was dreadfully in love, that bothered me to no end.

Here's how my mother-in-law helped out. As we were getting ready to drive off to our honeymoon resort, Mary stood out in the street and, with a voice like a foghorn, yelled out, "And remember, Gertrude, if you're unhappy, you come straight home to me."

•193

My mother-in-law's advice was generally bad, for she was paranoid. Once, over my protests, the family followed her advice and it turned out to be disastrous. I couldn't help but feel gratified, in a way, since my mother-in-law's First Law of Nature was that never, under any circumstances, was she to blame for anything that turned out bad. This time I felt I had her.

"Mary," I said gently, "you know that we were simply doing what you insisted we do."

Whereupon she said, "That makes it all your fault."

"Our fault? How so?"

"You should have known I didn't know what I was talking about."

•194

Once, when visiting with my mother-in-law, Gertrude and I had a violent argument (no uncommon occurrence) and, in a fit of anger, she beat me with her hand.

Her mother came running. "Stop, Gertrude, stop. Don't hit him like that. Don't hit him."

Even while I was busy trying to ward off the blows, I was conscious of a surprise. My mother-in-law was actually on my side. Unbelievable!

And then she said, "Stop it, Gertrude. You'll hurt your hand."

•195

When I was about to get married to Gertrude and was a little nervous about it, a friend of mine at school, named Stanley Ames, said to me, "Before you get married, consider your girlfriend's mother. If you don't like the mother, the chances are that eventually you won't like the daughter."

I was too much in love to pay attention, but he was right, and it is because of that piece of advice—which I didn't take—that I remember his name. And I pass it along to all of you.

My second wife, Janet, is sweet, tender, and loving. I met her mother in 1970, and this second mother-in-law of mine (who died in 1976) was also sweet, tender, and loving. I'll tell you a story about my second mother-in-law that is not funny, but I want to record it here because it touched me and gave me an experience I'd never had before.

•196

In 1973, before my divorce had come through and before I was able to marry Janet, she had a subarachnoid hemorrhage that had a good chance of altering her mental status and a fairly good chance of killing her. Naturally, I was distraught.

Her mother had been out of state, but she was back now and it was up to me to call her and give her the bad news.

I dreaded this, because I felt it only natural that her mother would consider that we had been "living in sin" and that this was a divine dispensation against her daughter and that it was my fault for luring her into that sort of life. I felt that she was going to let me have it and that I would only be able to bend my body to the storm and take it.

So I called her and through my tears, I told her.

There was a longish silence and then she said, very softly, "If anything happens to Janet, Isaac, I want to thank you for making her last few years so happy."

That's what I call a mother-in-law. From then on, when Janet lost her temper with her mother, I remained staunchly on her mother's side.

•197

I hate to go back to my first mother-in-law, but her idea of the greatest and most wonderful illness there was, was cancer. She was a real cancer fan and on a number of occasions, she announced very proudly that she had cancer. She never did, of course, not at all, not to the end of her long life, and that was probably a deep sorrow of hers.

She watched a new science program on television once and it happened to be all about cancer. She listened with delight, scarcely breathing, and she could hardly wait for a week to pass, so she could listen to it again.

She turned it on, settled herself comfortably, and behold, this time the program dealt with metallurgy. She listened for two minutes, then said, "It's not about cancer," and turned it off pettishly.

•198

Once when we were at my mother-in-law's, I spent the day visiting my various publishers (which is what I usually did when coming to New York in those days). I came back just before dinner and as I opened the door, I heard my mother-in-law say in great excitement, "And guess what it was, Gertrude."

Whereupon, without knowing the first thing about what the subject under discussion was, I said loudly, "Cancer!"

And my mother-in-law said triumphantly, "Right in the neck."

•199

One of the things my mother-in-law claimed to have which she really did have was arthritis. (Poor Gertrude inherited the tendency to it and suffered a good deal.)

When Stan got married, it turned out that his wife, Ruth, had a mother with extreme arthritis, to the point where she was virtually immobile. (Ruth, as far as I know, has not inherited it.)

Shortly after the marriage, Ruth's mother died.

My mother-in-law said, "Do you suppose she died of arthritis?" for it always struck her as an anomaly of nature for anyone to be sicker than she was.

I replied, "Yes, she did. Are you jealous, Mary?"

•200

A very similar thing happened with Stan. Stan and Ruth in their earlier days were great tennis buffs, playing the game virtually every day and sneering at me because I didn't know which end of a tennis racket one held while getting the ball to roll into the hole. They had to stop eventually, when Stan ruined his back and Ruth ruined her hip (and don't think I didn't tell them over and over again that it was all that putting with a tennis racket that did it).

One time long after that, Stan told me of a friend of his who had died on the tennis court and who was buried, in accordance with the instructions in his will, in his tennis costume.

Stan sighed, and I said, "Are you jealous, Stan?"

And he said, "Well, it's a good way to go."

"No, it isn't," I said strenuously. "A good way to go is to collapse at your typewriter with your nose stuck in the keys."

•201

Gertrude had a brother six years younger than herself, who was extremely handsome. Just as Gertrude looked like Olivia de Havilland, her brother, John, looked like Cary Grant. I never could understand how those two beauties were born to Mary and Henry, when Henry looked like Edward G. Robinson and Mary looked like nothing at all. John was the apple of Mary's eye. When he was born and she found she had a son, she dropped Gertrude at once, for Gertrude was only a daughter and she was a second-class citizen forever after. (What a miserable human being that Mary was.)

John was infantilized by his mother, who called him nothing but "Sonny." He also never managed to finish any project he started, but I won't try to psychoanalyze that.

However, he was a rather arrogant fellow who was well aware of the fact that he was smarter than most people and it amused him to make fun of any suitor that Gertrude brought home. In no time at all, he showed how stupid the suitor was and Gertrude, ashamed, would drop him.

Until she brought me home. She told me that I was the first person she brought home that Sonny couldn't make a fool of and that it was that that interested her in me.

"Oh, my goodness," I said in all honesty, "I didn't know he was trying."

•202

One of the reasons Mary didn't like me (one out of a great many) was that I made Sonny look bad. I was rapidly becoming successful with my writing and Sonny wasn't accomplishing anything at all.

So Mary said to me, "My Sonny is an *artist*. He is not a cheap businessman like you."

I said, "Mary, I'm a college professor and a novelist. Does that sound like a cheap businessman to you?"

That did not improve her opinion of me, somehow.

But let's get away from my in-laws for a while. Undoubtedly I'll think up more stories about them eventually.

•203

The harried housewife sprang to the telephone when it rang and listened with relief to the kindly voice in her ear. "How are you, darling?" it said. "What kind of a day are you having?"

"Oh, mother," said the housewife, breaking into bitter tears,

"I've had such a bad day. The baby won't eat and the washing machine broke down. I haven't had a chance to go shopping, and besides, I've just sprained my ankle and I have to hobble around. On top of that, the house is a mess and I'm supposed to have two couples to dinner tonight."

The mother was shocked and was at once all sympathy. "Oh, darling," she said, "sit down, relax, and close your eyes. I'll be over in half an hour. I'll do your shopping, clean up the house, and cook your dinner for you. I'll feed the baby and I'll call a repairman I know who'll be at your house to fix the washing machine promptly. Now stop crying. I'll do everything. In fact, I'll even call George at the office and tell him he ought to come home and help out for once."

"George?" said the housewife. "Who's George?"

"Why, George! Your husband!... Is this CAtskill 2-1374?"

"No, it's CAtskill 2-1375."

"Oh, I'm sorry. I guess I have the wrong number."

There was a short pause and the housewife said, "Does this mean you're not coming over?"

•204

I believe I saw the following in a Jules Feiffer strip.

A man is speaking into the telephone and you hear only his side of the conversation.

"Yes, mother, I've had a hard day. Gladys has been most difficult— I know I ought to be more firm, but it is hard. Well, you know how she is. Yes, I remember you warned me. I remember you told me she was a vile creature who would make my life miserable and you begged me not to marry her. You were perfectly right. You want to talk to her? All right."

He looks up from the telephone and calls to his wife in the next room, "Gladys, your mother wants to talk to you."

We must never forget that wives also have mothers-in-law, who can be every whit as irritating and evil as the husband's is. However, the wife's mother-in-law rarely appears in jokes, presumably because jokes are told primarily by men.

Almost every woman I know, although she will laugh heartily at jokes, will insist that she "can't ever remember them." That always puzzles me. They remember every article they ever bought, with its exact price and place of purchase—but they can't remember jokes.

As long as jokes are told almost exclusively by men, they will always retain a certain whiff of male chauvinist piggery.

•205

When Jewish comics tell denigrating jokes about Jews, they can be accused of anti-Semitism and self-hatred. I don't know. I think it's just an effort to laugh off something very painful. The comic writer Max Shulman, who was himself Jewish, of course, said, "Anti-Semitism consists of hating Jews more than is absolutely necessary."

Mentioning Max Shulman reminds me of a true story:

•206

My prolificity has always been a source of embarrassment to me. I write because I love to write, and publishers cooperate by publishing everything I write. The result is that by 1969 I had published a hundred books (and at this time of writing the number stands at 466, and still counting). It seems to amaze everyone, even other professionals—even me.

Once, when the number was only a hundred or so, I was introduced to a gentleman at a party. They said, "John Updike—Isaac Asimov."

I was very awed at having met a great contemporary writer, but I hesitated. It was conceivable that it was only John Updike, the local druggist, and I didn't want to make a fool of myself. Updike had no doubt about the name Isaac Asimov, however. There are no duplicates.

So he said, "Say, how do you write all those books?"

I was humiliated. It was my place to fawn on him, not vice versa. I made up my mind that the next time I met a famous writer I would not hesitate. Three days later, in the Boston University Library, I saw Max Shulman standing at the other side of the room.

I went there eagerly, all primed to fawn. I was going to say, "Mr. Shulman, I am Isaac Asimov, and I have read all your books and I love them. I laughed myself silly."

All I got to say, though, was, "Mr. Shulman, I am Isaac Asimov—"

And he interrupted, saying, "Say, how do you write all those books?"

I gave up.

•207

Said John to Mary, "I'll bet you ten cents I can kiss you on the lips without touching them."

"You're crazy," said Mary. "That's impossible. Here's a dime that says you can't."

The two dimes were placed on the mantelpiece and John then enfolded Mary and for ten minutes kissed her passionately, intimately, and moistly.

She broke away at last, panting and disheveled, and said, "You did nothing *but* touch my lips."

John pushed the dimes toward her and said, "So I lose."

•208

Mrs. Bryan, an ardent Catholic, finally persuaded her freethinking husband to come to church with her.

"Just keep an eye on me, and do exactly as I do," she said.

In the incense-laden atmosphere, Mr. Bryan laboriously rose, sat, genuflected, intoned, bent his head—all on cue from his wife.

The ventilation was poor, and Mr. Bryan found his brow wet with honest sweat. Surreptitiously, he flipped out his handkerchief and mopped his brow; then, when it was time to sit down again, he dropped it into his lap for later use.

Mrs. Bryan, out of the corner of her eye, noted something white in her husband's lap and whispered to him out of the side of her mouth, "For heaven's sake, Jim, is your fly open?"

And Mr. Bryan whispered back, "Why? Is it supposed to be?"

I have almost never met a Catholic priest I didn't like. This is terrible. I am unconvertible, of course, but still, life would be much easier if they were nasty, but they aren't.

•209

A couple of months ago, a Catholic priest gave a talk at the Dutch Treat Club. He was absolutely delightful and the talk was terrific.

Afterward, I said to him, "I notice that you are not wearing a clerical collar, Father. Why is that?"

He shook his head and said, "I only wear it at weddings and bar mitzvahs."

That broke me up. The only complaint I had against him was that he smoked. Ordinarily, I do not allow smoking at my table, but I felt that since he was a forced celibate, I couldn't very well deprive him of all pleasures.

•210

I was speaking at a Catholic college once, and the priest who was showing me around motioned me into an elevator ahead of him. In a fit of politeness, I motioned him, and we went into the Alphonse and Gaston routine of each trying to have the other go first.

Finally the priest stepped into the elevator and said to me, "All right, you win the humility sweepstakes this time."

•211

I told the previous tale to another priest once, and he said, "Ah, yes, we call it the 'I am the humblest man in the room, and I am proud of it' syndrome."

The stereotypical Irishman is fond of drinking and, for all I know, this may be accurate. The following ought to be told in a beautiful Irish brogue, though I heard it first from Emery Davis, who is no Irishman.

138

•212

Said McCarthy to O'Brien, "Did you hear about poor Houlihan?"

"No," said O'Brien. "What about poor Houlihan?"

"The poor man fell into a vat of beer and drowned."

"Saints preserve us," said O'Brien, shocked. "The poor fellow never had a chance."

"Yes, he did," said McCarthy. "He got out three times to go to the men's room."

I was a member of Mensa for many years; Mensa is an organization of high-IQ people. I never enjoyed my membership, however.

In the first place, I found that high-IQ people can be just as stupid as low-IQ people—much more stupid, in fact, because they think they are bright. They tend to be mind-proud, view themselves as a persecuted minority, and are, in general, unbearable.

The worst thing of all is that they are forever trying to challenge each other, and I was a particular target. The young kids at Mensa were forever trying to shoot the old man down, and I didn't want to play the game. Eventually I simply resigned.

Here's an example of the sort of thing that goes on. I attended a Mensa meeting not very many years ago because I was slated to speak there, and I must admit they do make a good audience.

•213

We were at the dinner table at that meeting and I did my best to entertain the others with some of my choice limericks and, of course, I was asked to improvise limericks for the names of some of the people present, and I tried.

When I had recited one that was, indeed, rather mediocre, one of the Mensans, nose high in the air, said, "Surely you can do better than that."

Whereupon, irritated, I said, "I surely can, but the important thing to remember is that you can't."

That's the kind of game I don't want to play, but as long as I've mentioned limericks, let's have a few more. I must say that my limerick books did very poorly, which didn't bother me, since I wrote them for amusement and not for profit. Anyway, here are some more.

•214

> At a nudist camp, sweet little Lillian
> Was slated to lead the cotillion.
> > That made her so proud
> > That to shine in the crowd,
> She painted her nipples vermilion.

•215

> I got into bed with Dolores,
> And her diaphragm proved to be porous.
> > The result of our sins
> > Was a fine pair of twins,
> Now the birth control people abhor us.

I tried this one out (trembling a bit) on a group of Planned Parenthood people to whom I was giving a talk. They loved it, and was I relieved!

I particularly like the intellectual type of limerick, in which you mention people who (it would seem) are difficult to rhyme. The following is an example of what I mean and is my favorite of this type:

•216

> To the ancient Greek writer, Herodotus,

Said a pretty young thing, "My how hard it is."
Said he, "Do you fear
I will hurt you, my dear?"
And she said, "Are you crazy? Thank God it is."

•217

There was once a remarkable stripper
Who'd undress to the very last zipper.
Before one—before all—
But one day in the fall,
She refused and said, "Not on Yom Kippur."

Sometimes you have to meet a challenge. Back in the fifties, I was challenged to write a limerick in which the first line was "A man with a prick of obsidian." I failed, but I kept working on it, on and off, and finally, after about twenty years, I came up with the following:

•218

A man with a prick of obsidian,
Of a length that was truly ophidian,
Was sufficiently gallant
To please girls with his talent,
Each day in the mid–post-meridian.

Ophidian, if you're curious, means "snakelike."

•219

The haughty philosopher, Plato,
Would unbend to a sweet young tomato.
Though she might be naive
Like you wouldn't believe,
He would patiently show her the way to.

•220

> There was an old fellow of Michigan,
> Who said, "How I wish I were rich again.
> > But each time I'm ahead
> > I fall into the bed
> Of that rotten old gold-digging bitch again."

•221

> A gourmet's delight is Priscilla,
> For her breath's a distinct sarsparilla.
> > One breast tastes of thyme,
> > The other of lime,
> And her vaginal flavor's vanilla.

I once recited this to a young woman named Priscilla and she smiled and said, "How did you know?"

•222

> Said a chic and attractive young Greek,
> "Would you like a nice peek that's unique?"
> > "Why, yes," Joe confessed,
> > So she quickly undressed,
> And showed him her sleek Greek physique.

•223

> There was a young woman named Sally
> Who loved an occasional dally.
> > She sat on the lap
> > Of a well-endowed chap,
> And said, "Ooh, you're right up my alley."

•224

A group of Mensans were contentedly finished with their meal and the game of Question-and-Answer was suggested. Each person in turn asked a question, and anyone who volunteered an answer that was wrong dropped out. If no one could answer, the questioner himself had to answer, and if he was wrong, he dropped out. Each dropout had to put $5 into the pot.

Eventually the matter boiled down to Thompson and Brown, and the erudition of each one boiled up so that both were held even for half an hour.

Finally Thompson said, "How does a gopher dig a hole without leaving a mound of sand at the lip?"

Brown thought about that and said, "I can't answer that. However, since it's your question, you had better answer it."

Thompson said coolly, as he reached for the accumulated pile of bills, "Easy. The gopher starts at the bottom of the hole and that's where he leaves the sand."

"Hold on," said Brown heatedly, grasping Thompson's wrist to prevent him from taking the pot. "How does the gopher get to the bottom of the hole in the first place?"

"That's your question," said Thompson sweetly, and took the money.

•225

Gertrude was once engaged in her favorite pleasure of telling me all my faults. She had about a thousand of them and she carefully listed them all. I listened patiently, and finally I said, "Look, Gertrude, you're telling me all the horrible things I do, but is it possible that you have your faults also? Do you have one fault? A single fault? If so, tell me what it is."

Gertrude paused and thought deeply, trying to find a single fault she had and obviously failing. Finally inspiration struck.

She said, "Yes, I have one fault. I'm too nice."

Funny! In a million years I wouldn't have thought of that as one of her faults.

• • •

Old women in love are a recognized source of amusement in the world of jokedom. And not only there. In almost every Gilbert & Sullivan operetta, there is an elderly woman in love and the Victorian audience laughed heartily. And so, I'm afraid, do we. It's just another aspect of the male chauvinism of the funny story.

•226

An elderly woman of fairly gross tonnage was sitting on the beach. Her eye fell with hard calculation upon a young man whose gleaming and muscular body was at the peak of manly beauty.

She called to him. "Young man."

He approached, and she said to him, "Young man, at first glance you may think I'm nothing but a fat old woman. However, it so happens that I am a widow of inordinate wealth. If you will consent to be my companion—in every sense of the word—I am prepared to see to it that you will live a life of luxury. Your every worldly care will be satisfied.

"However, I must make sure that you are a man of judgment. You will notice that I am wearing a diamond ring. Please glance at it from your present distance and estimate its weight. If you guess correctly, my offer stands."

The young man, looking at the woman with tremendous distaste, decided to end the charade at once. He said, "Your ring weighs eight hundred pounds."

"Wrong," said the woman, "but close enough."

One of the great values of being a firm and convinced humanist is that one need not fear hell. I am completely convinced that hell does not exist except in the mind of pious sadists. Does that mean I can freely commit all sorts of wrongs and evils since I need fear no punishment? Not at all. Even if we disregard the punishments dictated by the law, there is the punishment of my own conscience. I have a set of ethical standards and I try to live by them without being driven by the fear of hell or, for that matter, the hope of heaven.

However, in the world of jokedom, hell and heaven exist.

•227

Mark Twain once said, "Heaven for climate; hell for company."

•228

A man died and found himself in a wonderful place of comfort and beauty. A servant waited on him and fulfilled every need. He was a little surprised at finding himself in such bliss, for he had led a normally sinful life—but he accepted the situation.

After a long, long time, however, he got tired of eating delicious meals, of listening to wonderful music, of embracing lithe and lissome young women. So he said to his servant, "Isn't there any work I can do?"

The servant shook his head. "Our people don't work. They merely enjoy themselves."

"Well, frankly, I've had enough enjoyment. I would like to work. I would like to raise a sweat. I would like to feel tired. I would even like a little pain now and then."

The servant shook his head. "Quite impossible. Such things take place only in the—uh—other place."

"Well, damn it," said the man, "I think I would prefer to be in hell, in that case."

"But sir," said the servant, "you *are* in hell."

•229

It may be the thought of the previous story, which I first read many years ago, and which impressed me enormously, that led me to have the dream I had in the course of this last year.

I dreamed that I had died and that I found myself in a beautiful place, perfect in all respects, with angels singing with supernal beauty and charm, and the Recording Angel advancing to see me with a smile on his brightly radiant face.

"Greetings, Isaac," he said.

I said, "Pardon me, but there's some mistake. I don't belong here. I'm an atheist, did you know that?"

The Recording Angel said, "We know very well that you're an atheist, but it is we who decide who comes here, not you. I welcome you."

"I see," I said, and looked about me at all the perfection, decided I didn't want it, turned to the Recording Angel, and said, "In that case, do you have a typewriter I can use?"

—And I woke up.

I think I know why I woke up at that moment. Had I remained in my dream, the Recording Angel would have told me that there were no typewriters and no other tools with which to write, not even pen and paper. And I would have realized that heaven might be heaven in every aspect, but if it meant I could not write—I was in hell.

You may think that is odd of me, and my first wife, Gertrude, was, for one, very disapproving.

•230

Gertrude shook her head at me back in the late sixties, when I had pointed out in glee that my hundredth book would be out in not too long a time.

"Isaac," she said, "what good does it do you to write a hundred books, if you spend your whole life bent over your typewriter and let all its wonders pass you by? When you die, you will realize your entire life was wasted."

"Not at all," I said. "If I publish a hundred books and then die, you just lean over my deathbed to catch my last words. They will be, 'Damn, only a hundred.'"

•231

Actually, my 466th book has arrived recently and I have about 20 more in press. If I can only manage to live and work a few more years, I will reach the 500 mark, and if you think that that will satisfy me, it won't.

Do you know the Faustian bargain? Faust said to Mephistopheles that if the latter could somehow conquer Faust's restless spirit and so bemuse him with gifts that Faust would say, "Oh, passing moment, thou art so fair. Linger a while," then Mephistopheles could collect his soul.

If there were indeed a Mephistopheles, I have a deal I would like to make with him. Let him arrange to have me living in good health indefinitely until such time as I said, "I have written enough. I will now stop." *Then* he can have my soul, but it will be a long, long wait that he will have for it.

•232

I was once being interviewed by Barbara Walters in three segments, all at once, though they were to be run on three separate days.

In between two of the segments, she asked me how many books I had written, and I told her. She said, "Don't you ever want to do anything but write?"

"No," I said.

"Don't you want to go hunting? Fishing? Dancing? Hiking?"

And I said, "No! No! No! and No!"

She said, "But what would you do if the doctor gave you only six months to live?"

I said, "Type faster."

This was widely quoted, but the "six months" was changed to "six minutes," which bothered me. It's "six months."

•233

The elderly minister looked severely at the worshipers gathered in the church and said, "What a fearful thought it is that everyone in this congregation must, sooner or later, die and face the dreadful Judgment of the Almighty."

Everyone in the church stirred uneasily and looked fearful, except for one little man in the front row, who giggled.

The minister flushed, bent his glance at the little man, and said, "I say, every person in this congregation must sooner or later face the Judgment."

Again the little man giggled.

The minister now addressed the little man directly. "You, there, in the front row. May I ask what you find so amusing about my statement?"

And the little man said, "I am not amused, Reverend. I am relieved. I am not a member of this congregation."

It seems to me that every group has a neighboring group concerning whom they tell "stupid jokes." Here in the United States we tell Italian jokes and Polish jokes. The English tell Irish jokes, the Canadians tell Newfoundland jokes, and so on.

They're all vile canards, for no group is stupid as a group. There are stupid people and smart people in every group—a truism the damned human race never seems to learn.

And yet some of these jokes make me laugh. For instance, the Norwegians and Swedes are two such peaceable peoples that it is amusing to be told they tell jokes about each other. Here is one that is interchangeable. It can as easily be a Swede talking as a Norwegian.

•234

Said one Norwegian to another, "Do you know how you save a Swede from drowning?"

"No," said the other.

"Good," said the first.

•235

Said an earnest young man, "I don't know why people tell Polish jokes. The Poles are no more stupid than any other group. In fact, the stupidest person I ever met was Jewish—a Polish Jew."

There was a period some years ago when light bulb jokes were all the fashion. You asked how many people of one sort or another it took to screw in a light bulb and then made use of the stereotype.

•236

Q: How many Poles does it take to screw in a light bulb?
A: Five. One to stand on the ladder and hold the bulb in the socket, and four to turn the ladder.

•237

Q: How many WASPs does it take to screw in a light bulb?
A: Two. One to screw in the bulb, and one to mix the martinis.

•238

Q: How many psychiatrists does it take to screw in a light bulb?
A: One, but the light bulb has to *want* to be screwed in.

•239

A bee is buzzing about its business, going from flower to flower, collecting nectar and busily daubing itself with pollen. On its head it is wearing a tiny yarmulke, the kind of skullcap routinely worn by Jews.

Another bee came buzzing up and said, "Why ever are you wearing a yarmulke?"

To which the first bee replies, "Because I don't want anyone should, God forbid, mistake me for a WASP."

WASP is an acronym for "White Anglo-Saxon Protestant," but it is broadened to include anyone of northwest European descent.

My dear wife, Janet, has two Swedish grandparents plus one who is Danish and one who is English, so that she falls

149

perfectly into the WASP category. She claims that in the world of jokedom, WASPs are mercilessly stigmatized by Jewish comedians. As an example:

•240

Q: Why are WASPs poor lovers?
A: Because by the time they hang up their jackets and pants on separate hangers and give them each a good brushing and put shoe trees in their shoes, the young lady involved has lost interest.

Of course, WASPs are renowned stereotypically for their sangfroid and their coolness under pressure. For that reason, the following story should be told with a British accent, if you can manage it.

•241

Mrs. Alexander Chumley-Smythe of London called her husband in the City and said, "My dear, there is a fearful brute of a gorilla in the beech tree in the garden, mopping and mowing and making a spectacle of itself. I scarcely know what to do."

"Stay calm, old dear," said Chumley-Smythe, "and I will be right home."

So he was, and having observed the gorilla, and having agreed that it seemed a fearsome animal, he said, "Not to worry, my dear, we shall simply get in touch with some sound gorilla-trapping organization."

Turning to the London yellow pages, he looked under the heading of "Gorilla Trapping" and dialed the firm of Fortescue and Chichester. There was an immediate answer: "Fortescue here."

Chumley-Smythe told his story and Fortescue said, "Ah, yes, I will be right there. Hold tight and do not let the brute escape."

Fortescue was there within half an hour, and in his truck he had a ladder, an enormous dog, a rifle, and a large pair of manacles. He said, "My partner, Chichester, is engaged in trapping a gorilla in Basingstoke, so I wonder if you can help me."

"Certainly," said Chumley-Smythe. "What is it you wish me to do?"

Fortescue said, "I shall climb into the tree, using the ladder. I shall then most vigorously shake the branch on which the gorilla is sitting. This will shake him off and, as soon as he hits the ground, this ferocious gorilla hound will instantly seize the beast by his testicles, which will give him something to think about, you may be sure. With the brute pinned in this fashion, you have only to place these large manacles upon his wrists and, when I come down from the tree, we will be all set."

"That seems simple enough," said Chumley-Smythe, "but for what purpose have you brought this rifle?"

Fortescue slapped his forehead in disgust and said, "Dear, dear, I'll be forgetting my head next. Why, this rifle is the most important part. While I am shaking the branch on which the gorilla is sitting, he may be shaking the one on which I am sitting. You stand there with the rifle and if, by some mischance, it should be I that fall out of the tree, then, without waiting a moment—shoot the dog!"

Every new development in the news brings with it new jokes, many of which are so topical that they vanish almost at once. An example from years ago has staying power; but the one after that, dealing with the war in the Persian Gulf, can't possibly.

•242

Q: Why do the Poles specialize in sausages while the Arabs specialize in oil?

A: Because the Poles had first choice.

•243

The Poles sent a thousand men to the Gulf to take part in the war that was briefly raging there, and the Mexicans don't know what to do with them.

Animal stories are quite common and are almost invariably anthropomorphic—that is, the animals act exactly as though they were human beings. Such stories go back to the earliest times (Aesop's fables, for instance) and have not relinquished their hold on us even today as, for instance, in Joel Chandler Harris's Uncle Remus stories, and the contemporary *Watership Down* by Richard Adams.

•244

The two bulls of Farmer Jones had long since passed the point where they could attend to the cows of the herd. They had been retired and they asked nothing better than to eat their grass in peace and quiet.

The day came, therefore, when Farmer Jones brought in a virile young bull of surpassing talents to service the herd.

One of the old bulls watched the young one at his indiscriminate work and began to snort, bellow, and paw the ground.

The second bull said, "What is this, old man? Are you getting young ideas?"

"Not at all," whispered the first. "I just don't want that youngster there to get the idea I'm a cow."

In my time, I have given a number of commencement addresses—a couple of dozen, I think. These, like all my talks, are off the cuff, and that sometimes makes my sponsors nervous. Nor am I above trying to tease the president of the college, at times.

•245

At a college in south central Pennsylvania, the commencement exercises were starting. The academic procession was walking in to Edward Elgar's "Pomp and Circumstance" (without which, apparently, no such exercise would be allowed to take place). The procession included first the students, then the professors—and at the end of the long, long line came the president of the college on the right, and the speaker (Isaac Asimov) on the left.

Out of sheer deviltry, I muttered to the president out of the right corner of my mouth, "By the way, what shall I speak about?"

The scoundrel took it quite calmly. He muttered to me out of the left corner of his mouth, "About twenty minutes."

The next story I told with great success at a commencement—but only because I was getting an honorary degree. It goes as follows:

•246

A Texan walked into the offices of the president of a small Texas college and said, "I would like to donate a million dollars tax free to this institution."

The president's eyes opened wide and he said, "That is a kindly notion, sir. We will be pleased to accept it."

"There's a condition. I would like to have an honorary degree."

"No problem," said the president. "That can be arranged."

"For my horse," said the Texan.

And now the president got to his feet in shock. "For your *horse?*"

"Yes, my mare, Betsy. She's carried me for many years and I owe her a lot. I would like to have her receive a Tr.D., a Doctor of Transportation."

"But we can't give an honorary degree to a horse."

"I'm sorry to hear you say so, because in that case I can't give you a million dollars."

"Well, wait a minute," said the president, sweating profusely. "Let me consult the board of trustees."

'The board was convened in a hurry and listened to the story in various grades of shock and disbelief, all except the oldest trustee, whose eyes were closed and who seemed asleep.

One trustee expressed the general opinion, "We can't give a horse an honorary degree, no matter how much money is involved."

At this point, the oldest trustee opened his eyes and said, "For God's sake, take the money and give the horse his degree."

Said the president, "Don't you think that would be a disgrace to us?"

"Of course not," said the oldest trustee. "It would be an honor. It would be the first time we ever gave a degree to a *whole* horse."

•247

I spoke at a college commencement once and the president asked me to speak for fifteen minutes.

"Sure," I said agreeably. I got up and said, "The president has asked me to speak for fifteen minutes, so you won't be stuck with me for any longer than that."

After the talk was over, a student came to me in great excitement and said, "When you said you were going to speak for fifteen minutes, I started my stopwatch, which I happened to have with me, and it turned out you spoke for fourteen minutes and thirty-six seconds, and you never looked at your watch once. How did you manage that?"

I grinned and said, "Sheer genius, young man. Sheer genius."

•248

In my early days as a speaker, I spoke at a chemical firm in Philadelphia. I was given strict instructions because I was to be on closed-circuit TV. They showed me a mess of cards, which said ten minutes, five minutes, three minutes, two minutes, and one minute, and I was told that I must adjust my talk so that I was finished at the one-minute mark. I said, "Sure."

But then I gave my talk and was naturally caught up in it and forgot all about my instructions.

At the end, the man in charge said to me, "That was amazing. You didn't seem the least bit hurried or nervous as the time cards were shown you and yet you finished just as the one-minute card came to its end."

And I said in all honesty, "What time cards?"

I had never seen a single one of them.

•249

The diner in a midtown restaurant rose in a fearful state of fury and shouted at the waiter, "By the Lord Harry, this steak is unfit to eat. I'm going into the kitchen and I'll shove it down the chef's throat."

The waiter, lifting his eyebrows disdainfully, said, "I beg you, sir, to control yourself and be possessed of patience. There is, at present, a beef stew and a coconut custard pie who are in line ahead of you."

Jewish restaurants are, by stereotype, known for the insolence of the waiters and the unreasonableness of the clients. My favorite Jewish restaurant story is the following:

•250

Mr. Ginsberg went into Ratner's Dairy Restaurant every day at precisely twelve and he invariably ordered the same thing, a large bowl of matzo-ball soup. So routine was this event over the decades that every noon, as Ginsberg seated himself—always in the same seat, which was saved for him—the waiter deftly slipped a large bowl of piping fresh matzo-ball soup before him and watched with gratification as Ginsberg began to inhale it with the greatest of gusto.

But on this particular day, Ginsberg did no such thing. He merely sat and stared at the soup.

After an agonizing few minutes, the waiter approached. "What's the matter, Mr. Ginsberg, is the soup too cold for you? I'll heat it up."

Ginsberg growled, "Taste it!"

The waiter said, "I don't have to taste it. Just tell me. Is it too hot? I'll fan it. Does it need salt? Pepper? I'll fix it."

Ginsberg growled, "Taste it, I tell you."

"All right. All right. Don't get mad. I'll taste it." The waiter's eyes wandered over the table. "But where's the spoon?"

And Ginsberg shouted in fury, "*A-ha-a-a-a.*"

•251

A gentile once wandered into a Jewish restaurant and ordered roast chicken. It arrived complete with potatoes and a few sundries, and the diner looked at it without much favor.

He said to the waiter, "Don't I get a green vegetable?"

And the waiter said, "And what color is the sour pickle? Purple?"

•252

Another gentile once wandered into a Jewish restaurant and ordered roast chicken.

The waiter said, "Take my advice and have the boiled beef today."

"No, thank you," said the diner. "Roast chicken is what I want."

"Listen to me. The roast chicken is not for you. Have the boiled beef."

"What is this? Don't you suppose I know what I want? Bring me the roast chicken at once."

"I will not do that. I know better than you what you should have."

"Look," said the diner, striking the table a resounding blow, "get me the manager."

The manager, drawn by the noise, came bustling over. "What's the matter? What's going on?"

The waiter turned to him and said, "Listen. This guy didn't come here to eat. He came here to give me an argument."

•253

A Greek gentleman, eating in a Chinese restaurant, ordered fried rice, and the waiter, smiling and courteous, said, "Ah, yes, flied lice."

This struck the diner as excruciatingly funny and he ordered fried rice whenever he came in just to hear the waiter say "flied lice"—at which he would laugh heartily. He took to bringing in friends so that they might hear this, too, and little by little the waiter realized he was a source of fun and mockery.

Well, waiters have their feelings, too. This one took his life savings and invested it in a course on elocution and public speaking, and one day when the Greek gentleman arrived with several of his friends and ordered fried rice, the waiter said blandly, "Ah, yes, fr-r-ried r-r-r-ice."

And as the Greek sat there nonplussed, the Chinese waiter cried out in triumph, "How you like that, you Gleek plick?"

•254

A young man was driving his date on an outing along a country road in England when they came upon a truck in the road ahead, moving at a very gentle pace and remaining firmly in the middle of the road.

The young man leaned out of his car window and shouted up ahead, "I say. Let us pass, will you?"

The truck driver shouted back cheerfully, "Can't, guv'ner. Got a delicate delivery to make and I can't change my speed; nor what I can't get to one side, either."

"Well, *damn* your delivery. Let us pass," shouted the young man.

The truck driver's face darkened. "Narsty language, is it, sir? Well, I don't hold with narsty language myself, specially seeing as what you've got a lady with you. So I won't use none myself, like as what you've gone and done, but shall satisfy myself with a simple—but heartfelt—fuck you."

Those last two words are the ultimate in disdain. They have lost all sexual connotation and merely express disgust and contempt. You hear them, day in and day out, from everyone. Even my dear wife Janet— well, let me tell you the story.

•255

I have never been known for my sartorial splendor and my dear wife, Janet, finds herself compelled to comb my hair for me, and brush me off, and insist I take off one article of clothing and put on another on the silly grounds that the first one "doesn't match." In short, she wears herself out in the vain effort to make me look presentable, and this wears me out, too, because I don't care if I look presentable or not.

Finally I said, "Janet, in the Bible, the prophet Samuel, disappointed in King Saul, has decided to find another king and he comes to the house of Jesse of Bethlehem because God had sent him there for the purpose of finding the new king. Jesse had seven sons in the house, all of them strong and handsome and obvious king material, but Samuel would have none of them.

"There was an eighth son, the youngest, who was out watching the sheep, and *he* was the one Samuel wanted. He was, in fact, David, for as the Bible said, 'The Lord seeth not as man seeth; for man looketh on the outward appearance, but the Lord looketh on the heart.'"

I quoted this passage to Janet to show her that it wasn't important to look presentable and she started riffling the pages of the Bible.

I said to her, "What are you looking for, Janet?"

She said, "That other biblical quotation—fuck you."

•256

This reminds me of the telegram sent off in a rage which, with appropriate telegraphic brevity, read: FUCK YOU! INSULTING LETTER FOLLOWS!

•257

A nasty practical joke is to send a telegram to a friend which reads THINGS MAY YET BE ALL RIGHT. IGNORE PREVIOUS TELEGRAM. The point of the joke is that no previous telegram was sent.

•258

The terrible-tempered Mr. Anderson, having missed an easy putt, shouted, "Oh, fuck!"

A young lady in the party said, "You needn't use vile language."

Anderson stared at her angrily and said, "Oh, come on. I'm sure you've heard the word many times before."

"I have," said the young lady, "but never in anger."

Men are very sensitive about the size and potency of their genital equipment. A joke indicating a lack in these respects might get a smile out of men, but women lean back and laugh loud and long. Try this one on mixed company and see for yourself:

•259

Emery Davis said to me once, "I'm getting stronger as I'm getting older. When I was young, I simply could not bend my penis when it was erect; but now I can do so easily."

•260

Two little boys were urinating behind the barn and one said, "I wish I had a big one like my big brother. He holds his with four fingers."

Said the second little boy, "But you're holding yours with four fingers."

"Sure," said the first, "but I'm pissing on three of them."

Much less frequent are the jokes making fun of women's genital equipment (a strange turnabout from the usual male chauvinism of jokes).

•261

A woman who was having a one-night stand with a man she had casually picked up said rather contemptuously, "You have a very small organ."

To which the man replied, "It merely seems small because it has been asked to play in a cathedral."

•262

I once had occasion to talk to Gertrude in the last year of her life because there was a question concerning the children.

She behaved quite calmly, till I said (rather foolishly), "Do you realize that in a little while we will be celebrating our golden wedding?"

"What golden wedding?" she demanded suspiciously.

"Well, on July 26, 1992, we will be celebrating our golden wedding, since we were married on July 26, 1942."

"Ah," said Gertrude reminiscently, "that was a black day in my life."

I was a little irritated, and I said, "By a curious coincidence, it was a black day in my life, too."

Whereupon she shrieked, "Are you trying to say that it was a bad thing for you to marry me? If you don't admit right now that marrying me was the best thing you ever did, you're going to die and go straight to hell."

I said, "Gertrude, don't talk about my dying. If I die, your alimony stops."

There was a short pause, and then Gertrude said, in a totally different voice, "By the way, how do you feel?"

The next joke is unusual in that when I told it, very recently, everyone began shrieking at the next to the last line and I never got to give the last line. It made me feel bad. Here's the joke:

•263

When my mother was in her nursing home during the last year of her life, I called her frequently and she was always delighted to hear from me and seized the opportunity of telling me the latest news. She said to me:

"Yesterday, I was speaking to an old woman of ninety-four"—my mother was seventy-seven at the time—"and in the middle of the conversation, she just dropped dead. Oh, Isaac, everything happens to your mother."

At which point, everyone started laughing heartily and I didn't get the chance to deliver the last line, which was, "Gee, Ma, something also happened to the old lady."

•264

John Barrymore, whose Hamlet was famous, was once asked, "Do you think, Mr. Barrymore, that Shakespeare intended us to suppose that Hamlet had had sexual relations with Ophelia?"

"I don't know about Shakespeare's intentions," said Barrymore, "but I always did."

Naturally, Shakespeare, as the greatest writer who ever lived, must come in for his share of jokes, usually at the expense of others, however. After all, if there was anyone who was unassailable, surely it was Shakespeare.

•265

A woman who had seen *Hamlet* for the first time was asked her opinion about it.

"I thought very little of it," she said. "This man, Shakespeare, did nothing but string together a lot of quotations."

•266

I wrote a book once in which I had occasion to quote a longish speech from Shakespeare's *The Tempest*. I quoted it, then went on with my own writing.

When I went over the manuscript, I crossed out Shakespeare's passage. I could not endure the switch from my own writing, to Shakespeare's magnificent poetry, and then back to my own writing.

I grumbled, "He and I know the same words. It's just a matter of putting them together right. Why can't I do it as well as he does?"

In my first book, I included a number of historical anecdotes. I certainly didn't use them all up. I shall scatter quite a few through this book.

•267

When Alexander the Great was invading giant Persia and winning every battle, the Persian monarch in desperation offered to cede him the western half of his empire.

One of Alexander's generals, Parmenion, aware of the uncertainty of war, was willing to settle for that and said, "I would accept the terms, were I Alexander."

To which Alexander, who was playing for all, said, "And so would I, were I Parmenion."

•268

Edward VII of England was notorious for his numerous amours and his entirely hedonistic life. There was nothing his queen, Alexandra, could do about it because, aside from seeing to it that heirs to the throne were born, he ignored her completely. When he died, she is reported to have said philosophically, "Well, now at least I know where he is."

This reminds me of the following, which is not a historical anecdote, but then I stubbornly refuse to make this book orderly. I am following my own stream of consciousness.

•269

Mr. Jones had come home from a hard day of work and was appalled when his wife reminded him that they had arranged to visit a friend's house for dinner and bridge.

"I'm too tired to budge," he protested.

"It can't be helped," said Mrs. Jones, her eyes dangerous.

So Jones was forced to shower, change clothes, and drag himself off to the friend's house. He was largely silent during the meal, clearly in a bad humor. In the bridge game he was paired off with the hostess and proceeded to play one lousy game, so that he and the hostess lost steadily.

Finally he got up and muttered, "Got to go to the men's room."

Nor did he bother to close the door of the men's room, and the sound of water tinkling into water was clear and distinct.

Mrs. Jones, unendurably embarrassed, said, "Please excuse my husband. He has had a very hard day."

And the hostess said, "No need for excuses. I don't mind. This is the first moment since we started playing bridge that I know what he has in his hand."

•270

St. Augustine, in his wild youth, is supposed to have prayed, "Lord, grant me chastity and continence—but not just yet."

•271

The Roman Emperor Augustus is supposed to have noticed a younger man who had a strong resemblance to himself. He called in the young man and said, "Did I ever meet your mother?"

"Not to my knowledge, O Augustus," said the young man, "but I believe my grandfather knew your mother."

•272

William Schwenck Gilbert, half of the Gilbert & Sullivan team, had a terrible temper. He lived in London at a time when there were two kinds of public transportation. There were carriages with two wheels called hansom cabs because they had first been designed by one Joseph Hansom, and carriages with four wheels that were called four-wheelers.

One time Gilbert was standing outside the entrance of a hotel when a portly gentleman came out and, mistaking him for a door-man, said, "My good man, call me a carriage."

At which Gilbert scowled and said, "You're a four-wheeler."

The man said, "What do you mean, fellow?"

And Gilbert replied, "Well, you asked me to call you a carriage, and I couldn't very well call you hansom."

•273

Gilbert wrote a comic opera which he called *Ruddygore*. This created a sensation, for the British of the time considered *bloody* to be an unbearably uncouth expression. Since *gore* refers to blood, and since *ruddy* was a well-known euphemism for "bloody," the name of the operetta was equivalent to "bloody-blood" and there were loud protests. Gilbert held firm, but went as far as changing the *y* to *i* and making it *Ruddigore*.

In the early days of the performance, someone asked Gilbert how "Bloodygore" was getting along.

Gilbert's face darkened. "It's *Ruddigore*."

"That's the same thing."

"No, it isn't" said Gilbert. "If I said I admired your blooming countenance, would that be saying the same as 'I like your bloody cheek?' Well, it's not, and I don't."

•274

Gilbert is supposed to have asked the whereabouts of one of the girls in the chorus.

"She's around behind," he was told.

"I know she has," said Gilbert, "but where is she?"

•275

Gilbert had no marital problems, for his wife early learned to give in to him at every point. After his death, she said, "It's a lot easier being Mr. Gilbert's widow than being Mr. Gilbert's wife."

•276

Robert Benchley, the great American wit, had an experience similar to that of the man who asked Gilbert to call him a carriage, but in this case, of course, it was Benchley who had the last word. Stepping out of a hotel, he asked a man in an ornate uniform to call him a taxi.

"Sir," said the uniformed man in a dudgeon, "I happen to be a rear admiral in the United States Navy."

"That's all right," said Benchley. "Call me a battleship, then."

•277

George Gershwin was praising his father one day. He said, "And on top of all his virtues, he's so modest about me."

•278

My father was also full of virtues, but he was never modest about me. When I was a little boy of about five and had taught myself to read, he bought me a little English dictionary, without telling me how it worked. I studied it carefully and, since I knew the alphabet, I discovered it was a list of words in alphabetical order, and I amused myself by finding some words I knew.

When I told my father of my great discovery, he was overwhelmed with pleasure and could not wait to boast about me to his half-brother-in-law, my Uncle Joe.

With me present, he said, "I gave him a dictionary and he worked out how to look things up all by himself. You can give him any word you want and he will find it for you."

My Uncle Joe said sourly, "Impossible!"

And within fifteen seconds, I was holding up the dictionary and pointing. I had found the word *impossible*. My beaming father couldn't have asked for anything better.

•279

Eventually, I astonished my father more and more. Once, looking at one of my science books, he said, "Where did you learn all these things, Isaac?"

"From you, Papa," I said.

"From me? I don't know anything at all about this."

"That's not the point, Papa. You taught me to value knowledge and all these things in my books are only details."

•280

The Greek poet Bion took a sea voyage once, and the crew consisted of a group of particularly profane and dissolute men. A storm came up and the crew began to call loudly upon all the gods to deliver them.

"Don't attract their attention," said Bion. "It's better that they *not* know you're here."

Anyone who studies German is bound to notice an outstanding peculiarity of the language. The verb tends to come at the end of the sentence, so that while in English we say, "He went to the store," in Germany you say, "He to the store went." So:

•281

A German was giving an impassioned speech at the United Nations and the interpreter was silent.

"What's he saying?" someone whispered to the interpreter.

"I don't know yet," said the interpreter. "I'm waiting for the verb."

Writers, actors, and creative people generally are believed to be alcoholics, to a great extent. Certainly a good many of the writers I know have no objection to imbibing. Probably it's the result of the insecurity of the life and of the general ebullience expected of a creative person.

Oddly enough, the two most ebullient of all the science fiction writers, Harlan Ellison and myself, don't drink. We have other addictions: Writing is mine and fighting with editors is his. Anyway:

•282

A well-known actor, very much the worse for wear, staggered onto the stage on cue (probably having been pushed) and looked about him with a vacant stare.

The prompter stage-whispered, "Do you want the next line?"
Whereupon the actor said, "Next line, hell. What's the *play?*"

•283

I was giving a talk at a college down in Maryland, and I was told that a week earlier a very famous writer had spoken.

I felt it would only be polite to affect modesty. I said, "I couldn't possibly do better than he."

The person speaking to me said, "Will you be able to stand up?"

"Of course," I said, rather surprised.

"Then you win. When he came out, before saying a single word, he fell on his nose, dead drunk."

•284

The dean of women, addressing her charges, concluded, "And remember, young ladies, you represent not only your own honor but that of the school. When importuned by young men, ask yourself: Is an hour's pleasure worth a lifetime of disgrace? Now, are there any questions?"

A young lady raised her hand instantly and said, "Tell me, how do you make it last an hour?"

•285

Said the young man with satisfaction, "Yesterday, I finally got my girl to say that little word, 'Yes.'"

"Congratulations," said his friend. "When's the wedding?"

"What wedding?"

Time for more limericks:

When a young woman named Stephanie defied me to rhyme her name, I came up with the following:

•286

Said Joe, "When I leave my young Stephanie,

Her cries of unhappiness deafen me.
　　　But I make no apology,
　　　I rely on technology,
And screw her by wireless telephony."

•287

There was an old fellow named Paul
Whose prick was exceedingly small.
　　　When in bed with a lay
　　　He could screw her all day
Without touching the vaginal wall.

When I had a triple bypass in December of 1983, I was told they would have to stop my heart for hours and place me in a heart-lung machine. I was afraid they would skimp on the oxygen and that my brain might experience a shortage and lose some of its brilliance. (Years later, there were reports that there was real danger of that, so I wasn't just being silly.)

I asked my internist, Paul Esserman, to impress everyone concerned that my brain had an exceedingly fine edge and that I didn't want it blunted in the least, so that they were to make sure it would get plenty of oxygen. Paul promised and said he would show up when it was over and test me to make sure all was well.

•288

Sure enough, when I started swimming out of the anesthetic in the recovery room, I found him bending over me and I said, "Hello, Paùl."

And, by the way of testing me, he said, "Make me up a limerick, Isaac."

I began at once: "There was an old doctor named Paul/whose prick was exceedingly small—"

"That's enough," said Paul austerely. "You pass."

I was asked by *Newsday* to write an article on my bypass operation and I included that story. I thought it was safe because Paul was on a vacation trip somewhere. However, when he came back, all his patients sent him clippings of the article, and he threatened to sue me for "patient malpractice."

Happy ending, though, in one way. My writing since my operation has in no way deteriorated, so nothing has happened to my brain.

Another story about the bypass:

•289

My cardiologist, Peter Pasternack, recommended a surgeon (who was enormously skillful, as it turned out) and said that, as an example of the trust that he, the cardiologist, had in the surgeon, he had allowed the surgeon to operate on his mother the year before.

But I don't write mysteries for nothing. I saw the logical flaw in the argument. I said, "Do you love your mother, Peter?"

"Very much," he said.

I included that story in my article as well. Afterward, I thought I might have offended Peter, so I asked him if it was all right.

"Oh, yes. In fact, my mother was in seventh heaven. She showed all her friends where it said, in print, in a newspaper, that her son loved her very much."

•290

I have no ability to see myself in a mawkish light. No matter how much trouble I've had (barring the death of a loved one), I somehow manage to stress the lighter side of it.

Nevertheless, I was shaken when a young man said to me, "I read the article on your triple bypass, Dr. Asimov. I laughed all the way through."

But back to limericks:

•291

Shyly said a young woman named Mabel,
"How delighted I am that I'm able
　　　To screw on a bed
　　　—Or a sofa, instead,
—Or the grass—or the floor—or the table."

•292

There was a young woman of Brest
Who had a magnificent chest.
　　　When asked if she posed
　　　With her nipples disclosed,
She replied, "Yes—and all of the rest."

•293

His first night, Adam said to his dear,
"Darling Eve, you had better stand clear.
　　　Since touched by your hand
　　　It's begun to expand,
And I don't know how far 'twill uprear."

My very favorite limerick of all those I constructed was entitled "John Ciardi and I," since I wrote it for a book which he
co-authored. Here it is:

•294

There is something about satyriasis
That arouses psychiatrists' biases.
　　　But we're both of us pleased
　　　We're in this way diseased.
As the damsel who's waiting to try us is.

Notice that I have here a perfect triple rhyme, with the last
one entirely unexpected. I love reciting it but before I do, I

always ask the audience if anyone is present who doesn't know the meaning of the word *satyriasis*.

There are always a few who don't and I say, "It's the masculine equivalent of nymphomania," and everyone is at once satisfied.

Except that once, only once, a woman's hand shot up and she asked, "What's nymphomania?"

The audience held its breath waiting for me to define it, but all I said was, "Nymphomania is inordinate sexual desire in the female," and the questioner was quite satisfied.

•295

To moralists, sex is a sin
Yet Nature suggests we begin.
        She arranged it, no doubt,
        That a fellow juts out
In the place where a damsel juts in.

•296

"Here we are," said Attila the Hun.
"Won't you join us in all of the fun?
        We'll slaughter and pillage
        Every last helpless village.
Come quickly, the action's begun."

Did you notice that that one is absolutely clean?

•297

There was a young woman named Dawes
Whose costume was made all of gauze.
        When they turned on the light
        Behind her one night,
All the fellows broke into applause.

•298

During the American Civil War, a particular captured Confederate soldier was a hard man to handle.

Constantly, in his soft drawl, he would say, "Anyway, we beat the hell out of you sniveling Yankee dogs at Fredericksburg."

The Northern sergeant in charge could not punish the impertinent prisoner as he would have liked because there was a drive on at the time to make sure that prisoners were treated humanely. Finally, however, he could stand it no more.

He marched the prisoner out with a squad of soldiers and said, "Listen, you damned Reb, I don't care if it means my court-martial, but I'm going to have you shot if you don't swear allegiance to the United States."

The prisoner, weighing the murder in the sergeant's eyes, swore allegiance.

"Now," said the sergeant, "you did this before witnesses. You're a loyal American. If I hear any snide remarks about the American Army, you're a traitor. It may be against the articles of war to shoot prisoners, but it's perfectly all right to shoot traitors."

The ex-Confederate soldier thought about that for a while, then he said, "Okay, sergeant, but ain't it a stinking, filthy shame what them damned rebels did to us Yankees at Fredericksburg?"

•299

A visitor to a certain college paused to admire the new Hemingway Hall that had been built on campus.

"It's a pleasure to see a building named for Ernest Hemingway," he said.

"Actually," said his guide, "it's named for Joshua Hemingway. No relation."

The visitor was astonished. "Was Joshua Hemingway a writer, also?"

"Yes, indeed," said his guide. "He wrote a check."

• 300

This is the tale of the haughty family of Willoughby-ffinch of Somersetshire, who one and all were prostrated with grief and shame when the beautiful Millicent Willoughby-ffinch had the bad taste to fall in love with, and to marry, a handsome and athletic young man of appalling laboring background, by the name of Alfie Suggs.

Naturally, as any decent family of breeding would, they cut her off, and Mr. and Mrs. Suggs were forced to live a life of penury. Through it all, Millicent clung loyally to her husband.

Then came strokes of fate. A lucky business venture set Mr. Suggs on the road to prosperity and, with unexampled industry and pluck, he piled profit upon profit and grew rich. The Willoughby-ffinches, on the other hand, suffered reverses and grew poor.

Faithful Millicent, on her deathbed, begged her husband to be forgiving and repay the hardheartedness of her family with kindness, and, sorrowing, Alfie agreed. Consequently, when it was Alfie's turn to pass on, he left a sizable portion of his fortune to the Willoughby-ffinches on the sole condition—and this he could not resist—that they change their name legally to Suggs.

The fallen aristocrats had no choice but to accept this utter humiliation. They had their name changed and accepted the money. From then on they carefully spelled their name "Suggs"—but they pronounced it Willoughby-ffinch.

• 301

A certain British nobleman heard, with the greatest of indignation, that his son had taken up with a chorus girl and was living with her.

He wrote his son a terse letter: "If you do not abandon this creature and return home at once, I will cut off your allowance."

He received a letter in return which said, "If you do not double my allowance, I will marry her."

I know that I have said harsh things about critics, both in this book and elsewhere, but even a critic can melt my heart if he is sufficiently clever and can make me laugh. So as long as I wasn't the poor fellow who was victimized, I might as well tell you the following:

•302

Heywood Broun, among other things, reviewed stage plays, and he once excoriated an actor so thoroughly that the actor felt he had no recourse but to sue Broun for libel.

It was a hard-fought case, for Broun had indeed said some terrible things about the actor. Naturally, Broun's defense was that it was fair criticism and that no one could show that he had personal animosity against the actor that might have twisted his opinion.

In the end Broun won, but his lawyer warned him, saying, "Heywood, be very careful what you say about this man from now on. As a result of this case and all you had to go through, it will be easy for him to demonstrate personal animosity on your part next time."

The time came when Broun had to review another play which featured the actor. He gave it a moderate review and saved his reference to the actor for the last line. "As for so-and-so," he said, "his acting was not quite up to his usual standard."

•303

During the worst of the Cold War, Anderson, a salesman of rubber goods, had returned from Europe with an absolute winner of an order and could scarcely contain his sense of triumph. He had talked the Soviet Union into placing an order for 10 million condoms for its soldiers. Jubilantly, Anderson explained the effect this would have on the Soviet Union's birth rate, on its gold reserves (for, of course, they would have to pay in hard money), and on American industry.

The management of the firm was, however, taken aback and thoroughly upset, for Anderson, in his excitement, had overlooked one thing: the enormous size of the condoms which the Soviet Union had ordered. As the president of the firm said, "This indication of Russian virility would destroy the morale of American manhood and might corrupt the loyalty of American womanhood."

What to do? To fail to fill the order would be a slur on the firm's reputation that could not be countenanced; to fill it, on the other hand, would wreak havoc with America's world position. One thing, only, did everyone agree upon, and that was that Anderson must be demolished. After all, the blame was his.

Anderson, thinking faster than he ever had in his life, came up with the key suggestion and at once every tortured face cleared up and every frown in the room became a beaming smile. Anderson was not only reprieved from annihilation, but was given a promotion and, over the ensuing months, the 10 million condoms were manufactured and shipped.

Each and every one was made to order in the appalling size the Soviets had ordered, and each and every one carried in small and unobtrusive lettering the chaste word *Medium*.

•304

This reminds me of a time when I gave a lecture to the alumni of the medical school from which my internist, Paul, and my dear wife, Janet, had both received their degrees. It was at Paul's request.

Paul had graduated from the school with highest honors and everyone knew it, so I was searching for a way of capitalizing on that. I noticed that each alumnus and alumna wore an identification badge with name and year of graduation. Each had a letter, too, to indicate the month of the graduation: *J* for January and *A* for August.

Paul, I noticed, had the letter *M* after his name and I asked him about it, and he said that he had graduated under accelerated conditions during World War II and the *M* stood for May.

That was what I needed. In my talk, I referred to the cards and the letters, and said, "But my internist, Paul Esserman, has an *M* after his. I asked him what he meant and he said it stood for 'Mediocre.'"

It got the best laugh of the evening and Paul had another item in his projected lawsuit against me for patient malpractice.

•305

Young Father O'Houlihan showed every sign of being an ornament to the Church if you didn't mind his ferocious anti-English prejudice. In one of so Irish a background, it was to be expected that he feel a certain resentment against the English, and yet it behooved a priest to forgive his enemies and, at the very least, he ought to restrain open and violent expression of that prejudice.

Father O'Houlihan's superiors explained this to him, kindly but quite firmly, and the young priest was forced to agree. Not one word would he say against the English, he promised. With that he turned back to the youngsters whom he was regaling with tales from the Gospels.

"It was the Last Supper, children," he said, "and Jesus knew he would be betrayed and he said so. Naturally, all the apostles were shocked and each one wondered who the traitor might be. Even Judas Iscariot, that villain, pretended to be surprised and he said, 'Gorblime, guv'ner, but that's a nahsty accusation.'"

•306

Once, the Indian legends tell us, there was a cold lake in the mountains that separated two tribes. There was no way of going from one side of the lake to the other except by way of long and arduous mountain trails. Any attempt to swim across the freezing waters was sure death and neither tribe had yet invented the birch-bark canoe.

A handsome young brave of the tribe on the eastern shore of the lake fell in love with a beautiful maiden of the tribe on the western shore. Day after day, they came to the shores of the lake and called to each other mournfully across the waters. Day after day, their hopeless love grew stronger until finally the young brave could endure it no more. Come what might, he would manage to swim the lake.

So he jumped in and in a moment he was frozen stiff and sank dead to the silent bottom of the frigid lake.

All the Indians of both tribes mourned his passing and, in honor of the brave's character, they gave the lake the name it carries to this day—Lake Chippehanagonka, which in English means "Lake Stupid."

•307

There is a spot in Union Square where, day after day, chessboards are set up along the park benches and chess enthusiasts play endless games in silence. One day, a sudden rainstorm arose and the chess players seized their men and boards and scampered for shelter, invading the vestibule of a fancy apartment house that had been built in the area. They set up their boards there.

The doorman, appalled, ordered them out. When they refused to budge, he called the police.

A policeman arrived, took in the situation at a glance, and shook his head sorrowfully.

"Sorry," he said, "I can't do anything about this."

"Why not?" demanded the doorman.

"Because," said the policeman, "I have no intention of pulling your chess nuts out of the foyer."

You may have noticed that that was a pun, sprung upon you without warning. Undoubtedly, you did not laugh; you groaned. That is the traditional response to a pun—yet isn't it a fun game to play with the English language? One has to love the language as I do to appreciate such games.

Sometimes, in fact, I write stories (very short ones) whose sole purpose is to end with an outrageous pun. Here is a science fiction short, which I published, and which I will give you here in full.

•308

As is well known, in this thirtieth century of ours, space travel is fearfully dull and time-consuming. In search of diversion, many crew members defy the quarantine restrictions and pick up pets from the various habitable worlds they explore.

Jim Sloane had a rockette, which he called Teddy. It just sat there, looking like a rock, but sometimes it lifted a lower edge and sucked in powdered sugar. That was all it ate. No one ever saw it move, but every once in a while, it wasn't quite where people thought it was. There was a theory that it moved when no one was looking.

Bob Laverty had a heli-worm he called Dolly. It was green and carried on photosynthesis. Sometimes it moved to get into better light and when it did so it coiled its wormlike body and inched along very slowly like a turning helix.

One day, Jim Sloane challenged Bob Laverty to a race. "My Teddy," he said, "can beat your Dolly."

"Your Teddy," scoffed Laverty, "doesn't move."

"Bet!" said Sloane.

The whole crew got into the act. Even the captain risked half a credit. Everyone bet on Dolly. At least she moved.

Jim Sloane covered it all. He had been saving his salary through three trips and he put every millicredit of it on Teddy.

The race started at one end of the grand salon. At the other end, a heap of sugar had been placed for Teddy and a spotlight for Dolly. Dolly formed a coil at once and began to spiral its way very slowly toward the light. The watching crew cheered it on.

Teddy just sat there without budging.

"Sugar, Teddy. Sugar," said Sloane, pointing. Teddy did not move. It looked more like a rock than ever, but Sloane did not seem concerned.

Finally, when Dolly had spiraled halfway across the salon, Jim Sloane said casually to his rockette, "If you don't get out there, Teddy, I'm going to get a hammer and chip you into pebbles."

That was when people first discovered that rockettes could read minds. That was also when people first discovered that rockettes could teleport.

Sloane had no sooner made his threat when Teddy simply disappeared from his place and reappeared on top of the sugar.

Sloane won, of course, and he counted his winnings slowly and luxuriously.

Laverty said bitterly, "You *knew* the damn thing could teleport."

"No, I didn't," said Sloane, "but I knew he would win. It was a sure thing."

"How come?"

"It's an old saying everyone knows. Sloane's Teddy wins the race."

Did you groan? Did you also notice that the story was quite interesting in itself, and that you were sucked into it so that the final pun came with entire unexpectedness? If you think it's easy to do this sort of thing, I urge you to try.

Here is one more of that sort of thing. Just one more:

•309

It was extremely unusual for a Foy to be dying on earth. They were the highest social class on their planet (which had a name that was pronounced—as nearly as earthly throats could make the sounds—Sortibackenstrete) and were virtually immortal.

Every Foy, of course, came to a voluntary death eventually, and this one had given up because of an ill-starred love affair, if you can call it a love affair where five individuals, in order to reproduce, must indulge in a yearlong mental contact. Apparently, the Foy had not fit into the contact after several months of trying, and it had broken his heart—or hearts, for he had five.

All Foys had five large hearts and there was speculation that it was this that made them virtually immortal.

Maude Briscoe, earth's most renowned surgeon, wanted those hearts. "It can't be just their number and size, Ray," she said to her chief assistant. "It has to be something physiological or biochemical. I must have them."

"I don't know if we can manage that," said Ray Johnson. "I've been speaking to him earnestly, trying to overcome the Foy taboo against dismemberment after death. I've had to lie to him, Maude."

"Lie?"

"I told him that after death, there would be a dirge sung for him by the world-famous choir led by Harold J. Gassenbaum. I told him that, by earthly belief, this would mean that his astral essence would be instantaneously wafted back, through hyperspace, to his home planet of Sortib-what's-it's-name—provided he would sign a release allowing you, Maude, to have his hearts for scientific investigation."

"Don't tell me he believed that."

"Well, you know this modern attitude about accepting the myths and beliefs of intelligent aliens. It wouldn't have been polite for him not to believe me. Besides, the Foys have a profound admiration for earthly science and I think this one is a little flattered that we should want his hearts. He promised to consider the suggestion and I hope he decides soon because he can't live more than another day or so, and we must have his permission by interstellar law, and the hearts must be fresh—Ah, his signal."

Ray Johnson moved in with smooth and noiseless speed.

"Yes?" he whispered, unobtrusively turning on the holographic recording device in case the Foy wished to grant permission.

The Foy's large, gnarled, rather treelike body lay motionless on the bed. His bulging eyes palpitated—all five of them—as they rose, each on its stalk, and turned toward Ray. The Foy's voice had a strange tone and the lipless edges of his open round mouth did not move, but the words formed perfectly. His eyes were making the Foyan gestures of assent as he said,

"Give my big hearts to Maude, Ray. Dismember me for Harold's choir. Tell all the Foys on Sortibackenstrete that I will soon be there—"

Absolutely outrageous. Ed Ferman, the editor of *Fantasy and Science Fiction,* read the story, which I had carefully arranged so that the second page ended with the words "as he said," and the Foy's final statement was then on the top of the third page. Ed couldn't make out where the heck I was going and he finished page two in utter bewilderment, then turned to page three, got it all at once, and broke into wild laughter. After that, he had to take the story. (Writing is such fun!)

•310

A certain banker, renowned for his business acumen and for his talent at making three dollars flourish where only one had peeped forth, had the misfortune to lose an eye.

To replace it, he ordered a glass eye of the very finest make from Germany's premier producers of optical equipment. Made to accurate measure, and matched precisely with his remaining eye, it was the banker's boast that no one who did not know which eye was glass could tell which it was by cursory inspection alone.

On occasion, at social gatherings, he would dare strangers to guess which was the glass eye. No one was ever certain, and if they guessed, they did so only at a venture.

On one occasion, a man not personally known to the banker spoke up and said, "Why, that offers no problem at all. It is your left eye that is glass. I would bet a thousand dollars on it cheerfully."

The banker said, "You are right. But how could you tell?"

"Easy," said the man. "I have dealt with your bank and so I knew it had to be the left eye which was not yours by nature, for that is the one with the faint gleam of human kindness in it."

•311

A certain eye specialist is supposed to have successfully treated the great surrealist painter Salvador Dali. For his fee, the specialist requested that Dali paint something for him, on a subject of Dali's own choosing.

The grateful Dali therefore painted an enormous eye in meticulous detail and, in its very pupil, he placed a small but perfect portrait of the doctor.

The ophthalmologist looked at the painting with awe and astonishment and said, "Well, Mr. Dali, I can only say that I am glad I am not a proctologist."

This joke doesn't work, of course, unless you realize that a proctologist is a doctor who specializes in disorders of the anus and neighboring regions.

•312

A psychiatrist and a proctologist hired a suite of offices for themselves and put up a sign, THE DEPARTMENT OF ODDS AND ENDS.

•313

Mr. Jones was having proctological troubles for the first time in five years, so he decided to visit the doctor, who had treated him before and whom he hadn't seen since.

When he entered the office, he said jovially, "Hello, Doctor, I have an appointment with you." The doctor, however, did not seem to recognize him.

In a thoroughly businesslike way, the doctor said, "Please assume the position."

Jones knew the position very well. He got on his elbows and knees on the examination table and kept his legs well apart. The proctologist took one look, broke into a smile, and said, "Mr. Jones. Greetings. I didn't recognize you at first."

I recently read a thick book of one-liners—that is, single lines intended to be humorous or sardonic. It was a waste of time, for only about one one-liner in a hundred induced as much as a smile. This is not to say one-liners are bad; some comedians are experts at it, and some listeners like them. It's just that I prefer humor in the form of anecdotes. However, I suppose I ought to give you an example of a one-liner that *did* induce a smile in me.

•314

Organic farming is a lot of shit.

•315

The actress Ilka Chase married the actor Louis Calhern. It was an unsuitable marriage, apparently, and didn't last long, but in the interval, Miss Chase had had a vast number of business cards made up reading, "Mrs. Louis Calhern."

When she heard that Mr. Calhern was getting married again, she sent all the cards to the new bride, along with a message: "I hope this gets to you while you can still use them."

Show-business marriages are often spectacularly brief. Ethel Merman and Ernest Borgnine married—and stayed married only one night. What happened, I cannot imagine. When

Miss Merman wrote on her life, she left out that one night altogether.

English is full of close synonyms with different shades of meaning. A good dictionary will carefully try to distinguish between these shades but rarely in the heartfelt way that you find in the following:

•316

Worry is the first time you find you can't do it the second time; panic is the second time you find you can't do it the first time.

•317

An Englishman, a Frenchman, and a Russian were once discussing the meaning of true happiness.

The Englishman said, "True happiness, my friends, is rising early on a frosty fall morning, getting on top of a good horse, and galloping off behind the hounds in pursuit of the fox. A hard ride over fields and fences and rivulets until the fox is brought down. A ride back with the ears and the tail and then sitting before a roaring fire with a glass of good port. Ah, that is true happiness."

The Frenchman said, "That is not true happiness. That is merely animal pleasure. True happiness is meeting with the love of your life, having an excellent meal in a topnotch restaurant with champagne, and then retiring to a wonderful hotel room, where you can make frantic and impassioned love all night long. Ah, that is true happiness."

The Russian said, "That is not true happiness. That is merely a good time. True happiness comes when you are sitting in your apartment after a hard day at the factory, your little Ivan on your knee, and reading your copy of *Pravda*. There comes a knock at the door. Three men in ill-fitting brown suits come storming in and say, 'Stepan Stepanovich,' and you say, 'He lives in the rooms upstairs.' Ah, *that* is true happiness."

•318

In the bad old Stalinist days in the Soviet Union, the teacher was involved with the class that was learning English.

"Today," he said, "we will study the beautiful English word *catastrophe*. Is there anyone who knows the meaning and can give me an example?"

At once, little Boris raised his hand. "Teacher, if my mother were to lose a button from her best dress, that would be a catastrophe."

"Not quite," said the teacher. "It would be a loss, but it would not be a catastrophe. Anyone else?"

Up went Sonia's hand. "Teacher, if I fell and made my knee bleed, that would be a catastrophe."

"Not quite," said the teacher. "It would be a misfortune, but it would not be a catastrophe. Anyone else?"

No one seemed willing to try until from the back of the room little Ivan raised his hand. The teacher was astonished, for Ivan was undoubtedly the least successful student in his class.

Ivan said, "Teacher, if our great leader, Comrade Stalin, were to die, that would be a catastrophe."

The teacher said, "Perfectly right. If our great leader, Comrade Stalin, were to die, that would indeed be a catastrophe, not only for our own country but for all peace-loving nations everywhere. How did you work it out, Ivan?"

Ivan said, "What else could Comrade Stalin's death be? It wouldn't be a loss— It wouldn't be a misfortune—"

•319

A certain gorilla was once taught to play golf. It wasn't easy to train him to hold the club, to swing at the ball accurately, and to follow through, but the task was done. The proud trainer presented the gorilla to the golf club and before an enormous crowd of spectators, the powerful animal addressed the ball. It was clear that the gorilla's muscles were a great help, for the ball went screaming down the fairway, straight and true, in a huge 497-yard flight, landing three feet from the hole.

The gorilla jumped with delight, then loped forward to where the ball now reposed. It was followed by the enormous crowd. The trainer handed him the putter, the gorilla addressed the ball, and sent it screaming for another 497-yard flight—

•320

Back in the days when the New York Mets broke all records for floundering, a horse applied for a position on the club. Casey Stengel, the club's manager in those woebegone days, was thunderstruck, but reasoning that some of his players were no more intelligent than so many horses, he decided to let the animal try out.

Naturally, the tryout was carried on in utter secrecy, for it would not do to let the press get wind of this prematurely. They were having enough fun with the hapless Mets as it was.

In the empty ballpark, then, the horse walked up to the plate. Rearing himself on his hind legs, he displayed two forehooves that had been rounded out so that he could hold a baseball bat between them.

Calmly, the horse faced the pitcher, swinging his bat with professional aplomb. The pitcher hurled the ball and the horse let it go by. He let another go by. Then, with the third ball, he swung magnificently, and the ball went blazing through the hole between second base and shortstop for an obvious extra-base hit. The horse watched it motionlessly.

Casey Stengel, in huge excitement, jumped up and down, shouting, "Run, damn you, run."

But the horse tossed the bat to one side and said, "Don't be silly. Who ever heard of a horse running bases?"

•321

Julius Caesar was once asked what kind of death was the best one. He gave the best conceivable answer, for he said, "A sudden one." (The next day he was assassinated—suddenly.)

Here are two female chauvinist jokes told me by a woman. This shows that if they didn't resign from joke-telling they wouldn't leave it to the male chauvinists.

•322

For a long time, human beings have puzzled over certain mysteries and finally they decided to put those questions directly to God.

"Tell us, O Lord," they implored, "why are women possessed of bodies that are so soft and smooth?"

"So that men will love them, my children."

"And why are women so tender and affectionate?"

"So that men will love them, my children."

"But why are they so silly and stupid?"

"So that they will love men, my children."

•323

Three men encountered a genie, who offered to give them each one wish.

The first man said, "O genie, make me ten times as smart as I am."

"Your wish is granted," said the genie. "You are now highly intelligent."

The second man said, "O genie, make me a hundred times as smart as I am."

"Your wish is granted," said the genie. "You are now a genius."

The third man said, "O genie, make me a thousand times as smart as I am."

"Your wish is granted," said the genie. "You are now a woman."

•324

Napoleon liked to pose as an enlightened monarch, but he had his moments, and was especially short-tempered if anyone ridiculed him. When a German publisher permitted himself to put out an anti-Napoleon broadside, Napoleon had him executed.

It was not long after that that the British poet Thomas Campbell, addressing a convocation of writers, raised his glass in a toast to "Napoleon Bonaparte."

There was a loud outcry of repulsion, and Campbell said, "Gentlemen, I admit that Napoleon is a monster who has bent all Europe to his will and enslaved it, that he is fighting our own nation to the death, that he is therefore the wicked and mortal enemy of every one of us. But, after all, gentlemen, he has just shot a publisher."

And the whole audience broke into applause.

•325

George IV of Great Britain hated his wife with surpassing intensity and she returned it with interest. There were prolonged and rather disgusting divorce proceedings between them and the entire nation took an emotional part in it.

When Napoleon died at St. Helena in 1821, the news was brought to George IV. "Your greatest enemy is dead," he was told.

"Oh, is she?" said George.

•326

The crusty old Roman, Cato the Censor, was asked if he did not feel cheated that Rome, as the end of his long and illustrious career was coming to a close, had never put up a statue to him.

"No," he said. "I would rather have no statue and have people asking 'Why?' than have a statue and have people asking 'Why?'"

•327

After the death of Robert Burns, Scotland's most famous poet and one of the greatest of all time, there was considerable appreciation of his talents. He had had only a short life, spent entirely in penury, but now they were putting up a statue to him, and his mother was there to witness it.

"Oh, Robbie," she said, weeping. "You asked for bread and now they give you a stone."

•328

Philip III of Spain noticed a young man in the street, reading a book and laughing uproariously. The king said gravely, "That man is either crazy, or he is reading *Don Quixote*."

As it happened, the young man was indeed reading *Don Quixote,* the first modern novel, the funniest, and the best. I have read it five times and laughed uproariously each time.

And, talking about literature, John Ciardi, the poet, looked less like the popular conception of a poet than any human being ever invented. He was tall and stout, with large, craggy features, a magnificent nose, and a rolling baritone voice.

•329

One winter, when three inches of snow overlaid the ground, Ciardi ventured to drive into Central Park on Sunday at dawn. He was promptly stopped by a policeman, who began making out a ticket, explaining that Ciardi had crossed the white line on the highway and was driving on the wrong side.

"What white line?" said Ciardi, mystified.

"It's there," said the policeman calmly, "under the snow."

"I couldn't see it," protested Ciardi. "Besides, I'm the only one in the park, so what harm did I do?"

But you can't argue with a cop intent on making up his ticket quota.

"Name?" said the cop. "Address?" and, finally, "Occupation?"

At the last, the tortured and frustrated Ciardi, leaning his craggy face out the window said in stentorian tones, "I'm a *poet,* goddamn it."

The policeman was not taken aback. He even won the exchange by saying, "Does that mean you're self-employed?"

When John told me this story in a state of towering indignation, I told him that he had missed his chance. He should have answered the last question with, "No, I'm research poet for Union Carbide." The policeman would undoubtedly have been dumb enough to write that down.

•330

I spent two weeks at the Breadloaf Writers Conference in the summer of 1971. John Ciardi was its director and when I took my leave, I shook hands with him and said in my cute jocular way, "Farewell, O minor poet."

He didn't blink an eye but responded at once. "Farewell, O major pain in the ass."

•331

I encountered a huge mystery at Breadloaf. I pride myself on being an early riser. I'd wake up at the crack of dawn, perform my ablutions, and be down at the dining room even before breakfast was served. When it was served, you can bet I was the first one to help myself to the goodies.

The only thing that bothered me was that while I was getting ready, I would invariably hear the banging of the door to the lecturer's building (I was one of the lecturers). I could only conclude that someone was beating me to breakfast, but when I got down there I was the only person in the place.

It bothered me. I could not understand the mystery until finally, as a result of listening to the other lecturers talk, I made it out. The other lecturers maintained a harem and there was usually some woman spending the night with one of them. It was the woman who left very early so as not to be seen and she didn't go to breakfast, but back to her own room for a little more sleep.

I was glad to know this, but I was not tempted to start a harem of my own. What would I have said to my dear wife, Janet?

•332

John Ciardi, who was born a Catholic, told me the following one, for which I disclaim responsibility.

A woman was taken in adultery and a group of men approached Jesus and said to him, "This woman was taken in adultery and by the law she should be stoned to death. But what say you?"

Jesus thought and said, "I say that he among you who is without sin should throw the first stone."

At that, all the gathered multitude tossed their stones away and crept off, shamefaced—at least, all but one middle-aged woman who hefted half a brick in her hand. Taking careful aim, she sent it flying, struck the woman taken in adultery in the forehead, and felled her.

Shaking his head, Jesus walked over to the woman who had thrown the brick and said, "Sometimes you piss me off, Mom."

•333

There's no accounting for collectors, and John Ciardi collected Etruscan earthenware fertility symbols. In ancient times, when an Etruscan woman wanted a child, or perhaps a lot of children, she would place on the altar of the god to whom she was praying a little molded earthenware model of the male generative organ. (Gods tend to be stupid and they need all the help they can get to understand what it is a petitioner wants.)

Ciardi had a bunch of these things lined up in a glass-fronted bookcase.

However, when the ladies of the town came to visit, Judith, John's wife, took away all the figurines and disposed of them in a safe place so as not to jar ladylike sensibilities. The only trouble was that half the time Judith couldn't remember where she had put them and Ciardi had to institute a search.

One time, he came back and found the ladies there and the figurines gone and in a state of fury yelled out, "Goddamn it, Judith, what have you done with my genitals?"

•334

Maurice Chevalier, at reaching the age of seventy, was asked how he felt now that he had reached that age. "I much prefer it," he said, "to the alternative."

I agreed with him very heartily when I first heard that story and was considerably younger. Now that I have reached the seventies myself, I am less certain about the extent of preference to the alternative. Being old is no fun—unless one is a jokester. There is always that.

•335

Mrs. Smith, standing at the window in her palatial home in Beverly Hills, watched the new owners of the next estate busying themselves about their home. The grass was being mowed, bushes were being planted, renovations were being made.

"Ah," Mrs. Smith said with a reminiscent sigh. "To be nouveau riche again."

•336

The traveler, stopping for directions, stared curiously about the primitive farmhouse, which, while clean and neat enough, seemed utterly without modern conveniences.

Except for one thing. Over the kitchen sink, suspended from an electric cord, there hung a bare light bulb. Although dusk was closing in, it was not glowing.

Curious, the traveler asked, "Does that electric light work?"

"Don't know," answered the farmer.

"Haven't you ever tried to turn it on?" asked the traveler, astonished.

"No," said the farmer. "We ain't never run out of kerosene yet."

•337

The strong man at the circus squeezed a lemon, and squeezed and squeezed until the last drop had pushed its way outward. He held up the dried lemon rind and said, "I will give fifty dollars to anyone who can squeeze another drop out of this lemon."

At this a little fellow, not much over five feet high and thin as a rail, piped up, "I'll accept that offer, mister."

Everyone stared as the strong man handed him the lemon rind. The little man's small hands seized at it and he began to squeeze—and squeeze—and squeeze—and behold, a drop squeezed out.

The strong man, flabbergasted, passed over a $50 bill and said, "I'll give you a hundred if you squeeze out another and if you can't, give me back the fifty."

"All right," said the little man cheerfully, and he squeezed—and squeezed—and squeezed—and, behold, another drop squeezed out.

"Say," said the strong man as he passed over a $100 bill. "What do you do for a living?"

"I," said the little man, "am the regional representative of the United Jewish Appeal."

Jews laugh inordinately at that one, having encountered the squeezers of the United Jewish Appeal.

•338

Those of us who have labored to obtain our Ph.D.s must sometimes wonder if anyone in the world can possibly be interested in the learned dissertation over which we have sweated, even though it is carefully filed in the library of the institution at which the degree was earned.

There is the story of the scholar who, years ago, produced a dissertation that was loudly hailed as the best written and most valuable in a generation. A copy was reverently placed in the library files and the scholar, as an experiment, placed a crisp $20 bill among its pages. Every year he returned to the library and took down the dissertation. Every year, it fell open to the stuffed page. Every year, the $20 bill was still there—untouched.

•339

My own Ph.D. dissertation has never been touched by anyone, not even by me, and justly so, for it was a remarkably unimportant piece of work. Once only, though, was it treated with disdain.

Shortly after getting my doctorate, I applied for a job at a Brooklyn chemical firm. I was turned down, and with what seemed to me to be contempt. I had given my interviewer a copy of my Ph.D. dissertation as evidence of the quality of my work and he eventually sent it back to me with the words, "I am returning your pamphlet."

You don't call a dissertation a pamphlet. I foamed at the mouth, but what could I do?

Well, thirty years later, that same Brooklyn chemical firm asked me to favor them with a talk. They offered a substantial fee, but I absolutely refused to oblige them unless they added a thousand dollars to it. They finally did, and I gave the talk.

That additional thousand was for my hurt feelings, but let me tell you, it wasn't enough.

•340

An irate woman once told Churchill, when he was a young man and temporarily sporting a small mustache, "Young man, I like neither your politics nor your mustache."

To which Churchill replied, "Madam, you are not likely to come into contact with either."

•341

Churchill was quite stout in later life and there is a story that a woman, tapping him on his protruding abdomen, said, "Winnie, if this were on a woman, we'd know what to think."

And Churchill replied, "Half an hour ago, madam, it *was* on a woman, and now what do you think?"

•342

A deputation of women came to Churchill in order to protest his overconsumption of spiritous liquors. They said, "Mr. Churchill, if all the spirits you have drunk in your life were poured into this room, they would fill it to here."

Churchill regarded the imaginary line they had traced on the wall, and his eyes then went up to the ceiling, and he sighed. "So much to do; so little done."

•343

When Churchill was in his eighties and celebrating his birthday, a newspaper photographer said reverentially, "I hope I'll be photographing you on your hundredth birthday, Mr. Churchill."

"Why not?" said Churchill. "You look like a healthy young man. You ought to survive that long."

•344

An eminent heart specialist was at a glittering social function and was in animated conversation with a lovely young thing wearing a great deal of makeup and the barest minimum of clothing. It was only a few minutes too late that the good doctor became aware that his wife, whom he thought was safely in the next room, was watching him with a steely glare.

Clearing his throat, the doctor said, "Ah, my dear, that young lady over there and I were just indulging in a purely professional consultation."

"So I can well imagine," said his wife icily, "but was it your profession, or hers?"

•345

A young man came into a house of prostitution and said to the madam, "I would like to have a young woman, but I have a particular way—"

The madam interrupted him. "Sir, this is a refined and high-quality establishment and no man is require to state his preferences. We have women well skilled and well trained in the art of love, and they will oblige you in any way you wish. I will recommend you to one of my experienced young women, Euphrosyne."

The young man said, "Thank you," and followed a rather statuesque woman up the stairs.

In a minute and a half he was downstairs again, and the madam said, "Is that all the time you took?"

The young man said forlornly, "She wouldn't do it."

The madam reeled with shock. "Wouldn't do it? I can't understand it. All I can say, then, is that the honor of the establishment is at stake. As you can see, sir, I am past my first youth, and my sinews are not as strong, or my joints as flexible, as they once were. Nevertheless, I will myself personally oblige you in any fashion you wish. How do you want it?"

And the young man said, "On credit."

•346

A farm girl brought a bull to a pasture in order that it might service the cow there. The farm boy in charge of the cow joined her and they watched the process.

After a while, the farm boy turned to the farm girl and said, "That just makes me itch to do the same thing. How about it?"

And the farm girl said indifferently, "Go ahead. It's your cow."

•347

Mr. Jones sat moist-eyed over his beer in the bar, and the man next to him said, "You look troubled, my friend. What is it?"

Jones sighed deeply. "I married a girl and I've had an unhappy marriage ever since. You have no idea how miserable my life is. I would never have married that girl, either, if I had not been advised to do so in the strongest terms."

"Who advised you?"

And Jones said, "The girl."

•348

Back in the old days when men were men, and often fools, the doughty young Shelby Beauregard was fighting his first duel. He aimed carefully and missed. Fortunately, the other fellow missed, too, and honor was satisfied.

Nevertheless, a friend berated Shelby. "How could you miss?" he was asked. "When you aimed at a target you hit the bull's eye every time."

"Sure," said Shelby, "but the target was never pointing a pistol at me."

•349

Moskowitz and Finkelstein, in an excess of rage at each other, decided to fight a duel. Each of them brought a pistol and practiced and, needless to say, each was worried sick.

Nevertheless, on the appointed hour, Moskowitz appeared at the appointed place with his second. He waited, but Finkelstein did not show up. Suddenly a youngster came running up and thrust a note into Moskowitz's hands.

It read, "Dear Moskowitz: My wife is not well, so I may not be able to show up. However, don't let that stop you. You shoot."

•350

Jose Ferrer was once preparing to do his Cyrano de Bergerac and, for some reason, failed to put on his grotesque nose. However, he was so immersed in his part, which he carried through with such bravura, that no one in the audience apparently noticed that the nose was missing. Nor did Jose.

•351

Spencer Tracy once absolutely refused to grow a three-day beard that was needed for the part he was doing.

"But Mr. Tracy," they said, "you must have the beard for the part."

"I'll *act* the beard," growled Tracy. And apparently he did—successfully.

•352

I was once walking down the hall at Doubleday with my then-editor, Lawrence P. Ashmead. Another editor, a very sweet guy named Ferris Mack, passed by and said, "Can't stop to talk, Asimov. I'm on my way to meet a real writer."

And I called after him, "Take Ashmead with you and let him meet a real editor."

•353

I don't fly. I simply don't like to. People are often quick to assume that if I just flew in an airplane once, I would get over my fears and thenceforth fly in them regularly.

I tell them, "No, I won't, because I once flew in an airplane and it didn't change my mind."

"How did you come to fly in an airplane?"

So I told them I had been stationed in Hawaii in 1946 and I was to be sent to Virginia. I asked if I might cross the Pacific by ship and the United States by train, and my travel orders were so written.

A sergeant came to get me, piled me and my duffel bag into his jeep, and took me to the airport.

"Sergeant," I said, "my travel orders say—"

And the sergeant said, "Don't give me a hard time, soldier. Get in that plane."

What could I do? I got in the plane and it flew me to San Francisco. But I've never been in a plane since.

•354

A nervous man was boarding a plane for the first time. He said to the stewardess, "Please ask the pilot to fly very low, and very, very slowly."

•355

My nephew, Eric, told me this story, which he swore to me was true.

He was on a plane, and it had achieved high and steady flight so that it was on automatic pilot. The pilot stretched, yawned, and said, "What I need now is a cup of coffee and a blow job." What the pilot didn't know was that the public address system was on and that his words rang out throughout the plane.

A stewardess ran forward pell-mell to tell the pilot to shut off the system before he committed further indiscretions.

And as she ran, a passenger called out, "Don't forget, miss. He wants coffee, also."

•356

A certain hippie, a little weary of his love beads, decided to trade them in for a white robe and set himself up as an Eastern swami. He advertised his renown in various underground newspapers and even-

ISAAC ASIMOV

tually gathered a group of disciples who now sat reverently about him while he remained lost in meditation.

Finally the newly made swami said, "Life is like six matzo balls floating in a bowl of ice-cold Kool-Aid."

The disciples nodded respectfully—except for one, who said, "But swami, why is life like six matzo balls floating in a bowl of Kool-Aid?"

At this, the ex-hippie lifted his head, fixed the questioner with an icy stare, and said, "Listen, buddy, did you come here to learn or to argue?"

•357

I have never heard a kind word about Hollywood, but the unkindest of all is this: In Hollywood, it is not enough to succeed; your friends have to fail.

•358

Yogi Berra, who was once a great Yankee catcher, is the Dorothy Parker of baseball. All sorts of great lines are attributed to him that have caught the public's fancy. With respect to a baseball game, he said, "It's never over till it's over."

•359

Once when something happened that had happened before, Yogi said, "It's déjà vu all over again."

•360

Yogi also said, "You can observe a great deal just by watching."

•361

Once Yogi Berra, in his younger days, was in a batting slump. The manager felt this was because he was cutting at too many bad balls. He therefore called Yogi to one side during an idle day in the schedule and gave him an intensive course in judging incoming baseballs to determine whether they were outside the strike zone and therefore ought to be allowed to pass as balls.

Yogi's batting promptly grew worse, and when the manager asked him what was wrong, he said, "It's this judging of balls. I just can't hit and think at the same time."

●362

Goldfarb and Bloom, both rather advanced in years, were returning home from their afternoon checkers game when Goldfarb asked thoughtfully, "Bloom, how long is it since you've had sex?"

"A long time," admitted Bloom.

"You ever think of it?"

"Now and then."

"So do I. You know what? Tonight I'm going to suggest it to my wife. Who knows? Maybe we can manage."

"All right," said Bloom. "Let me know how you make out. And meanwhile, I'll try to, also."

So the next day, Bloom said to Goldfarb, "Well, Goldfarb, how did you make out last night with sex?"

And Goldfarb stopped dead, hit his forehead with his hand, and said, "Oh, my, I forgot."

●363

Just as American villages invariably have a village idiot, the Jewish shtetls in Eastern Europe invariably had their schlemiel, whose every action led to disaster.

You can imagine, then, the furor that took place in this small Eastern European town in the old days when a well-known schlemiel dropped his piece of buttered bread—as a schlemiel is bound to do— but had it land on the carpet with the butter side *up*.

Was it possible that schlemieldom had deserted the poor man? The wisest men in town held a hurried consultation and decided that it was not so. The schlemiel was still a schlemiel—more so than ever, in fact. What had happened, as the learned rabbi pointed out, was that he had buttered the wrong side of the bread.

•364

The schlemiel must be distinguished from the schlimazel. The schlemiel is clumsy and stupid and brings all sorts of misfortune to pass. The schlimazel is merely a person who has bad luck. Thus, as it is said, "The schlemiel spills hot soup all over the schlimazel's pants."

Jokes travel. They pass on for thousands of miles with no trouble in this modern age of ours. What bothers me is that sometimes one of *my* witticisms travels and then resurfaces—years later, perhaps—and is attributed either to that great man "anonymous" or, worse yet, to some named individual. I have two examples.

•365

During the days when I was a graduate student in the early forties, we were dealing with chemistry in which there were a great many units used in measuring various quantities—in particular, the entire metric system. A friend of mine, Mario Castillo, and I therefore whiled away one lunch period by making up units and I finally came up with the "millihelen," which is enough beauty to launch one ship. (After all, Helen of Troy had a "face that launched a thousand ships.")

Years later, I saw "millihelen" in *Time,* and it wasn't attributed to me, either.

•366

I always hate references to the "good old days" because I don't think they were "good." If there are no antibiotics, no internal plumbing, and no refrigeration, you can have it; I don't want it.

One time, though, my first wife, Gertrude, sighed and said, "I wish it were a hundred years ago when it was easy to get servants." I understood her feeling, for we had been trying to get a cleaning woman without success. (That was because all the potential cleaning women were themselves looking for cleaning women.)

I said, "No, Gertrude, it would be horrible a hundred years ago."
She said, "Why?"
I said, "Because we'd be the servants."
Years later, that turned up in the *Old Farmer's Almanac,* attributed to someone else.

•367

I have arguments in that respect with people during my lectures. I'm pro-technology and lots of young people aren't. They want the good old days. I once asked a young man if he thought he would be happier in ancient Athens, sitting in the agora, and chewing the fat with Socrates.

"Of course," he said.

I said, "Only a few Athenian aristocrats had the chance at that. Most Athenians were artisans or slaves. Do you want to take a chance at being one of those?" And he sat down.

There's the same stupidity that people display when they talk about the transmigration of souls. They always imagine they were once Napoleon or Cleopatra, when the fact is that 95 percent of the human race at all times were peasants, slaves, servants, starving wretches, and everything that was bad.

I refuse to let myself be transmigrated. I have had a very happy and successful life, and if I, after death, enter another soul, the odds are that my new life would be far worse than the one I am now approaching the end of. I don't want to go through that. I am perfectly willing to quit while I am ahead.

•368

Moskowitz and Finkelstein met in the garment district.

"Well," said Moskowitz. "How's business?"

"Fooie," said Finkelstein.

And Moskowitz said, "That's not bad for this time of year."

•369

Easterners are not particularly fond of the Texan stereotype. They tell a way of finding Texas without a map (provided there are no Texans within hearing). You travel west till you smell shit. You are then in Oklahoma. You turn south and when you step in the shit, you're in Texas.

•370

An airplane flying from Houston to Chicago had a very close call. For a while it seemed as though it were doomed to crash to fiery destruction, but at the last minute the pilot got it under control and landed safely. Out of the plane came 200 midgets.

An onlooker said, "I never saw so many midgets in my life."

Said another, "Those aren't midgets. Those are Texans with the shit scared out of them."

•371

An easterner was visiting Texas and could not believe the huge scale on which everything was built: the size of the parking lots, the size of the airfields, the size of the hamburgers, the size of the drinks—everything.

After doing his best to consume the enormous portions served him in the hotel restaurant, he asked how to get to the men's room. He was given the direction and made off briskly. Somehow he took the wrong turning, opened the door that led to the swimming pool, and fell in.

Whereupon he screamed, "Don't flush! Don't flush!"

•372

A Texan had just had a baby son, and he was passing out enormous cigars.

"Likeliest little varmint you ever saw," he said proudly. "He weighs twenty-seven pounds."

Two weeks later, a friend met him and said, "How's the kid?"

"Fine," said the Texan. "The little tyke weighs sixteen pounds."

The friend looked puzzled. "Why, when he was born you said he weighed twenty-seven pounds."

"I know," said the Texan, "but we had him circumcised."

New York has its stereotype, too. Thus:

•373

Q: How many New Yorkers does it take to screw in a light bulb?
A: What the hell business is that of yours?

•374

The school year was over and the faculty heaved their usual sigh of relief. Professor Murray of English literature said to his colleague, Professor Cardozo of romance languages, "I had an interesting experience during the year. A Miss Brentwood came to see me in the middle of the year and said intensely, 'Professor Murray, I'd do anything to get a passing mark in this course. I mean, literally anything.' She was a strikingly beautiful girl and I must admit I was tempted, but her school record was abominable and I did manage to cling to my integrity. I said, 'Miss Brentwood, I suggest you study.' That, of course, was the last thing she would do and in the end I was forced to give her a failing mark."

"Amazing," said Professor Cardozo, "for precisely the same thing happened to me. I, too, had to flunk Miss Brentwood. Do you suppose she tried it with all her professors?"

"Possibly," said Professor Murray. "Shall we look up her record and see?"

No sooner said than done. They scanned the record and Professor Cardozo said, "Interesting. An F in my course and in yours and, indeed, in all of them but one. In one course, she got an A."

"And which course was that?"

"Professor Hingman's course in professional ethics."

•375

Of all the Hollywood horrors, one of the worst was Harry Cohn, who apparently was hated by all who dealt with him or even heard of him. On the day of his funeral, the crowds that came were enormous.

One onlooker said, "I suppose they're all here to make sure he's dead."

Another said, "It just proves that if you give people what they want, they'll buy tickets."

•376

The story is that after the rabbi had given his eulogy over the body of Harry Cohn, he asked if there was anyone who would like to stand up and tell some fond remembrances of the man, or make a tribute to his memory.

The vast audience was untouched. No one responded. Again and again, the rabbi urged them to forget any petty dislikes and to remember only that a soul and a brother had gone into the hereafter, and still no one moved.

Finally a little man stood up and said, "I'll say something."

The rabbi smiled and said, "Come up here, sir."

Up went the little man on the stage, gazed at the audience, and finally said, "His brother was almost as bad."

•377

A man who had the misfortune of being totally bald was naturally teased about it at times.

A friend ran his hand over the bald head and said, "It feels just like my wife's behind."

The bald man passed his own hand over his head and said, "My God, so it does."

•378

My friend Emory Davis, the band leader, has a beautiful head of skin. He said, "God made only a few perfect heads. The rest he covered with hair."

•379

Of all the presidents we have had, Calvin Coolidge may have had the least charisma. He was known for his silence. He had a very quiet five-plus years in the presidency and managed to get out in time for the bursting of the bubble in the administration of his successor, Herbert Hoover.

In 1933 Coolidge died, and when Dorothy Parker heard the news, she said, "How can they tell?"

•380

One story is told about Coolidge that does not feature his taciturnity. Therefore it may be apocryphal.

He and Mrs. Coolidge were being shown around a government chicken farm and Mrs. Coolidge, watching a rooster at work, asked if he mounted the hens more than once a day.

"Of course, ma'am," said the guide. "It does its work dozens of times a day."

"Tell that to the president," said Mrs. Coolidge.

He did so. Coolidge thought a moment and said, "Same hen all the time?"

"Oh, no," said the guide, "a different hen each time."

And Coolidge said, "Tell that to my wife."

•381

Mr. Arbuthnot was busily packing.

"Where are you going?" asked Mrs. Arbuthnot.

"To Australia, woman, and don't try to stop me."

"But why are you going to Australia?"

"Because I hear that in that country men are at a premium and women will gladly pay ten dollars for a night of love."

At this, Mrs. Arbuthnot also began packing.

"And where are you going?" asked Mr. Arbuthnot.

"To Australia."

"Why?"

"I am curious to see how you intend to manage to live on ten dollars a month."

•382

A talk was given in the Old West to a crowd of hard-bitten prospectors and cowboys. It was something less than a success and the speaker was a little disconcerted afterward to notice that several men in the audience were closely inspecting their revolvers and checking their ammunition.

With a nervous attempt at a chuckle, he asked one who was sighting along the barrel, "Surely, you don't intend to use that thing on me, do you?"

"Nope," said the cowboy. "That would be impolite. We aim to use it on the guy who brung you."

•383

The closest I ever came to giving a bad talk was in 1957, shortly after the first satellite was launched into space by the Soviet Union. I was to speak at a Catholic church and my agent had assured them I was a very funny fellow. He did not, however, tell *me* I was supposed to be. What I wanted to do was talk on the importance of science education in the United States. I wasn't planning to be funny.

What's more, they locked me in a room for an hour before the talk and left me with nothing to read but liturgical books that I didn't want to read. By the time they released me, I was morose indeed. About halfway through my serious talk, the guy running the show put a piece of paper on my desk. I thought it might be an emergency call from home and my heart palpitated. I opened it while still talking, and all it said was, "Be funny."

I stopped my talk in midsentence, announced I would accept no fee, and that I would now go home. The audience, however, yelled for me to continue, so I did, with a lighter heart, and I was paid my fee.

However, as soon as I got home, I fired my agent.

•384

It is reported that George Bernard Shaw once sent two tickets to the opening night of one of his plays to Winston Churchill, along with the message, "Dear Winston: Here are two tickets for yourself and a friend, assuming you have a friend."

Winston returned the tickets with the note, "Dear Bernard. A prior engagement prevents my attending opening night. Please replace these with tickets for the second night, assuming there is a second night."

•385

In 1971, I was utterly flabbergasted to receive in the mail from the New York City Bureau of Motor Vehicles a "second notice" concerning a parking violation I had committed. My fine was increased to $20 and I was threatened with the loss of my driver's license.

My indignation was aroused by the fact that I had never received any "first notice" and, indeed, that I had not committed any parking violation.

I called my lawyer, Bob Zicklin. "Do I have to pay the fine," I demanded heatedly, "or do I have some recourse?"

"Of course you have a recourse," said Bob soothingly. "This is a government of law and not of arbitrary power. You write a letter to the bureau explaining the situation and they will set a date for the hearing. On that date, you go to the place they will tell you to go, wait until it is your turn to be heard. That will probably take most of the day. When you are before the magistrate, you tell the whole story in detail. They, of course, will not believe you, and *then* you pay the fine."

So I paid the fine by return mail.

Bob Zicklin's partner, Donald Laventhall, told me the story all lawyers love to tell.

A banker, a doctor, and a lawyer went swimming in water they didn't realize was shark-infested. The sharks came and gobbled down the banker and the doctor. One of them, however, lifted the lawyer gently in his teeth, swam to shore, and delivered him, unharmed, on the sand.

Very naturally, I asked, "Why?"

"Professional courtesy," said Donald gravely.

More limericks:

•386

> A methodical fellow named Wade
> Could recall every girl that he'd laid.
> > He recorded each poke,
> > Every thrust, every stroke,
> And precisely how much he'd been paid.

•387

> There was a young woman named Linda
> Who did it in front of the winda.
> > The guys passing by
> > Would give her the eye,
> But she didn't allow it to hinda.

There's always the danger that some wiseguy will say,

"What did she do in front of the window?" My answer is always,

"She combed her hair."

•388

> There was once a great knight named Sir Lancelot
> Who placed Queen Guinevere in a trance a lot.
> > But what bothered the king
> > Was he managed the thing
> By serenely removing his pants a lot.

•389

There was a young lass named Vanessa
Who said to her father confessor,
"When the fellows surround me
Pursue me and hound me,
Do you think I give in to them? Yes, sir."

•390

A publisher once (name of Knopf),
Alas, never knew when to stopf.
He lay down on the hipf
Of a charming young pipf,
And now he's a charming old popf.

•391

An astronomer said, "What's the use!
Our classical knowledge is loose.
There can be nothing stupider
Than to name that world Jupiter,
When we all know it should be called Zeus."

Another clean one. I just couldn't resist the rhyme.

•392

The Homeric young fighter Achilles
Was great with the fair Trojan fillies
But Paris said, "We'll
Just aim at his heel."
Now Achilles is pushing up lilies.

Another clean one, but classical. I'll finish with three versions
of Mother Goose:

•393

> They say Jack and his best girlfriend, Jill,
> One nice day went and climbed up a hill.
> > Was it water they're after?
> > Then why all the laughter?
> And how come Jill made sure of her pill?

•394

> Where is Little Boy Blue this fine morn?
> In the haystack as sure as you're born.
> > But he isn't asleep;
> > He's with Little Bo-Peep;
> And just look where he's putting his horn.

And my favorite:

•395

> "As for screwing," said Little Miss Muffet,
> "I proclaim here and now that I love it.
> > I defy the authority
> > Of the Moral Majority.
> They can take all their preaching and stuff it."

The following is not a funny remark. It is a riposte—a quick and slashing retort that instantly buries the verbal opponent. To understand it we must know that Benjamin Disraeli, the British statesman, was Jewish by birth. His family converted to Christianity when he was twelve in order that he might have greater opportunities for advancement. This did not alter the fact, however—at least to bigots—that Disraeli was Jewish.

•396

An Irish member of Parliament, in the course of an attack on Disraeli, referred slightingly and contemptuously to the fact that he was a Jew. Disraeli got slowly to his feet and said, "Yes, I am a Jew, and when the ancestors of the right honorable gentleman who has just spoken were brutal savages in an unknown island, mine were priests in the Temple of Solomon."

I have an acute dislike for Noel Coward. Effete and snobbish, he made sneering remarks about wounded soldiers from Brooklyn during World War II. No one can possibly sneer at Brooklyn and remain in my good graces. I therefore tell the following with great pleasure:

•397

The author Edna Ferber was fond of wearing mannish suits. On one occasion, Noel Coward lifted his nose and said, "You look almost like a man, Edna."

To which Miss Ferber replied, "And so do you, Noel."

•398

Joseph DiMaggio is, in my opinion, the greatest baseball player who ever lived. For a time, he was married to Marilyn Monroe, who may well be the most famous sex object of all time.

Shortly after their marriage, Miss Monroe went on a tour which proved enormously successful. When she came back, she reported the details to her husband, glowing. "Thousands of people," she said, "You never heard such applause."

And Joe said quietly, "Yes, I did."

•399

In the fourth century B.C., Demosthenes and Phocion were bitter rivals in Athens. Demosthenes, possibly the greatest orator of all time, had the better of it, but Phocion was no babe in the woods.

One time, Demostehenes said to Phocion, "Someday you will drive the Athenians out of their minds and they will kill you."

And Phocion replied, "And if they are ever in their right minds, they will kill you."

•400

Diogenes, also of the fourth century B.C., is the most famous misanthrope of all time. His opinion of the human race was abysmally low (and, I sometimes think, accurate) and he eschewed all luxuries, living as simply—and as honestly—as he could.

One time, as he was making a frugal meal of beans, he was addressed by Aristippus of Cyrene, who had a very comfortable position at the court of Dionysius, the king of Syracuse.

Aristippus said, "Just think, Diogenes, that if you could only learn to flatter Dionysius, you wouldn't have to live on beans."

And Diogenes replied, "Just think, Aristippus, if you could only learn to live on beans, you wouldn't have to flatter Dionysius."

•401

William Gladstone and Benjamin Disraeli were the great British opponents of the late nineteenth century. During one of their debates, Gladstone stated that Disraeli couldn't possibly be sure of his facts. To which Disraeli replied, "I wish I were as sure of anything as my opponent is of everything."

•402

When I worked at the Philadelphia Navy Yard during World War II, I was part, for a period of time, of a car pool, and there was much bantering going on back and forth.

One of the young men, who struck me as a little too self-assured about the things he felt he knew, refused to express an opinion on some particular subject. "I don't know enough," he said, "to give an opinion."

To which I replied dryly, "That never stopped you before."

•403

Arthur Miller, the famous playwright, was once standing in a bar alone, nursing his drink and lost in thought. Another man entered, very nattily dressed and perfumed, advanced to the bar, and stared at Miller curiously.

Finally the light dawned, and he cried out, "Miller. Arthur Miller! It's been years since I met you. Don't you remember Solly Fishbein from the old high school? I'm Solly."

By a great effort of memory, Miller seemed to remember a Solly Fishbein. "Yes, yes," he mumbled, "of course—"

"Boy, it's good to see you," cried old Solly. "How many years has it been? Wow! Those were the days, hey? And here I am now, married, two kids, in the clothing business and making a damned good thing out of it, too. We were out in Jamaica last year, and we're going to Europe next year. Living it up, I tell you. And my two kids— brightest in the world. The older one is at M.I.T.—"

He rattled on exuberantly while Miller listened patiently, smiling and nodding at appropriate moments.

Finally old Solly slowed down and said, "And how's the world been treating you, Arthur? What've you been doing?"

"I write," said Miller briefly.

"Oh? What kind of things do you write, Arthur? Advertising?"

"Not really," said Miller with increasing discomfort. "I write plays."

"Plays?" Solly thought awhile. "Ever do anything that's been produced? Anything I might have seen, Arthur?"

"Well," said Miller. "I suppose the play I wrote that's best known is *Death of a Salesman*."

"*Death of a—*" There was a long pause and now finally Solly said in a subdued voice, "Pardon me, Arthur Miller, but are you *Arthur Miller*?"

•404

The scene is a lonely castle on a dark windswept night in the depths of Transylvania. Our lovely heroine, in her restless sleep, is unaware that through the open window has come a figure of deepest menace.

His cloak, which a moment before had opened in the shape of bat's wings, is now closed about him. His chalk-white face is without emotion, but his eyes sparkle in the moonlight and his lips are moist and dark.

Slowly he advances on her.

The beautiful girl stirs in her sleep. Her eyes open, her mouth twisting in terror. However, she hasn't lived in Transylvania without learning something. Just as the vampire—for that is what it is—is about to sweep down on her, she whips a crucifix from under her pillow and holds it up.

The vampire laughs and says, "Look, lady, unless you have a Star of David, let me get about my business, will you?"

•405

The time was the late nineteenth century, when Ireland still groaned under the hand of the absentee English landlords and their brutal agents. It was a time when desperate measures were sometimes taken, and Dennis and Patrick had made up their minds that one agent, a man of unexampled villainy, would have to die.

They had studied his habits thoroughly and they well knew that once a week he went to visit a girlfriend and would come back along a lonely stretch of road at exactly midnight. Well before midnight on an appropriate day, they lay in wait for him, each with his knife.

But midnight approached, came, and went, and there was no sign of the agent.

Finally Dennis said, "He is late. He should have been by here near an hour ago."

And Patrick said, "That he should. I surely hope nothing has happened to the darling man."

•406

Mr. Jones had died and, as he had been an exemplary man, there was no difficulty in assigning him to heaven. But as the Recording Angel was about to make the necessary notations, Jones held up his hand.

"A moment, sir."

"Yes, Mr. Jones?"

"Before you send me to heaven, would it be possible for me to get just a glimpse of hell—just that I might see, for even a brief moment, what it is I will not be subjected to?"

The Recording Angel turned away from his word processor. "I suppose this can be arranged, even though it is not usual. Of course, you won't be able to stay long."

"A moment or two is all I ask."

There was a whizzing sensation, and Mr. Jones suddenly found himself in a dark, smoky atmosphere, lit by a fitful dim red glare. There was the sound of loud music in the air as though a rock and roll band of unexampled virtuosity was playing, and all around were dim figures, drinking, laughing, and dancing.

Mr. Jones seemed disconcerted, "Why, sir, this looks and sounds like a nightclub."

"I suppose you could call it that."

"But is all of hell like this?"

"Much of it is, of course, but rock and roll is not to everyone's tastes. We have gambling casinos, rococo ballrooms—"

Mr. Jones grew excited. "Disgusting. If hell is like this, quick, take me to heaven."

Again there was a whizzing sensation and Mr. Jones found himself in a room filled with pearly light. There, surrounded by bare, unadorned walls, seated at a wooden table, were seven men reading with deep concentration out of what seemed to be books of meditative philosophy.

"What's this?" asked Jones.

"Heaven," said the Recording Angel.

"But is this all? There's not even music."

"Listen," said the Recording Angel, "for four priests, two ministers, and a rabbi, you think we're going to invest in a band?"

I told this to a Jewish woman who laughed only moderately, to my disappointment. She said thoughtfully, "Only one rabbi?"

What could I do but answer solemnly, "Actually, they had trouble finding even one."

•407

Morris Bernstein had died and gone to heaven.

Almost the first person he saw there was the aged rabbi who had taught him in Hebrew school when he was young, and who had passed away nearly thirty years before. He recognized him at once, of course, and remembering those dear school days, he rushed over.

"Rabbi Cohen, Rabbi Cohen, do you remember me? I'm Morris Bernstein, and you taught me Hebrew once. Remember?" (Morris was quite aware that at the rabbi's aged side was a beautiful woman.)

The rabbi stared at Morris and said, "Yes, I remember you. You were a good student and I'm glad you've honored my teaching by qualifying for heaven."

Morris said, "And I'm glad that your own well-known piety and holiness has resulted in your being rewarded in this magnificent way," and his eye wandered to the tall, gorgeous redheaded feminine wonder who was now clutching the rabbi's withered arm.

The rabbi said, "Alas, Morris, this woman is not my reward. She was evil, and I am her punishment."

•408

A minister and a lawyer happened to die simultaneously in separate parts of the country and they showed up together for processing purposes in the anteroom of heaven.

Part of the process was being assigned dwelling places in heaven and the minister found himself in a narrow, unfurnished cell. He could not help but notice that the lawyer was being awarded a palatial mansion, and he raised his voice in protest.

He said, "Why am I getting a narrow, unfurnished cell, I who am a man of the cloth, and this lawyer, who devoted his life to secular pursuits, gets a mansion?"

"Well," said the Recording Angel, "we have millions of ministers here and it's impossible to give them more than the bare necessities. This other fellow, however, is a great triumph for heaven. He's our first lawyer."

•409

In various places in the city, one may find the terse sign, JESUS SAVES! put up by those who are interested in salvation.

Underneath one of them in the subway, a keen financial mind wrote, "But Moses invests!"

•410

A recent immigrant from Russia, needing directions, accosted a policeman and inquired politely in Yiddish as to where he might find the post office. The policeman drew a blank and merely stared at him helplessly.

Whereupon the immigrant repeated his request in Russian, and got just as little response.

The immigrant, furious, cried out, "What kind of land is this in which the people speak neither Jewish nor gentile?"

Self-assurance is not necessarily a lovable characteristic, especially when it is undeserved. An unreasonably self-assured person is a blowhard. However, if a person wishes to be an achiever, he has to know what he can do.

•411

I am self-assured and I know what I can do.

About twenty years ago, I wrote a medium-length story called "The Gods Themselves." My editor read it and said, "I want you to expand it into a novel."

I did not want to do that, because such expansion usually involves a matter of pumping a lot of hot air into it and ruins it.

So I said, "Look here. This story involves earth and an alternate universe and it ends without a true resolution. Why don't I write a second story, set in the alternate universe, and tell it again, still ending without a true resolution. Then I'll write a third story, back on earth, and produce the resolution."

I had made all that up on the spur of the moment, and my editor, knowing me, suspected that that was what I had done. He said, "Are you sure you can do that?"

"Of course," I said. "Unless I discover that I'm not Isaac Asimov."

You will be relieved to know that I wrote the additional stories exactly as I promised, combining the three into a novel, *The Gods Themselves,* and it won the two top awards in science fiction, the Hugo and the Nebula.

What's more, *The Gods Themselves* is my favorite science fiction novel among those I wrote, even if it isn't the most lucrative. After all, money isn't everything.

Still, if you want self-assurance, here is the granddaddy of them all.

•412

In 1916, Einstein worked out the general theory of relativity. Among other things, it predicted that a light beam passing through a gravitational field would be curved in its path by a certain amount.

This could be tested by waiting for a solar eclipse and observing the stars in the near neighborhood of the eclipsed sun. Their light beams, skimming by the sun, would be bent and the stars would appear to be farther from the Sun than they ought to be by a very small amount.

In 1919, after World War I was over, this was put to the test and Einstein proved to be correct. (Only marginally so, to be sure, but many other tests in the three-quarters of a century since have amply supported his theory.)

After the solar eclipse observation was carried through, someone asked Einstein how he would have felt if the test had *not* supported the theory.

Einstein replied, "In that case, I would have been sorry for the Lord God trying to work without it, for the theory *is* correct."

Of course, there are always factors that work to reduce my self-assurance.

I've been on talk shows in my time and have reached the point where my face looks distantly familiar to some people who are otherwise perfect strangers. Being human, I occasionally get a feeling of self-importance over this, and the following exchange (perfectly true) was most salutary in this respect:

•413

An elderly woman and myself were alone in an elevator. She looked at me fixedly, then said, "You're someone famous, aren't you? Who are you?"

I smiled fatuously and said, "I'm Isaac Asimov."

And she said sharply, "Who?" and lost interest.

•414

I was on a talk show once in which a showgirl, tall and of unearthly beauty, sat on my left, and you can well imagine that I was completely aware of her presence.

I behaved myself until the interviewer, in response to something I said, said, "You're a romantic, Asimov."

At which I turned to the young woman at my side and, forgetting I was on television (as I invariably do), said, "Talking about romantic, dear, what are you doing after the show?"

I meant nothing by it, I assure you. It was simply a bit of flirtatiousness on my part. However, my first wife, Gertrude, was watching and, since our marriage was moving its rocky way toward complete breakdown, she decided to take offense and I think it hastened the divorce.

•415

I was on another talk show at about that same time and David Frost initiated the proceedings by saying, "Dr. Asimov, do you believe in God?"

I had not yet reached the point where I was willing to admit my atheism to a large television audience, so I stalled by saying, "Whose?"

He said, "I mean the Judeo-Christian God of Western tradition. You know that very well, Dr. Asimov."

I stalled again. "I haven't given it much thought."

Said Frost, "I don't believe that. I'm sure a person of your wide knowledge and attainments would have sought to find God."

Whereupon I saw my chance and seized it. I said, "God is smarter than I am. Let him try to find me."

In the laughter that followed, the subject was dropped.

•416

That wasn't the end of it, however. I was quite certain that God, even if he existed, would not mind an honest atheist. He might, however, grow irritated over a wiseguy atheist. My talk with Frost had only been a taping. What would happen on the day it was really to appear?

I found out on that day. For twenty-one years I had suffered occasionally from the fearful pain of kidney stones and the day on which I appeared on television with my wiseguy crack about God finding me, I had my worst (and last) attack.

There's no use trying to describe the bitter, unrelenting pain one experiences in such an attack. All I could do was clutch my abdomen, stagger about, and gasp, "All right, God. You've found me. Now let me go."

Eventually he did, and the pain subsided just in time for me to catch the program. The Old Man may be short-tempered, but he's never been malignant—at least not to me, and not so far.

When I was young and did something foolish—as happened occasionally—my exasperated father would explode and shout at me, "*Goyische kup*," which meant that I had "the brains of a gentile." So now you know enough to understand the following joke.

•417

Moses and St. Peter agreed that earth was wallowing in sin and they decided to come down to the old planet and put on a supernatural show that would perhaps win humanity to repentance and virtue.

They came down to the seashore and a huge and enormous crowd gathered around the two strangers who were so tall, so impressive, and who had countenances glowing with all the fire of heaven.

They held out their arms above the crowd, exhorting them to repentance, and said in unison, "And to show what the Lord can do, we will now proceed to walk on water."

And, turning, they walked out into the ocean. Moses did remain on the surface, but St. Peter, as he walked outward, sank lower and lower. There was a stir in the crowd and Moses turned to see what was happening. There was St. Peter, up to his waist in water.

Whereupon Moses cried out, "Peter! Walk on the rocks, *goyische kup.*"

Jews who hear this joke for the first time laugh uproariously, but largely because of the last two words. Without it, it would fizzle. One might point out that St. Peter was just as Jewish as Moses, but it would be criminal to spoil the joke. For that matter, some people tell the story substituting Jesus for St. Peter, but Jesus was just as Jewish as Moses, too.

Insomnia is one of those laugh-inducing illnesses. It's in no way life threatening so people can laugh while quite ignoring the fact that insomniacs really have a miserable time of it.

•418

There was a man who had insomnia so bad he couldn't even fall asleep when it was time to wake up.

•419

There was a man who had insomnia so bad he couldn't even fall asleep when the TV set was on.

•420

I have long noticed that if I am sitting in a crowded room, on a hard wooden chair, with people rustling their papers and a speaker droning on about something or other, it is torture to try to stay awake.

And then, having kept myself awake through a long talk, I go home and get into my warm, soft, comfortable bed, with the lights out and absolute quiet everywhere—and I can't sleep.

•421

A speaker had once delivered himself of an interminably long address and after he was done one of the listeners worked up the nerve to mention it.

"That was a very long speech," he said.

"Well," said the speaker, "there was no clock in the hall, so I couldn't check the time I was taking."

"Ah," said the other, "but there was a calendar on the wall."

•422

Mr. Brown was an enormous figure in the world of finance and, from humble beginnings, he had risen to a position of billionairish eminence. A newspaper reporter, interviewing him, asked the reason for his success.

"The frigidity of my wife," said Brown with a growl.

"The frigidity of your wife?" said the newspaperman in astonishment. "What can that have to do with it?"

"Simple," said Brown. "I wake up early in the morning, anxious for some action. My wife refuses. So I wash, dress, and go to the office with one thought in mind. If I can't screw my wife, I'm going to screw the rest of the world."

•423

Mr. Moskowitz's wife had recently died, and he had not been seen much in society since then. Finkelstein, concerned for an old friend, decided to drop in on him, unnannounced, and labor at cheering up the poor man.

He knocked gently at Moskowitz's apartment. Though he heard distinctly the sounds of occupancy within, it was quite a while before the door was opened. When it was, Moskowitz looked tense and there were obvious signs that a young lady was also present. It did not take much of Finkelstein's shrewd worldly wisdom to deduce that she was hiding in the bathroom.

Finkelstein said austerely, "Well, Moskowitz, I won't stay, under the circumstances. But I must tell you that for a man who has been so recently bereaved, you are acting in a singularly shocking manner."

Moskowitz shrugged and said, "Finkelstein, my old friend, in my present mood, stricken with grief as I am, do I know what I'm doing?"

•424

One of my favorite television programs is *The Golden Girls,* and of the three middle-aged women featured in it, my favorite is Rose, played by Betty White. She is completely lovable, but completely dim-witted, and is at her best when she is telling impossible tales of her hometown, St. Olaf's, Minnesota.

Rose said one time, "We had someone at St. Olaf's Hospital who had been sick for a long time and was so tired of it. He kept saying, "Please let me die. Please take out all these tubes. Please let me die." So in the end the doctors did it and they let him die, and we all felt terrible."

Dorothy, the sane one, said, "Why should you feel terrible, if the man wanted to die?"

"Well," said Rose earnestly, "we could never be sure, because in the very next bed was St. Olaf's meanest ventriloquist—"

•425

It was an enormous funeral that was winding its way through the streets of the town and, in every way, no sign of sorrow had been stinted, right down to the open cars filled with flowers.

A bystander, who had been away from the neighborhood for a while, nudged a neighbor. "Who died?" he whispered.

"Big Angelo's girlfriend," said the other.

"Big Angelo's girlfriend? But she was so young! What did she die of?"

"Gonorrhea."

"Gonorrhea! But that's impossible. No one dies of gonorrhea."

"You do when you give it to Big Angelo."

When it comes to male chauvinist jokes, there are very few that are more savage than the following. It is my observation, however, that women laugh at it surprisingly loudly and heartily. I really can't understand it. Here's the joke. Try it out yourself and see how the women react.

•426

A man, attending the flowers at a grave site, noticed a very curious funeral procession entering the cemetery. First there was a hearse followed by an open car laden with flowers; then a second hearse followed by a second open car laden with flowers; then a man with a Doberman pinscher on a leash; then seventy-five men in single file, all marching solemnly.

The man at the grave site felt his curiosity overcome him. He walked up to the man with the dog and said, "Please forgive me, but could you tell me why there are two hearses?"

"Easily. In the first hearse is my wife, who was bitten to death by a Doberman pinscher."

"And in the second?"

"My mother-in-law. She came to the rescue of my wife and was also bitten to death by a Doberman pinscher."

"*This* Doberman pinscher?"

"Yes. We felt it only appropriate that he should attend the funeral."

The man at the grave site drew a long breath and said, "That's a very valuable dog you have there. Would you be willing to rent him to me for a few days?"

"Of course," said the other, "but you'll have to get to the end of the line."

•427

I love cats and am willing to stroke any cat no matter how ill-tempered it looks—and I am almost never scratched.

However, I hate and fear dogs and no dog ever comes near me, no matter how friendly and happy it looks, even if it is a Chihuahua, without my edging nervously away.

Once, though, I was in an elevator with my dear wife, Janet, and a beautiful redhead entered with a Doberman pinscher. Whereupon I smiled at her with all the fetching flirtatiousness of which I was capable and said, "Nice dog," and patted the Doberman pinscher on its head.

Janet was not amused. She said that for the sake of the woman I was willing to place my hand on a man-eating dog. But I suppose no woman really understands how the male libido works.

•428

They say that to be poor is no disgrace. Well, it's no great honor, either.

•429

When Athens had an Athenian empire in the fifth century B.C. and controlled all the islands in the Aegean Sea, it assessed one small island a rather large sum in taxes.

When the island refused to pay, the Athenian commissioner said, "I have an important god on my side that will make you pay. He is called Force."

To which the islanders replied, "We have an equally important god on our side that will keep us from paying. He is called Destitution."

Some funny stories, in order to work, have to set up conditions that are simply unbelievable. However, here's one that made me laugh, so I'll give it to you, even though it's ridiculous:

•430

Mr. Smith enjoyed horseback riding and, on a visit to another city, thought he would rent a horse from a local livery stable.

The livery stable owner was perfectly willing to oblige, but there were difficulties. "I have only one horse available at this time," he said, "and it is such a peculiar one that you might not wish to use him."

"What is the nature of the peculiarity?" asked Smith.

"He is a religious horse! At least he was owned by a preacher, who for some reason trained him to start moving only at the exclamation 'Jesus Christ!' and to stop only at the exclamation 'Amen!' Nothing else will do and most riders find it difficult to remember these words in an emergency."

"Nonsense," said Smith. "That is but a trifle. Bring out the horse."

This the owner did. Smith vaulted easily into the saddle and tested the animal. He attempted to start him with the usual giddy-up, tongue clickings, rein slappings, and heel kickings, but nothing did any good. The horse remained as though graven in wood.

Finally Smith said, "Jesus Christ!" and the horse was galvanized into furious life. Smith said at once, "Amen!" and the horse stopped.

"No trouble," said Smith. "I'll bring him back in an hour."

He then cried, "Jesus Christ!" and the horse was off. It was a magnificent creature that carried Smith as easily as though he were weightless. It had a flawless movement and a beautiful stride. Smith, feeling as though he were flying, had never enjoyed a ride so much before.

—Until he suddenly realized that the horse, moving steadily forward, was approaching, at furious speed, what seemed to be the lip of a cliff.

"Whoa-a-a-a-h" cried the excited Smith. "Stop! You damned horse!"

Backward he heaved at the reins with all his might, but nothing was to any avail till at the last moment he remembered and cried, "Amen!" The horse skidded to a sudden halt, ending, motionless, with his front hooves at the very edge of the cliff.

Smith leaned forward over the neck of the horse and looked

down a half-mile drop to where the sea foamed furiously against huge rocks.

Awed, he cried out, "Jesus Chri-i-i-i-i—"

•431

Oscar Wilde was a poseur and what he said was never necessarily true. However, he was visiting at a friend's summer house and one morning he did not show up till it was nearly lunchtime.

His friend said, "What have you been doing all morning, Oscar?"

"Working," said Wilde.

"Accomplish anything?"

"Oh, yes, I inserted a comma in a poem I'm writing."

He then disappeared all afternoon.

When he showed up for dinner, his friend said, "More work?"

"Yes," said Oscar. "I removed that comma."

The reverse of the prolific writer is the sufferer from writer's block, a serious disease in which a writer can only stare hopelessly at a blank sheet of paper and finds himself either totally unable to write or able to write only a sentence or two before crumpling the paper. I've never experienced this personally, but I have lots of friends who have.

•432

One of my favorite cartoons is that of a writer sitting at his typewriter. The ashtray contains a mountain of cigarette stubs. The floor is an ocean of crumpled papers. The writer is unshaven and looks haggard and miserable. And there in front of him is his daughter. She is talking and the caption reads:

"Daddy, tell me a story."

•433

A much happier cartoon shows a writer at his typewriter, drinking a cup of coffee and looking out the window at a swirling snowstorm.

In the snowstorm are various people dashing out of their houses to their cars, which, presumably, will take them to their commuter trains.

The writer, smiling, has his cup of coffee high in the air and the caption reads:

"Bon voyage."

I once told Herb Graff the following story, one that serves to keep me humble. Of all the stories I've told him, this is his favorite and he has lunched out on it innumerable times. It has the advantage of being perfectly true.

•434

Back in the early seventies, I had just joined the Gilbert & Sullivan Society and was waiting for the festivities to begin. I didn't know the gentleman at my right, who was a bit older than I was, and he clearly didn't know me. A young man came up to me and asked very politely for my autograph, which I was glad to give. There then followed this conversation between myself and the man beside me.

STRANGER (curiously): "Why did he ask you for your autograph?"

I (modestly): "I guess he recognized me."

STRANGER (naturally): "Who are you?"

I: "I am Isaac Asimov."

STRANGER (at sea): "But why did he ask you for your autograph?"

I (sighing inwardly): "I'm a writer."

STRANGER (perking up amazingly): "My son is a writer. He has just published his second book. He has published two novels" (holding up two proud fingers) "on sports."

I: "Wonderful."

STRANGER: "What do you write?"

I (cautiously): "Different things."

STRANGER: "Do you write books?"

I (wishing he'd stop): "Yes."

STRANGER: "How many have you written?"

I (at my wit's end): "A few."

STRANGER: "Come on. How many?"

I (suddenly annoyed and anxious to put an end to it by telling him the truth): "One hundred and twenty."

STRANGER (totally unfazed): "Any of them on sports?"

I: "No."

STRANGER (triumphant): "My son has written two novels on sports."

I (totally crushed): "Wonderful."

•435

My beautiful daughter knows me very well.

When I lived in Newton, Massachusetts, it was necessary for me, nearly every day, to walk a block and a half to the mailbox and post some letters. Invariably, I would do so while deep in thought, and as I walked away I would realize that I didn't remember whether I had noticed if the letters had dropped into the bowels of the box. So I, just as invariably, went back and looked into the opening again.

Robyn frequently accompanied me on my little walk, and on this occasion (she being about seven, I suppose) had one of her little girlfriends with her.

They watched me mail the letters, walk away, then turn back and stare into the opening.

Robyn's friend said to her, "Why does he do that?"

Robyn knew why. She said, "Because he's crazy."

•436

Now let's move ahead in time. Robyn and I were discussing college entrance and I said, "Don't worry about the costs, Robyn. I've got enough money to pay for it."

And then a stab of uncertainty suddenly struck me. (As an editor once said to me, "If you're rich and have a daughter on whom you dote, what is there for her not to like?")

So I said to Robyn uncertainly, "Robyn, would you still love me even if I were poor?"

And Robyn answered, "Sure, Dad. You'd still be crazy, wouldn't you?"

•437

Let's move still further ahead. Robyn is now twenty-two and is taking graduate courses at Boston University. I went to Boston to talk at the university and I rather expected to see her in the audience. However, the hall was crowded, and I didn't spy her, and once I began to give my talk, with my usual concentration on the task at hand, I forgot about her.

After the talk, a number of students crowded about me to ask questions and I was answering with great vivacity, as I usually do, and with only the vaguest awareness of my surroundings.

Very casually, I noted a beautiful, blond-haired, blue-eyed young woman standing quietly nearby, but my eyes slid over her without pause. This happened several times, until a vague feeling of having missed something pervaded me. I turned back to the young woman, stared awhile as I gathered my otherwise busy perceptions, and finally said with a distinct question mark in my voice, "Robyn?"

And Robyn, for it was she, turned to a friend next to her, held out her arms helplessly, and said, "See! How many minutes did it take for him to recognize me?"

•438

I once came to Boston University to take Robyn out to a steak house for dinner. She asked me if it would be all right to take her roommate, too. I said sure, and she brought along five roommates.

Every one of them was twenty-one years old; every one of them was beautiful; and I kissed every one of them.

One of the young ladies said, "Oh, Dr. Asimov, you behave just as Robyn said you would."

"What do you mean?" I said.

"Well, you kissed us all."

I said, "Don't the other daddies kiss you all, too?"

"No," they all chorused. "Robyn said you would be the only one."

That was something, so as we crossed the parking lot to enter the steak house I said, "Remember, girls, I don't have enough money to pay for all of you, so just order salads."

Whereupon Robyn stopped dead, turned to me, and said, "Dad.

These girls don't know your sense of humor. Now, you take it back. You're going to spoil their time."

Every last one of them ordered a huge steak, when I'm sure their ordinary dinners consisted of a few marshmallows and a milkshake.

•439

I was once watching the show *Laverne and Shirley,* of which I was very fond, and in this particular episode, Shirley's ne'er-do-well father shows up and Shirley, in a fit of nostalgia, plays a record which went, "You're the end of the rainbow, my pot of gold; you're Daddy's little girl to have and to hold—"

I just melted and the tears rolled down my cheeks and when the program was over I felt I just had to call Robyn at Boston University. Usually, when I call, I get one of the other girls, who has to scrape her up from wherever she's hiding. This time, however, Robyn answered directly.

"Hello, Dad," she said very gravely.

"Hello, Robyn." I paused, not knowing how to put it. "You didn't happen to watch *Laverne and Shirley* just now, did you?"

"One moment, Dad," she said. "Girls. My dad wants to know if we watched *Laverne and Shirley.*"

And there were incredible howls of laughter.

I was puzzled. I said, "What's going on, Robyn?"

"Well," she said, "we were watching *Laverne and Shirley* and when Shirley began playing the record about the pot of gold, I said, 'Oh, my God, my dad is going to call up as soon as this is over.' And you did."

—But I don't care. She loves me anyway.

One can sometimes overhear astonishing statements, but I can tell you one right now that must have struck an entire subway car of individuals dumb with amazement:

•440

When I was actively working in the biochemistry department at the medical school, one of the graduate students, a young woman, was working assiduously on the determination of certain enzymes present in the prostate gland, a small organ found only in males near the penis.

She was correlating the quantity of enzyme present with the existence of cancer in order to develop a method (if possible) of the early diagnosis of prostatic cancer. All work with organs is tricky, however, for there are variations from individual to individual and in the physical condition of the prostates obtained from cadavers.

I met the young woman, rather unexpectedly, in a subway car one morning and noted that she looked worried.

"What's the matter?" I asked.

And the young woman, in an ordinary speaking voice, said, "Oh, my prostate is acting up," and a dreadful hush fell over everyone present in the car.

•441

About a dozen years earlier than that I was a fresh young graduate student at Columbia, and in the synthetic organic chemistry laboratory at the desk immediately to my left was a very pretty blond student who attracted me enormously.

We were working on organic compounds that smelled very unlike roses, but we were used to it and didn't mind. It clung to our clothes and caused a certain amount of consternation among others who had not immersed themselves in the laboratory.

The young woman said to me one morning, "The people in the subway car don't like me because I smell so bad."

I was horrified. How could a young woman like that smell bad, no matter what chemicals saturated her clothing? I said indignantly, "That's terrible."

"No," she said, "that's good. I always get a seat because my end of the car empties out."

•442

It is amazing that even in graduate school, students had only a vague hold on the English language. I was presenting a small theory I had concerning the materials we were working with, and a fellow student interrupted me to say, "I doubt the veracity of that statement."

I stared at him coldly and said, "Morris, you are welcome to doubt the accuracy of my statement, but I won't permit you to doubt its veracity."

•443

A group of ultra-Orthodox Chasidic Jews were perturbed over the state of the world and decided that the only chance of averting the anger of the Lord was to attempt to convert more of mankind to Chasidism. For the purpose, they chose young Herschel to travel to Africa, where he might begin the good work with some primitive African tribe who might benefit most from enlightenment.

Herschel, with utter faith in the protection of the Holy One, took an unlicensed air flight into central Africa and parachuted down into an area untrodden by white men. There he found a tribe that was utterly primitive. Patiently, he learned their language and then began to strive to inculcate them with the premises of Chasidism.

This, however, annoyed the tribesmen, who found their own religion ample for their purposes. They therefore decided to sacrifice Herschel to their gods with all appropriate tortures.

Herschel saw his fate approaching with complete equanimity, even cheerfulness. He had faith in God and if God saw fit for his own purposes to have Herschel tortured to death, that was acceptable.

As the tribesmen made their preparations, they were astonished and impressed at Herschel's attitude. They had never seen such calm bravery.

The chief said to Herschel, "We simply can't torture so brave a man. We will give you a fighting chance. If you can achieve three great trials, we will not only turn you free, but everyone in the tribe, from myself down to the least, will become Chasidic Jews."

Herschel said, "Done! What are the three great trials?"

"First," said the chief, "you must walk through a pit of deadly mamba snakes, whose smallest bite is certain death. If you survive, you must extract the infected tooth of a ferocious lioness we have caged in the jungle, and you must do it with your bare hands. If you survive that, then you must satisfy, in full, the enormous cravings of the tribal nymphomaniac."

"Very well," said Herschel. "Let the first trial begin."

The chief, with the entire tribe following, every man and woman fascinated, led the way to a pit in which dozens of deadly mamba snakes writhed, jaws open, fangs dripping. They hissed horribly.

Without a tremor, Herschel, smiling, walked into the pit and every member of the tribe turned away in horror. When they heard no shriek of agony, they turned again in surprise and found Herschel, still smiling, at the other end of the pit and the mambas crowded to either side. They had parted before him like the waters of the Red Sea.

Excitedly, the tribe followed the chief off to the jungle, where the agonized roaring of the caged lioness with the infected tooth could be heard.

Still smiling, Herschel entered the jungle. The tribe heard the door to the cage creak open and the roaring rise to a maniacal frenzy. They waited, breathless, for the cry of a human being as he was torn to bits, but instead they heard only the lioness's roar growing softer and softer and finally subsiding into a rumbling purr.

After a long interval, Herschel emerged unharmed, not even scratched, and, still smiling, he said, "Okay, fellows, now where's the lady with the bad tooth?"

The limericks I have inserted in this book up to this point have all been of my own composition. However, I am not the only limericist in the world, and I would like to include a few more now that I did not make up, but can only wish I had. Here they are:

•444

Once Titian, while mixing rose madder,
Spied his model high up on a ladder.
      Her position to Titian
      Suggested coition,
So he climbed up the ladder and had 'er.

•445

I sat next to the Duchess at tea;
It was just as I feared it would be.
      Her rumblings abdominal
      Were truly phenomenal,
And everyone thought it was me.

It has been suggested that the previous limerick was written by President Woodrow Wilson. Perhaps! He also is credited with the next one, and the unusual thing is that both are terribly clever and amusing, even though they are clean.

•446

At beauty, I am not a star.
There are others more handsome by far.
      But my face, I don't mind it,
      Because I'm behind it.
It's the people out front that I jar.

•447

To his bride said the lynx-eyed detective,
"Can it be that my eyesight's defective?
      Has your east tit the least bit
      The best of your west tit?
Or is it a trick of perspective?"

•448

There was a young plumber of Leigh
Who was plumbing a girl by the sea.
      Said the maid, "Cease your plumbing,
      I think someone's coming."
Said the plumber, still plumbing, "It's me!"

I have long thought that the limerick is especially adapted to the English language and that, in fact, it would not be a successful verse form in another. However, I may be wrong. At least I have seen a version of the preceding limerick in French and it was just as funny in that language.

•449

In the Garden of Eden lay Adam,
Complacently stroking his madam.
    And loud was his mirth
    For he knew that on earth
There were only two balls—and he had 'em.

It must be an unsophisticated person, or an intellectually blind member of the religious right, to believe that the Garden of Eden, Adam, Eve, and a talking serpent ever existed. However, in the world of jokedom they exist:

•450

Eve had just been fashioned from Adam's rib and God said, "Now, be fruitful and multiply."

"How do I do that?" asked Adam.

"Just take Eve into the bushes there. I have placed the proper instincts within you and you will know what to do."

Off they went into the bushes and, within a minute, Adam was back.

"Lord," he said, "what's a headache?"

•451

There was a young lady named Alice,
Who pissed in a Catholic chalice.
    The padre agreed
    'Twas done out of need,
And not out of Protestant malice.

•452

There was a young man from Australia
Who painted his rear like a dahlia.
            The color was fine,
            Likewise the design.
The aroma—ah, that was a failure.

•453

I met a lewd nude in Bermuda,
Who thought she was shrewd; I was shrewder.
            She thought it quite crude
            To be wooed in the nude;
I was cruder; pursued her; and screwed 'er.

•454

There was a young lady from Kew,
Who said, as the bishop withdrew,
            "Oh, the Vicar is quicker
            And thicker and slicker
And four inches longer than you."

•455

There was a young girl of Darjeeling
Who could dance with such exquisite feeling,
            That no murmur was heard,
            Not a sound, not a word,
But the fly-buttons hitting the ceiling.

•456

A modern young lady named Hall
Attended a birth control ball.
            She was loaded with pessaries
            And other accessories—
But no one approached her at all.

•457

Nymphomaniacal Jill
Tried a dynamite stick for a thrill;
They found her vagina
In North Carolina,
And bits of her tits in Brazil.

A better known version of this limerick is:

•458

Nymphomaniacal Alice
Used a dynamite stick as a phallus.
They found her vagina
In North Carolina,
And part of her anus in Dallas.

•459

There was a young lady of Kent
Who said that she knew what it meant
When men asked her to dine
And plied her with wine.
She knew what it meant, but she went.

•460

Rosalina, a pretty young lass,
Had a truly magnificent ass;
Not rounded and pink,
As you possibly think—
It was gray, had long ears, and ate grass.

•461

There was an old monk of Siberia,
Whose existence grew drearier and drearier.

He did to a nun,
What he shouldn't have done,
And now she's a Mother Superior.

•462

A certain old colonel named Randy,
One morning awoke with a dandy.
He said to his aide,
"Go, fetch me a maid,
Or a goat, or just anything handy."

•463

There once was a monarch of Spain
Who was terribly haughty and vain.
When women were nigh,
He'd unbutton his fly,
And have them with sneers of disdain.

One last limerick is included here, simply because it makes fun of limericks:

•464

There was a young man of Japan,
Whose limericks never would scan,
When asked why that was
He answered, "Because
I always squeeze as many syllables into the last line as ever possibly I can."

•465

Women are peculiar. I once went with Gertrude to see a revival of the old silent classic *Son of the Sheik,* with Rudolf Valentino. As we seated ourselves, Gertrude, who had never seen Valentino in action, but only in movie stills, said, "I never could see what anyone saw in Valentino. He never struck me as the least desirable."

She kept on mumbling in this fashion until Valentino appeared on the screen and then she went, "Whoo," and she watched him throughout the picture with a red face and burning eyes. I heard nothing further about his being undesirable.

•466

Janet is just as bad. One day we went to see *The Pirates of Penzance* on its first performance in Central Park. We had seen it at least a dozen times, so Janet was not expecting much. And then the pirate ship appeared with Keven Kline as the pirate captain. He looked like Errol Flynn only much better and Janet went, "Wow!" I doubt that she heard a note of the play, but she sure kept her eyes on Kline.

•467

Once, when Robyn was twelve, she said to me, "I've got nothing to read."

So I pulled down one of my books of short stories and opened it to "The Ugly Little Boy" and said, "Here, read this."

"The Ugly Little Boy" is a very unusual Asimov story. I am noted for the cerebral qualities of my stories, but every once in a long while I make use of emotion just to show people I can do it if I want to, and "The Ugly Little Boy" is incredibly emotional.

Robyn went off to read it and emerged from her room every once in a while to tell me how good the story was and how much she was enjoying it. I nodded and waited.

Sure enough, she didn't emerge after a while for quite a time, and when she did come out, her face was red and streaked, and her eyes were swollen. She looked at me accusingly and said, "You didn't tell me it was going to be sa-a-a-ad."

And I said, "Oh, Robyn," and she crawled into my lap and cried herself out till she could cry no more and I kept patting her.

Years later I told the story to Janet and said, "What kind of daddy am I? There she was crying her eyes out and I was enjoying it."

And Janet said, "Perfectly normal. You're a writer first, and a daddy second."

•468

But let us get back to Herschel, the young Chassid who underwent the three trials in central Africa.

After he had left that tribe, he heard rumors that, in a certain spot to the southwest, there was a native tribe that was already Jewish. In fact, the story was that the tribe was descended from fugitives from Nebuchadrezzar, Jews who fled into Egypt at the time of the destruction of the first Temple, and then penetrated farther into Africa. For 2,000 years, they had dwelt in the jungles and were now, through intermarriage, indistinguishable from surrounding tribes. Still (the story went) they retained their Jewish heritage.

Filled with excitement, Herschel battled through the jungle trail to find them. He came finally upon a tribe that did indeed seem to have something Mediterranean about their cast of features. Cautiously he questioned them, but was disappointed to find that there seemed nothing Jewish about their customs and beliefs.

Downcast indeed, he could only conclude that he had found the wrong tribe, but as he prepared to journey on, he was invited to attend a great ceremony that night. He decided to accept the invitation. After all, something, some faint trace of Judaism, might show up, and he was expert enough to detect that if it did.

That night the drums beat and the tribesmen writhed in their dances. Finally, as the celebration reached its height, the shaman himself—the witch doctor—entered. He was tall and slender. His tall mask was most impressive. He wore a necklace of skulls and animal fangs, and a flaring grass skirt. He had rattles in either hand, and he leaped high, he whirled wildly, he skipped skillfully, and his muscles rippled.

And just as Herschel decided sadly there was nothing here to detain him, the woman next to him leaned toward him, smiling broadly to reveal her gleaming teeth, and said, "Well, mister, what do you think of my son, the doctor?"

•469

After Herschel returned to his small Eastern European town, the entire population clustered about him so that they might admire this adventurous traveler who had seen things that were completely strange and unimaginable.

One of them said, "Tell me, Herschel, what is the worst thing that happened to you in those heathen places?"

"The worst? Well, one time I roused the enemy of the tribe I was living with and they banded together and attacked me, throwing their spears at me. I did my best to evade the spears, calling on the Holy One for help, but one of the spears struck me and pinned me tightly to a tree. There they left me for the whole day before releasing me."

"Oh, Herschel," said an awed listener. "A whole day pinned to a tree. How it must have hurt."

"Not really," said Herschel. "Only when I laughed."

•470

Mrs. Finkelstein had arrived in the wilds of India in her search for the great Swami who had appeared in the foothills of the high Himalayas.

She was warned that the trip would be a dangerous one and fraught with all sort of perils, but she shook her head. "I must see the Swami. If it costs me my life, I must see him."

Everyone was impressed with Mrs. Finkelstein's determination and grit. They marveled at how such a woman, middle-aged and scrawny, could find it in herself to dare man and beast, heat and mountainous cold, in order to reach the Swami and find enlightenment.

They directed her and she traveled on and on, scrambling up the foothills of the high Himalayas till she found the cavern in which the Swami sat. Outside were his disciples, dressed in the usual saffron robes and with the usual bald heads of Buddhist monks.

They stared at Mrs. Finkelstein. "What is it you want, O woman from the great beyond?"

She said, "Listen. I've got to see the Swami."

Impressed by her great determination, they said, "Enter the abode of the great Swami."

This she did and stared at the Swami in his robes and turban, surrounded by dim light and by clouds of incense.

And she said, "All right, Melvin. Enough with this Swami silliness. Come on home."

•471

I encountered the Norse myths when I was a kid and I was very impressed by them, especially with the tale of Thor's foray into the land of the giants and his wrestling match with an old woman, Elli. The old woman, though she seemed barely strong enough to stand, somehow grew stronger as the wrestling match progressed, and stronger still, until she forced the great and mighty Thor, god of Thunder, down to one knee.

It turned out that Elli was merely a personification of old age. I was perhaps eight or nine when I read it, and I at once understood what old age must be, an understanding that has never left me. And now that Elli has me down on one knee, I can only say I didn't have to find it out when I was a little kid. I could have waited.

Here's a tale of Thor you won't find in the myths.

•472

Thor thought he would visit earth and amuse himself with an earth woman (a common practice among the pagan gods). He found one who was almost as large as he himself was, and who looked at him with a smile on her lips and fire in her eyes. It didn't take long to come to an understanding and Thor went to work with all the enthusiasm and capacity of a Norse god.

The night wore away in repeated bouts of passion and finally, as dawn was breaking, the god felt it would be only right to acquaint the woman with the great good fortune that had come her way. Standing up, he stroked his great red beard and said, "Know, O woman, that I am Thor."

Whereupon the woman looked up at him wearily and said, "*You're* Thor! Why, thuffering thathafrath, I'm tho thore I can't even thit up."

There's a similar story involving our own supernaturals which I ordinarily hesitate to tell. Naturally, it was told me by a gentile.

•473

God had had a heavy century and he looked tired. The archangel Gabriel, full of commiseration, said, "Lord, I think you could use a vacation. Go ahead, we'll take care of things while you're gone."

God shrugged his shoulders. "I'd be willing, but I can't think where to go."

"How about the planet earth? You used to go down there once in a while in old times."

God shuddered. "Not on your life. The last time I was there, about two thousand years ago, I had an affair with a little Jewish girl, and believe it or not, they're still talking about it."

When one learns a foreign language, the texts eventually get to the point where they tell you little anecdotes. I studied both French and German and read short and supposedly funny stories in both languages. Either the textbook editors had poor taste in humor or natural differences soured them for me. Here is an example of a story in a German text which has remained with me for over half a century, for its absolute failure to elicit a smile.

•474

Herr Schmidt came to call on Herr Mueller in the old days when there was no telephone to use first, and you had to take potluck. Schmidt's luck was not good.

He said to the maid who opened the door, "May I see Herr Schmidt?"

"I'm sorry. Herr Schmidt has gone out."

"Then may I see Frau Schmidt?"

"I'm sorry. Frau Schmidt has also gone out."

"Then may I sit by the fire and wait for one or the other to return?"

"I'm sorry. The fire has also gone out."

However—and this is the point—I read one story in my German text that I liked very much and here it is:

•475

A tall, fierce soldier walked into a barbershop in the old days when soldiers were really tall and fierce.

He said, "I want a shave. I want a close shave. And I don't want to be cut." He drew out his huge sword from its scabbard and laid it across his lap. He said, "In fact, if I am cut, however lightly, I will split the barber with this sword."

The barber, teeth chattering, said, "I'm sorry, but I have a cramp in my hand and I fear I could not do a good job. My first assistant will shave you."

The first assistant, turning green, said, "Unfortunately, I have a bad head cold and I do not wish to give it to you. The second assistant will shave you."

Whereupon the second assistant fainted dead away and that took care of him.

At this the teenage apprentice barber, Max, said cheerfully, "I will shave you, Lieutenant."

"Very well," said the soldier, "but see that you don't cut me."

"Not a chance," said Max as he mixed the lather. He applied it, sharpened his razor, and then, whistling blithely, shaved the soldier. When he was done, the soldier felt his cheeks and chin and said, "Young man, that was a perfect shave. Here is ten marks as your reward, but tell me, how is it you were brave enough to shave me and risk being killed by my sword?"

Max said with a broad smile, "I was in no danger, Lieutenant. It was you who were in danger. If at any time I had cut you, my razor would have been less than two inches from your throat."

•476

My hatred of critics does not prevent me from telling you about the critic who reviewed a production of *King Lear*. He said, "The actor playing the king seemed to be under the constant apprehension that someone else would play the ace."

•477

Two old men, each one over ninety, were sitting on a park bench.

One said, with a certain air of satisfaction, "Death seems to have forgotten us."

The other put his finger to his lips. "Ssh!"

•478

A woman said proudly, "Before I married my husband, I told him quite frankly of the various different love affairs I had had. I did not want to marry him under false pretenses."

"What honesty," said one of those who was listening to her.

"And what courage," said another.

"And what a memory," said a third.

•479

Four women were sitting on the porch at a summer resort, and one heaved a deep sigh. "Oh!"

The second responded with, "Oh, dear."

The third said, "Oh, dear me!"

And the fourth stood up angrily and said, "If all you're going to talk about are your children, I'm leaving."

In the Jewish mythology of my childhood, children were always "bad." Mothers, working hard in their slummish apartments, had no time for their numerous offspring and had to keep them in line with yells and blows. We children played in the street, because there was nowhere else to play. We got dirty because there was no way of preventing it. We ripped our clothes because accidents would happen. We were out of earshot when we were wanted because there was no way of knowing when we would be wanted. All this was held against us.

Since people often lived on the fourth floor with no elevators, there was no chance of running up and down the stairs for trivial reasons. If you wanted your son to run an errand at the grocery store, you had to yell for him out the window. If you were lucky and he answered, you threw down the necessary money wrapped up in a piece of paper. The streets were always full of discordant yelling.

•480

Mr. Moskowitz said to Mrs. Finkelstein, "Are you going out to shop?"

"Yes, I am."

"If you should see my son, Sammy, tell him to stop whatever it is he is doing and give him a good hock."

"But what if he's not doing anything bad?"

"In that case, it's not my son, Sammy."

Of course, when we said "bad" in those halcyon days, we didn't mean bad as in these days. Nowadays, bad children are involved with knives, guns, mayhem, murder, and drugs.

I was a "bad boy" at school because I whispered in class when we were suppose to sit in dead silence.

I was a "bad boy" at home because I fought with my sister. To me, fighting with my sister was inevitable; to live with her was to want to kill her.

To my mother, the fighting was more than she could bear. She would pull us apart, chastise each of us just as hard as she could, and then she would yell at us for an hour or two. The point she made was that nowhere else in the world did children fight. We were the only ones who did so and when we fought we made so much noise that people for blocks around were startled.

There was no chance at all of telling her that every set of

children in every family were forever at each other's throats and that my mother made much more noise yelling at us than ever we made fighting.

•481

My father worried when my sister was getting married because the boy she married was not Jewish.

My father said to me, "Do you think I ought to try to stop it?"

I said, "Papa, are you going crazy? Here's a nice fellow who wants to take Marcia off our hands and you want to *stop* him?"

My father gave it some thought and decided I was right.

•482

My mother, who had fought with Marcia every day of Marcia's life, got a little nervous as the day of Marcia's marriage drew near.

Stan consoled her. "Mama," he said, "remember! You're not gaining a son, you're losing a daughter."

My mother cheered up at once.

But my sister fooled us all. Her marriage was continually and exceedingly happy. All Marcia's characteristics that the family found unbearable, Nick didn't mind at all. What's more, they had two tall and stalwart sons, and the older, Larry, has already given Marcia a granddaughter. What's more, I'm very fond of Larry. I had him as a guest at the Trap-Door Spiders not too long ago, and he impressed everyone with his intelligence and aplomb.

•483

A senatorial candidate felt that it would be best for his political future if he demonstrated an interest in Native Americans.

He therefore visited a Navajo tribe and launched into an impassioned speech. The Navajos listened and shouted with fervor, "Ungah! Ungah!"

The candidate wound up to a tremendous peroration and, amid the repeated enthusiastic cries of "Ungah," came to a perspiring and breathless halt.

The chief of the tribe stepped forward and said, "Mr. Senator, we of the tribe are grateful for your interest in us and wish to bestow a gift on you. In yonder corral are the tribal horses. Go in and choose which one you wish to have as your own, but please, be careful not to step in the piles of ungah."

•484

King Christian X of Denmark remained in Copenhagen during the German occupation, but refused in any way to cooperate with the Nazis. Indeed, the Danish Jews were shipped to Sweden and saved from the Holocaust. When the Nazis tried to get the Danish Jews, before their escape, to wear yellow Stars of David so that they might be identified for easier maltreatment, King Christian put on a yellow Star of David himself and killed the project.

The German authorities, anxious to keep Denmark as a model example of the blessings of German occupation, did not attempt to exert their full brutality on the nation, but did attempt persuasion. In an attempt to get King Christian to agree to institute certain repressive measures, a German representative said, "But surely, Your Majesty, you Danes have a Jewish problem, too."

"As a matter of fact," said His Majesty, "we don't. We Danes insist on considering ourselves fully equal, in intelligence and achievement, to the Jews among us."

•485

During the same occupation, a German general was going through a museum in Copenhagen and was shown a restored Viking ship.

The general stared at it through his monocle and said, "Rather small, isn't it?"

"Yes," said the young lady serving as his guide. "German ships are much bigger, but with these small ships, we Danes managed to invade and conquer England."

And so they had, about the year 1000, in Hamlet's time.

•486

There is the belief that after the destruction of Israel, with its ten tribes, those ten tribes somehow established themselves in the depths of Asia and formed a powerful kingdom. Pure mythology.

Herschel, our old Chasidic friend, having completed his African journeys, went to China next, hot on the trail of the Ten Lost Tribes.

He finally found a Jewish tribe, clearly Mongolian in appearance, but with religious services that did seem to have resemblances to Judaism. Carefully, he learned the language and began to question the leader, who in some ways seemed to behave like a rabbi.

Herschel said to the leader, "Do you realize that your rites are reminiscent of those of Judaism?"

"That is no surprise," said the Mongol rabbi, "since we are Jews. But how could *you* tell?"

Herschel smiled and stroked his dark beard and then his long earlocks. His lips curled under his generously curving nose, and he said, "How could I tell? Because I'm Jewish myself."

"Funny," said the other, peering at him closely. "You don't look Jewish."

•487

I once saw a cartoon which showed two people staring at each other. One was a little man in a loincloth, looking like Mahatma Gandhi. The other was a stalwart man with a full feathered headdress looking like Sitting Bull. Both are speaking simultaneously, and the caption reads:

"Funny, but you don't look Indian."

•488

During World War II, when the Chinese were our allies and the Japanese were our foes, there was a great deal of talk about how one could distinguish between Chinese and Japanese in appearance.

With this in mind, the following cartoon appeared. Two Japanese are looking at a poster, obviously designed to indicate the difference in appearance between Americans (Japan's foes) and Germans (her allies). The American had a nondescript, wide-eyed, innocent look on his face. The German was a caricature with a bullet head, short hair, and a scowl of unutterable evil on his face.

In the caption, one Japanese says to the other:

"No use. All white men look the same to me."

•489

I once committed, quite unintentionally, a terrible faux pas. It came about this way.

At a party, I met a woman I didn't know. Her name was Jewish (say, Rosenblum) and she had a magnificent hooked nose. I was delighted. A woman who looked like that, I thought, must know Yiddish and that would give me an opportunity, which I rarely had, to tell some of my stories in Yiddish.

I tried it and was met with a blank look. She said, "I'm not Jewish by birth. My husband is Jewish and when I married, I converted to Judaism, but I don't know any Yiddish."

"My God," I said, "and when you converted, you even got yourself a reverse nose job."

I must have hurt her feelings terribly, but I had not meant to. It was just one of those things that escaped me before I had a chance to think.

•490

I am told that Eisenhower complained that after he had left the presidency, his golf game deteriorated. "Many more people beat me now that I am not president any longer," he said.

•491

A man and a woman met on the beach, fell in love with each other at first glance, and after three days, were married.

The wedding night was just as successful as it could be, but when the woman awoke the following morning, she found her husband dressing.

She said, "Where are you going?"

He said, "Darling, we married so rapidly, I had no chance to tell you that I'm a golf fiend. I play golf every day; I enter every tournament. I am afraid that you will rarely see me."

She nodded and said, "Well, that's all right. After all, we married so rapidly, I had no chance to tell you, either—I'm a hooker."

The man said, "That's nothing. Don't worry about that. It's easily corrected. You just hold the golf club like this—"

To those as ignorant of golf as I am, I suppose I ought to explain that when a golf ball curves in one direction rather than heading straight for the hole, it is a "slice." In the other direction it is a "hook." This joke was told to me, by the way, by a fellow I know who is the worst jokester in the world. But it shows you should listen. Even a terrible jokester may come up with a good one.

•492

Michael Faraday, a British scientist, who was one of the greatest of all time, used to give hugely successful lectures at which he demonstrated some of his discoveries. On this occasion, he showed that a magnet moving into a coil of wire, or moving out of it, set up an electric current in the wire. This marked an important discovery in the field of electromagnetism.

William Gladstone, the British statesman, observing the needle jerk as an indication of the electric current, is supposed to have said, "But Mr. Faraday, what is the use of this phenomenon?"

And Faraday is supposed to have answered, quite correctly, "Mr. Gladstone, in twenty years you will be taxing it."

•493

A similar story is told of Benjamin Franklin, who was present in Paris when the first public demonstration of a balloon was presented in 1783. Afterward, someone asked Franklin, "But what is the use of such a device?"

Franklin answered, "What is the use of a newborn baby?"

As I mentioned earlier in the book, I have been called by those who disapprove of me "a monster of vanity and arrogance." That's not at all so, and I am called that only by people who don't know me. What gives them the idea, however, is that I cannot prevent myself from saying things that feed the notion—simply because they are funny. Two examples occur to me:

•494

Oscar Levant, the pianist, is supposed to have said to his good friend George Gershwin, the musician (who was a real monster of vanity and arrogance), "George, if you had your life to live over, would you fall in love with yourself again?"

This was much repeated and, when I was working at the Philadelphia Navy Yard during World War II, a good friend of mine, Leonard Meisel, thought he'd try it on me.

"Isaac," he said, "if you had your life to live over, would you fall in love with yourself again?"

And I answered instantly, "Even sooner."

I think Leonard has repeated that little exchange ever since.

•495

Once someone pointed out a newspaper item to me. It referred to me as "Isaac Asimov, the Leonard Bernstein of science fiction."

To which I responded austerely, "I prefer to think that Leonard Bernstein is the Isaac Asimov of music."

•496

A famous movie star was once asked by an interviewer, "How many husbands have you had?"

To which the movie star said, "You mean, apart from my own?"

•497

I value the well-known eccentricity of writers.

Once, when I was teaching at the medical school, a stiff and humorless member of the faculty berated me for coming to school without a jacket or tie. (The school was then without air conditioning, and the summers were hot.) I listened politely, and paid no attention.

Another faculty member said to me, "Do you intend to continue to dress informally and lecture in that fashion?"

"Absolutely," I said. "I'm a writer, and writers are allowed to be eccentric."

•498

It's not surprising that I had trouble with the medical school. For one thing, I hated doing research because I found I was no good at it. I was the best lecturer in the school and I was an excellent science writer. (Not science fiction—I wrote that on my own time.)

I thought that my lecturing and writing were enough, but I was called on the carpet by the director.

When I became sufficiently annoyed with his lecturing me, I snapped at him, "Listen, as a writer, I am very nearly the best science writer in the world and I reflect glory on the school. As a researcher, I am merely mediocre and if there is one thing the school doesn't need, it is one more merely mediocre researcher."

This so infuriated the director that I was fired on the spot, but I managed to keep my title, which I still have. I am Professor of Biochemistry to this day.

•499

In the course of my fight with the school, I couldn't help but notice that I became a pariah. No one on the faculty cared to be seen talking to me, lest the school administration turn against him or her as well. Once, however, a fellow faculty member, making sure we were unobserved, said to me, "Isaac, the faculty is proud of you for your courage in fighting the administration for academic freedom."

I said, "There's no courage involved in it. Don't you know my definition of academic freedom?"

"No. What's your definition of academic freedom?"

I said, "Independent income."

Yes, indeed, the school did me an enormous favor, though I didn't know it at the time. They fired me in 1958 and I turned to writing full time, and since then my income has increased a hundredfold. Who can tell what life holds?

•500

A man tried to get a job as sexton at the local synagogue. The rabbi told him that he would make a good sexton, but alas, he could not read or write, and literacy would be needed in the course of his work.

The man left, disconsolate, found another job, and, by working very hard and making use of his native ability, he gradually advanced until finally he owned a small business.

Still working hard, he expanded his business until he was very rich. And he still could not read or write.

Once, when he was being interviewed by a newspaper reporter, the fact of his illiteracy came to be known.

The newspaper report said, "Imagine, sir, what you would have been if you could only read and write."

"I know what I would have been," said the man. "I would now be the sexton at a small synagogue."

•501

"Damn," said an ardent young man, reading a letter.

His friend, standing near him, said, "Bad news?"

"Disturbing news, anyway," said the young man. "It's from someone who says if I don't stay away from his wife, he'll kill me."

"In that case, if I were you, I would stay away from his wife."

"Gladly, but which one? The letter is anonymous."

• 502

Another telegraphic practical joke is to send one that reads: "Get out of town. All is discovered."

• 503

I was told (as a true story) that a refined-looking little old lady from Boston was heard to say, "Oh, *shit*, I just stepped in some doggy-do."

• 504

Three French children, aged six, seven, and eight, were walking along the street. They stopped at the sight of a pair of dogs copulating.

The six-year-old said, "Look at those dogs fighting."

The seven-year-old laughed and said, "You little ninny. They're screwing."

And the eight-year-old said gravely, "Yes, and dog-fashion at that."

• 505

Mr. Anderson's automobile suddenly developed a flat tire one night, immediately outside the strong iron fence that walled off the local mental institution.

Annoyed but resigned, Anderson jacked up the car and prepared to replace the wheel. He took off the hubcap, unscrewed the bolts, which he placed in the hubcap, which in turn was resting in the road, and placed the spare tire with its hub onto the axle.

He was about to reach for the hubcap with its bolts when a speeding car raced by and, even as Mr. Anderson jumped back for dear life, it ran over the hubcap, sent it spinning for two blocks, and sent the bolts flying in all directions.

There was no possibility of finding the bolts in the dark, and helplessly, Anderson realized he was standing there with a wheel on the axle, unbolted and useless.

While he wondered what to do, a man from the other side of the fence shouted, "Hey, mister."

Anderson looked up, surprised, and realized that he had attracted the attention of one of the mental inmates, who had been watching the procedures by the light of the street lamps.

Anderson said cautiously, "Yes? Is there something you want?"

"I just want to give you some advice. Look—just take off the other hubcaps and remove one bolt from each wheel and use them for that spare tire you have. The other wheels will be held by four bolts apiece and your spare by three. That will hold you till you get to the nearest repair shop, where you can get additional bolts and an additional hubcap.

"Great," said Anderson. "You're perfectly right. Now, why didn't I think of that?" Then, embarrassed, he said, "It's really amazing that, under the circumstances—uh—you could—"

"Because I'm in here?" said the inmate contemptuously. "That just means I'm crazy. It doesn't mean I'm stupid."

● 506

A man who had been in a mental home for some years finally seemed to have improved to the point where it was thought he might be released. The head of the institution, in a fit of commendable caution, decided, however, to interview him first.

"Tell me," he said, "if we release you, as we are considering doing, what do you intend to do with your life?"

The inmate said, "It would be wonderful to get back to real life and, if I do, I will certainly refrain from making my former mistake. I was a nuclear physicist, you know, and it was the stress of my work in weapons research that helped put me here. If I am released, I shall confine myself to work in pure theory, where I trust the situation will be less difficult and stressful."

"Marvelous," said the head of the institution.

"Or else," ruminated the inmate. "I might teach. There is something to be said for spending one's life in bringing up a new generation of scientists."

"Absolutely," said the head.

"Then again, I might write. There is considerable need for books on science for the general public. Or I might even write a novel based on my experiences in this fine institution."

"An interesting possibility," said the head.

"And finally, if none of these things appeals to me, I can always continue to be a teakettle."

•507

Prolific writers are (alas) not always appreciated. Edward Gibbon wrote the long and wonderful *Decline and Fall of the Roman Empire* in several volumes. He had given a copy of the first volume to the brother of George III, the Duke of Gloucester, not because the duke had the mental capacity to appreciate it (royalty rarely does) but as a gesture of respect.

When the second volume was published, he gave a copy of that to Gloucester also, and Gloucester's comment was, "Another damned thick square book! Always scribble, scribble, scribble, eh, Mr. Gibbon?"

•508

Here are a couple of additional stories about W. S. Gilbert of musical comedy fame.

A composer had died, and a friend of Gilbert's who hadn't heard of that asked after him and said, "He was a hard-working fellow, so I suppose he's still composing."

"Actually," said Gilbert, "right now he's decomposing."

•509

Gilbert never had any hesitation about giving an actor a dressing-down, if he felt he deserved it.

On one occasion he said loudly to an actor, "You are not prepared, sir. You are not prepared."

The actor, irritated, said, "I'll have you know that I know my lines."

"Perhaps you do," said Gilbert, "but it's my lines you don't know."

•510

Once at the Gilbert & Sullivan Society, I had occasion to quote a bit of Gilbert. In the audience was Priscilla Reeves, a beautiful mezzo-soprano who had sung in every G & S operetta and had done so marvelously. She took the occasion to correct my quotation and, needless to say, she was right and I was wrong.

The audience, one and all of whom were G & S experts, laughed heartily at my discomfiture.

I said, "That was Priscilla Reeves. She knows every word of Gilbert & Sullivan. [Pause.] Now she's working on the notes."

(It was a dirty lie, of course, but I got my laugh.)

•511

The Italians are always good for a laugh, usually because of their good-natured and civilized inefficiency. Giovanni Giolitti, who was prime minister of Italy now and then in the days before Mussolini, was asked if it was difficult to govern Italy.

"Not at all," said Giolitti. "It's just useless."

•512

Gladstone, whom I have mentioned in this book several times, was extremely pious and extremely sure of his own rightness in everything, including religion.

On one occasion, during a party at Gladstone's home when for a time he wasn't in the room—so that Mrs. Gladstone was presiding—a rather heated discussion arose over a certain biblical passage. Finally one of the party, growing tired of the increasingly futile dispute, said, "It doesn't matter. There is One above who knows all things and will explain it to us in due time."

Whereupon Mrs. Gladstone brightened and said, "Yes, indeed, and Mr. Gladstone will be coming downstairs in just a few minutes."

•513

Never in history was a nation ruled by such miserable thugs and hoodlums as was Nazi Germany, and, of them all, Hermann Göring was second only to Hitler. He was fat, sybaritic, self-absorbed, and increasingly useless as World War II proceeded.

There is a tale of a time when he was visiting Rome. While making his way through the crowd, the portly Göring stepped on the toe of an Italian gentleman, who grimaced in pain.

Göring stared at him haughtily and said, "I am Hermann Göring."

The Italian said, "As an excuse, that is insufficient, but as an explanation, it is entirely ample."

•514

A divorced man came across his ex-wife unexpectedly at a party. They fell to talking and the man discovered that his old rancor had entirely vanished. Indeed, his ex-wife was looking very good and he discovered that he recalled certain tender moments when the marriage was young and happy.

Softly he said, "Why don't you come home with me, dear, and we can make love again in memory of old times?"

Instantly she drew herself up stiffly and said, "Over my dead body."

The ex-husband shook his head and said, "Things haven't changed, have they?"

My sister-in-law is so entirely in love with Stan (and vice versa) that I'm sure there is no hope of ever prying them loose from each other. Ruth is one of the few women to whom I have never once had the urge to say anything flirtatious. However, I once said something that budged her very slightly. Here's the story:

•515

My brother's attitude toward the paper he works for, *Newsday*, is about equal to my attitude toward my typewriter. It fills his life, and when he comes home after a day's work, he bubbles over with tales of what went on at the paper, all of which he tells in great detail to Ruth.

Janet and I were visiting him once and we witnessed this ritual, and when it was done I said to Ruth:

"You know, Ruth, if you had married me instead of Stan, then not once in your whole life would you hear the phrase 'Today at *Newsday—*'"

And I swear that just for a few moments, her eyes flickered.

•516

Chemists synthesize marvelous chemicals these days. There is the story that one synthesized an aphrodisiac for men that was so powerful it had to be swallowed very quickly to avoid getting a stiff neck.

Some limericks were made up by friends of mine. Thus, here's one concocted by Anthony Boucher, once editor of *Fantasy and Science Fiction.*

•517

A spaceman and girl in free fall
Found a new way of heeding love's call.
     "I've been tumbled," she said,
     "On floor, sofa, and bed,
But never halfway up a wall."

So I made up one for Tony:

•518

There was a young fellow named Boucher,
Who, without any help from a voucher,
     Could approach any maid,
     Whether gladsome or staid,
And could bed her, or floor her, or couch 'er.

The science fiction writer Poul Anderson offers the following:

•519

There was a young girl with a bust
That aroused a French cavalier's lust.
　　　She was then heard to say
　　　About midnight, "Touché,
I didn't quite parry that thrust."

And now a few more classic limericks of uncertain origin.

•520

On the beautiful breasts of Miss Hale
Was tattooed the full price of her tail.
　　　On her lovely behind
　　　For the sake of the blind
Was the same information in braille.

•521

The sinister queen of Baroda
Used to live in a Chinese pagoda,
　　　Where the walls of the halls
　　　Were behung with the balls
And the tools of the fools who bestrode 'er.

•522

An old soldier who lived on his pension
Saw a Wac who was lovely past mention.
　　　He sighed, "My poor rod,
　　　In the old days, by God,
Would have risen and stood at attention."

•523

There once was a learned baboon
Who always played on the bassoon.
     For he said, "It appears
     That in billions of years,
I shall finally hit on a tune."

You want something bitter? Here's something bitter.

•524

The nuclear war had come and gone. Earth lay devastated and nearly lifeless. In a puddle of water were two tiny bacteria. One said to the other, "All over again—but this time, no brains."

•525

The movie actress was taking a shower and her young niece came into the bathroom to watch as the actress emerged and began to towel herself.

"Auntie?" said the little girl.

"Yes, dear?"

"Why am I so plain and you're so fancy?"

•526

General Grant, whatever his success as a general, was tone deaf. He used to say that he only knew two tunes. One was "Yankee Doodle."

"And the other?" asked a friend.

"Isn't 'Yankee Doodle,'" said Grant.

•527

Senator Charles Sumner of Massachusetts had all the haughtiness and self-assurance of a Boston Brahmin. Someone once said that Sumner did not believe in the Bible.

"Of course not," said another promptly. "He didn't write it."

•528

I once wrote a two-volume book on the Bible and the editors decided that they wanted to call it *Asimov's Guide to the Bible*. I protested, pointing out that I did not present myself as a biblical authority and the title made me sound too arrogant.

However, you can't talk to editors. The book jacket was prepared and shown to me, and there was my name on it.

I couldn't resist. I said, "How come *Bible* is in bigger letters than my name is?"

•529

In a later version of the book jacket of my *Guide to the Bible,* a passage of writing was placed within a square on the back.

My editor, Larry Ashmead, said to me, "They included a passage from the book, Isaac, but I read it and I'm sorry to say I don't like it."

I was absolutely stunned. Larry was so pro-Asimov that he embarrassed me. *Nothing* I wrote did he fail to like. How awful that passage must be if even Larry didn't like it.

"Let me see the book jacket," I said.

I read the passage in back and said, "Larry, this isn't mine. They just picked up something from somewhere to see what it would look like."

I have never been more flattered in my life.

•530

Every once in a while, someone would come to Larry Ashmead and ask him to recommend a writer who would do some particular job. Larry always recommended me no matter what the job was and I hated to turn him down. So one day I found myself condemned to write an essay on "Sex in Space" for a magazine called *Sexology.*

I did it and it appeared and some time afterward I agreed to talk at an elementary school, because it was in my old neighborhood. A little kid, perhaps ten years old, said, "I read one of your articles. It was called 'Sex in Space.'"

I winced and said, "You shouldn't have read that."

"I know," he said. "It was terrible."

At once, my writer's arrogance was brought into play. "Why was it terrible?" I demanded.

And the kid said, "It wasn't dirty enough."

•531

Moskowitz, finding he had left important papers at home, came back in the middle of the day. Taking little notice of the fact that his wife was flustered, he was about to leave again when his small son said, "Papa, there's a boogeyman in the closet."

Moskowitz shrugged the matter aside in annoyance and said, "Don't be silly, Sammy."

"There is, Papa, there is," said Sammy urgently. "There's a boogeyman in the closet. I saw him."

"Sammy," said Moskowitz, "come with me. We'll open the closet door and I'll show you there's no boogeyman there."

Together they went to the closet. Moskowitz pulled the door open and there, in his undershirt, stood a most discomfited Finkelstein, who was, as it happened, Moskowitz's best friend.

Moskowitz stared at him and finally said angrily, "Finkelstein, have you nothing better to do than hang around closets scaring little boys?"

•532

A less naive man than Moskowitz, on encountering a strange man in the closet of his bedroom, said angrily, "And what the hell are you doing here, you bum?"

To which the man replied with wistful hope, "Would you believe—voting?"

Humor can come from unexpected sources. Here's a case where a bit of successful humor turned away wrath.

•533

In the early seventies, I had an office in a rather downtrodden hotel on the Upper West Side of Manhattan. The hotel was in the process of renovations, which meant constant banging and clattering.

Ordinarily, I can work along despite noise (how else could I live and work in Manhattan?), but when someone came to the corridor immediately outside my office and began to bang endlessly, my cup of wrath finally overflowed.

I opened the door to investigate the matter, and there was a workman fiddling with the lights in the hall, and presumably planning to substitute other, better lights.

I walked up to him angrily. "Listen," I said, "how long do you expect to make this horrible noise that is making it impossible for me to work?"

The workman stopped, turned toward me, and said, "How long did it take Michelangelo to finish the Sistine Chapel?"

I burst into laughter and didn't mind the noise afterward. After all, it is delightful to have a laborer see his own work in the light of Michelangelo.

•534

A man walked into the office of a circus impresario and said, "I would like a job because I have a very unusual act."

The impresario looked at him sourly and said, "Let's see it."

The man moved up the ropes attached to the central pole of the great tent till he was far up in the air. He then jumped and, with his arms extended and his fingers wiggling, he swooped, veered, climbed, and finally let himself come down gently, gently, and landed.

The impresario said, "That's what you call unusual? Bird imitations?"

•535

I once caught a taxi and asked to be taken to Grand Central Station. Clearly, the cabbie didn't know where it was and it turned out he was fresh out of the Soviet Union and this was his first day on the job. Beyond the fact that he was in Manhattan, he knew nothing.

I didn't get mad. I remembered when my father came here from the Soviet Union and had to turn his hand to anything he could to feed the family. I said, "Do as I tell you," and talked him over to Grand Central Station.

When I got out, I said, "Learn the city as quickly as you can because there are few New York passengers who are as nice as I am and they will be annoyed with you if you don't know where you're going."

•536

Sometimes taxi drivers make me laugh and it is then my usual custom to double the tip.

One one occasion, I noticed the name of the driver was Michael P. O'Brien. I said, "I'd be willing to bet that the middle initial P. stands for Patrick."

The driver said, "You'd be right. It's Patrick." There was a short pause and then he added, "A great deal of originality went into thinking up that middle name."

I laughed and doubled his tip.

•537

I had lunch once at a French restaurant with two of my Doubleday editors, Timothy Seldes and Richard Winslow. I was anxious to have them agree to publish a book I wanted to do, so I was determined not to rock the boat in any way. When they ordered a drink, I ordered one, too. When they ordered a second drink, I ordered a second, too.

The result was foregone. Tim and Dick showed no signs whatever of having imbibed liquor, but I had gotten sloshed (which is why I don't drink). When they ordered a third drink, I tried to order one, too, but Tim said something quickly to the French waiter in French and the waiter leaned over me and said solicitously, "Would ze zhentleman like some bread and buttair?"

I finally got editorial permission to do my book and between that and the two drinks I was as happy as a lark. I left the restaurant to get a taxi that would take me to my next appointment. As the taxi driver pulled away, I said to him, for no reason other than drunken camaraderie, "I just had lunch with two editors."

The driver must have had his share of drunken passengers. He stopped the taxi with a jerk, turned to me with a look of concern, and said, "Did they get you to sign anything?"

I reassured him, and doubled his tip.

•538

I once said to Tim Seldes artlessly, "Tim, wasn't Gilbert Seldes, the writer, your father?"

"Yes," said Tim Seldes, eyes narrowed. He knew me and he suspected I was up to something.

"And wasn't George Seldes, the writer, your uncle?"

"Yes," said Tim, more suspicious than ever.

"And isn't Marion Seldes, the actress, your sister?"

"Yes," he said. "Why are you asking, Asimov?"

"Because I wanted to ask you how it felt to be the only member of the family that didn't have any talent."

He kicked me out of his office.

•539

Timothy Seldes had a beautiful secretary who was six feet tall, a full four inches taller than I was.

We were walking down the Doubleday corridor one day when she said, "Does it bother you, Isaac, to be walking with a woman who is taller than you are?"

"Not at all," I said. "You're only taller because we're vertical. If we were to lie down on our backs, I'd be taller than you."

•540

Beth Walker is the female half of Walker and Company, which has published seventy of my books so far. I have been flirting with her amiably for twenty years now because she combines what I like most in women. She is attractive and she has a sense of humor.

One time, not too long ago, she wished to express approval of the fact that I had lost some weight.

She tapped my abdomen and said, "Keep it down, Isaac. Keep it down."

Whereupon I said, "If I were younger and you did that, I wouldn't be able to."

•541

People seem to object to any remark I make that indicates I am aware of having grown old.

One young woman said to me, "Oh, no, Dr. Asimov, you're forever young inside."

I responded, "My inside may be forever young, but my outside is falling apart."

•542

Mrs. Moskowitz said to her husband of many years, "Jake, today is our wedding anniversary, and you have forgotten. You haven't brought me anything as a present."

Mr. Moskowitz said, "You are quite wrong, Becky. I have not forgotten and I have a present for you for the anniversary." And he handed her an official-looking document.

"What is this?" she asked.

"Read and you'll see," said Moskowitz. "It's a deed to a fancy cemetery plot in a posh cemetery."

At first blush it seemed a rather unromantic present, but after all, they were getting on in years and such matters must be taken into account.

Mrs. Moskowitz sighed and said, "Thank you, Jake," and that was that.

Came the next year and once again Mrs. Moskowitz said, "Well, Jake, today is our wedding anniversary. Did you get me something for this year?"

"What for?" asked Moskowitz. "You haven't used last year's present yet."

Although I am well known throughout the science fiction world for my flirtatiousness (I once got an elaborate plaque that read ISAAC ASIMOV, LOVABLE LECHER), my love life is not at all spectacular. I would like it to be, I'm sure, but the fact is that you can write 466 books or you can be a Don Juan—you cannot do both—and I made my choice long ago.

•543

Once, at the conclusion of a talk, a young man took advantage of the question-and-answer session to ask me, "Dr. Asimov, if you had to choose between women and writing, which would you choose?"

I grinned and said, "Well, I can type all day without getting tired."

•544

At the Rensselaerville Institute, a fellow member was Isidore Adler, a chemist who taught at the University of Maryland. He was a jock. He played tennis every chance he got. He went swimming. He went jogging.

His specialty was handball and, even though he was in his sixties and a grandfather, he had the stamina to beat the young fellows at the university. He would console them by saying, "It's very nice of you to let a grandfather win," and they would grind their teeth at him.

Also at the institute was a young woman (a mathematics teacher) called Winnie, who had an unbelievably explosive figure and could do belly dances such as you would not believe. However, she considered herself overweight and anxious to thin out a bit, so she asked Izzy if she might go jogging with him every morning before breakfast.

"Of course," he said, and every morning they jogged down the hill and through the little village, and up the hill again. Naturally, Izzy was a little faster than Winnie, so that every morning the villagers had the eye-popping pleasure of seeing an elderly, quite plain man running through the town with an unbelievable Valkyrie in hot pursuit.

God only knows what they made of it.

•545

Also at the institute was a grade school teacher, Mary Sayer, attractive, sweet, and with a spectacular figure. Naturally, I flirted with her for years and since she had a good sense of humor, she didn't mind.

I was at a science fiction convention once, one that was very crowded, and Janet had gone off somewhere to do something, and I waited and she didn't come back, and I started looking for her and couldn't find her, and in no time I was distraught.

And who should I bump into but Mary Sayer, who is a science fiction fan. Ordinarily, I would instantly have begun another round of flirtation, but now all I could think of was Janet. Mary, in consternation, asked why I looked so unhappy. I explained.

She said, "Don't wander about aimlessly. Go back to your room. Eventually she'll go there. She's a grown woman and won't be lost. Come, I'll take you."

And so she did, and we sat at opposite ends of the room and all I did was moan because Janet wasn't there.

And then I heard a key scrabbling at the lock and I knew that Janet was back. I was on my feet at once, anxious not to lose the chance of a lifetime. "Come here, Mary."

She came to me in puzzlement. I led her in front of the door, put my arm about her waist, bent her back, and placed a luscious smackeroo on her lips, just as the door opened and Janet walked in.

Janet said, "Oh, hello, Mary," walked to a chair, sat down, and said, "Boy, am I tired."

What could I do but let go of Mary?... I get no attention.

Later on I said, "Didn't you notice that I was kissing Mary when you walked in, Janet?"

"Sure," she said, "but I attached no importance to that. I knew it was just one of your silly games."

•546

Janet said to me once, when I complained that her attitude toward my flirtatiousness was too indifferent, "Of course I don't trust you, Isaac, but I trust all the other girls."

Personally, I think that's insulting.

•547

Musicians usually get the better of it. For instance, we always talk of Jerome Kern's "Ol' Man River."

Mrs. Hammerstein, who was the widow of Oscar Hammerstein, who wrote the lyrics, would not let that pass, however. Whenever she heard Jerome Kern credited, she would say firmly, "My husband wrote 'Ol' Man River.' What Kern wrote was 'da da dee-dah, da da da dee-dah—'"

•548

There is a story (which may not be true) that Ernest Hemingway used the word *fuck* in one of his books in the old days when the word was unprintable. The editors took the book to old man Charles Scribner to see if they dared make any alterations in Hemingway's copy. Scribner was in a hurry and said he would make the decision the next day. In order not to forget, the story goes, he wrote down in bold letters on the memo pad headed "Things to do" the word "Fuck!"

•549

I had a very bad time at Scribner's Bookstore a few years ago. I wanted a particular book and had only a few minutes before an important luncheon appointment. So I dashed into Scribner's, which I had never entered before, and paying no attention to the hushed and genteel atmosphere of the place, I demanded the book in a loud voice.

I was kicked out of the store.

I wrote an indignant letter to Charles Scribner (the son of the man who wrote "Fuck!" on his memo pad) and I got back a stiff reply to the effect that I had made a noisy nuisance of myself and it was right that I should have been kicked out of the store.

But there's not much you can do to a writer. I did two things: (1) I cursed the store, and (2) I wrote up the incident, first as a mystery story and second as an essay for the *New York Times*.

I was paid amply in both cases and, as for the store, thanks to my curse, it went out of business soon thereafter, and I hope that the rotten bum who kicked me out lost his job.

•550

A troubled man was consulting a psychiatrist.

"Doctor," he said, "I'm in serious trouble. When I am dancing with a beautiful young woman, when I have my arms about her, when I am breathing her perfume, when I am gazing at her lovely face, I seem entirely unmoved. I'm not aroused. Nothing happens. On the other hand, when I see my wife—and I must tell you, Doctor, that she is rather old and not really at all good-looking—I get an erection."

The psychiatrist said, "Quite normal, sir. Quite normal."

"Normal!" said the patient, flabbergasted. "To react to my ugly old wife and not to some beautiful young woman?"

"Of course," said the psychiatrist. "That's why we call the penis a prick."

•551

Mrs. Anderson and Mrs. Johnson were discussing their psychiatric experiences and Mrs. Anderson said, "I had a dream about six months ago—" and at once went off into the details of the dream with enthusiasm and vigor.

Mrs. Johnson gasped at the quirks and oddnesses of the dream, which ended with Mrs. Anderson, the dreamer, flying over the earth and bombarding it systematically with bananas that exploded into mushroom clouds, while vast orchestras were playing, "Come to Me, My Melancholy Baby."

When the tale of the dream was over, Mrs. Johnson said, "And what did your psychiatrist say to that?"

"Nothing," said Mrs. Anderson gloomily. "I never told him."

"You never told him? Why not?"

"Do you think I wanted him to think I was crazy?"

•552

There is a story that once the Greek shipping magnate Aristotle Onassis entered a restaurant with his entourage and seated himself.

A young man attempted to approach and was, of course, fended off. Onassis, however, interested in the earnestness on the face of the young man, gestured that he might speak to him.

The young man said, "Mr. Onassis, I'm with a young woman here whom I'm trying to impress. I have not much in the way of looks, or charm, or money, but if, when you leave, you just stop at my table and say, 'Hi, Al, how are you?' she will be so impressed that—well I love her, you see."

Onassis, touched, said, "Very well. I'll take care of it."

And when he left, he stopped for a moment at the young man's table and said, "Hi, Al, how are you?"

The young man leaned back, put his arm around the girl's shoulder, and said, "I've told you a million times, Onassis, not to bother me when I'm with a woman. Fuck off."

•553

Henry VIII of England once ordered one of his courtiers to carry a message to Francis I of France. The message was an angry one and the courtier was nervous.

He said, "Francis, if angered, may decide to cut off my head."

"Have no fear," said King Henry, "for if he does, I will cut off the heads of a hundred Frenchmen in my dominion."

"So you may, Your Majesty," said the courtier, "but of all the heads you cut off, not one will fit on my shoulders."

•554

Mr. Wellesley boarded a bus and managed to snaffle the last available seat. He put his six-year-old son, Johnny, on his lap.

At the next stop, an attractive young woman boarded the bus and looked about vainly for a seat.

Mr. Wellesley whispered into his son's ear, "Now, Johnny, be a gentleman. Stand up and offer the young woman your seat."

•555

A certain merchant, having struck it rich indeed, moved into a palatial home and seized the opportunity to impress his old associates, all of whom remained in moderate circumstances.

"It takes four people—four people," said the nouveau riche, "to take care of my morning bath."

"Four people," marveled an old associate. "But what can there be for the four people to do?"

"Well," said the merchant, "the first one draws the water. The tub has to be filled to just the right height, of course. The second one tests the temperature; I'm very particular about that. The third one decides on which bath salts I will use that day and adds just the right amount to the water. So you see I need all three."

"But you mentioned four people. What does the fourth one do?"

"Oh," said the merchant, "the fourth one takes my bath for me."

•556

I'm a great one for singing in the shower—and sometimes out of it. People often say to me, "You've got a good voice."

My answer, invariably, given with a sigh, is, "It used to be. I myself am younger than springtime, but my voice was born in 1920."

•557

Once our entertainer failed us at the Dutch Treat Club and I was called and asked if I could do something on short notice.

I said, "You bet," and the next day I got up after lunch and announced that I would tell the story of the bombardment of Fort McHenry during the War of 1812 and would then sing all four stanzas of "The Star-Spangled Banner," which was written to commemorate the occasion.

275

The audience groaned loudly, and Herb Graff rose and closed the door to the kitchen, from which came the loud noise of conversation and the clashing of pots and pans.

I said, "Thank you, Herb, for closing the door."

And he said, "It was at the request of the kitchen staff."

•558

However, I fooled the bums. The tale of the War of 1812 is an exciting one, and none of the people there had ever really listened to the words of the first stanza of "The Star-Spangled Banner," or had known that there were three other stanzas. I sang my little heart out and when I finished I got a roaring, standing ovation.

I was accompanied in my singing by Al Hague, who is best known for his role as the piano teacher in the television program *Fame.* He said to me at the conclusion, "You've got a good sense of relative pitch, Isaac. Once you get started, you hit every note exactly. The trouble is you don't know where to get started. You sang each of the four stanzas in a different key."

•559

The honeymoon couple had had a blissful first night together, and the bridegroom, sighing happily, said, "Darling, now that we are married and obviously well mated, the details of your past life are not important. Still, I am curious. Am I the first man who ever slept with you?"

And the bride said, "Well, if you doze off, you will be."

•560

One of the outstanding "appeasers" in the thirties—those disgraceful men who were stupid enough to think that Hitler could be made to behave himself if he were given what he wanted—was Sir Samuel Hoare.

A man meeting Hoare said to him, "Ah, there, Sir Samuel, glad to see you. How are you? And how is Mrs. W.?"

•561

Mr. Jones was very pleased with his new secretary.

"I've got a real gem," he said to one of his cronies.

"Really?" said his friend. "How fast can she type?"

"Actually, she types quite slowly," said Jones.

"Then what makes her a gem?"

"She also runs quite slowly."

•562

In the old days, when train travel was the chief method of getting around, some of them were pretty slow.

One of these slow trains came to a dead halt, and a passenger, annoyed at the rate of progress, said irascibly to the conductor, "Do you mind telling me why we have stopped?"

The conductor said, "There's a cow on the tracks."

The cow was finally gotten rid of and the train resumed its slow, slow progress over the countryside. In about fifteen minutes, though, it came to a halt again.

"Good God," said the passenger to the conductor, "don't tell me we caught up with that cow again."

•563

On another such slow train, a young woman passenger said to the conductor, "See here, conductor, aren't we ever going to reach Chicago? You can see I'm far gone in pregnancy. Well, if we don't get to Chicago soon, you'll have to help deliver the baby."

The conductor stared at her in horror. "But madam, you shouldn't have gotten on the train in this condition."

And the woman replied, "I didn't."

•564

Moskowitz, staring at the day's headlines, suddenly shouted, "Moses was an idiot."

Finkelstein, horrified at the blasphemy, said, "Moskowitz, how can you say Moses was an idiot?"

"Well, wasn't he? For forty years he kept the children of Israel wandering in the desert and then he finally brought them to the only Middle Eastern country without oil."

•565

A Greek, a Chinaman, a Frenchman, a German, an American, and an Englishman were shipwrecked on a tropical island that offered all the necessary facilities for life. After three months, time hung heavy on their hands, so the Greek started a restaurant, the Chinaman a laundry, and the Frenchman six political parties. The German rounded up the natives and began to drill them into an army, while the American manufactured weapons to sell to them.

As for the Englishman, he was still waiting to be introduced.

•566

A big, burly fellow got into one of those compartments they have on British trains and found that the only other occupant was a thin, weedy little fellow.

The big man pulled out a huge black cigar and said in a gruff voice that obviously would brook no opposition. "I suppose you won't mind if I light my cigar."

"Not at all," said the thin little man, "provided you won't mind if I throw up."

•567

At a political rally in Great Britain, the solidly conservative candidate said sternly, "I was born an Englishman, I have lived an Englishman, and I hope before God to die an Englishman."

And a voice from the audience, thick with a Scottish burr, cried out, "Man, have you no ambition?"

•568

In a graft-ridden corrupt dictatorship, which shall be nameless, a long line of depressed city dwellers was inching forward to collect their day's ration of second-rate hamburger meat.

One of the men in the line muttered to his friend behind him, "It is all the fault of that scoundrel who rules us. He and his cronies grow rich, while the people starve. I can stand this no longer. I shall get the rifle I hid when they took away our arms. I will go to the presidential palace and, though it cost me my life, I shall shoot and kill him."

He left at a grim run, but two hours later he was back. His friend, who had inched forward a block and a half in the interval, let him into the line and said, "How did you make out?"

The would-be assassin scowled and said, "You call *this* a line?"

It's amazing the responses you can get to jokes. I told the foregoing story to an apparently sensible woman and she did not laugh. Instead, accepting it as history rather than as nonsense, she said, "Where did this happen?"

"Nowhere," I said. "It's just a story."

She paid no attention and said, "It must have been East Germany."

"Actually," I said truthfully, "when I was told the story, it was placed in Israel."

She jumped. "Impossible. It had to be in East Germany."

And nothing would budge her. It was quite a while before I had the heart to tell the story again.

•569

An actor was doing *Hamlet* and doing a very poor job—so poor that the audience was growing increasingly restless. The booing and catcalls began and increased in vehemence and loudness.

Finally the actor came to the front of the stage and addressed the audience.

"Ladies and gentlemen, please do not blame the actors if you're not satisfied. We're not the ones who wrote this shit."

•570

An astronaut was asked what he thought of just before takeoff.

He said, "I think that I'm sitting on a complex device made up of over seven thousand separate parts, each one of which was manufactured by the lowest bidder."

•571

My family and friends often use me as a kind of walking encyclopedia. My beautiful daughter, Robyn, had found this out by the age of ten. I was off in New York for a few days and Gertrude's brother, John, was visiting. Gertrude and John got into an argument over something they could not resolve, so they sent Robyn upstairs to get the appropriate volume of the *Encyclopedia Britannica*.

Robyn was most reluctant to do this and halfway up the stairs she shouted, "It's too bad Daddy isn't here. You could just ask him."

•572

My friend Lin Carter of the Trap-Door Spiders called me once and said, "Isaac, who said, 'Liberty, Liberty, what crimes are committed in thy name?'"

And I answered without hesitation, "Madame Jeanne Roland, on her way to the guillotine in 1793."

Lin was astonished at this and dined out on the incident for a long time.

•573

A few months ago, my friend L. Sprague de Camp called me from Texas, where he now lives.

"Isaac," he said, "I need to know the wavelengths of the ultrasonic waves emitted by bats in flight and I can't find the information. I thought you might know offhand."

"I'm sorry, Sprague," I said, "I don't know the answer offhand, but I will go through my reference library and see if I can find it. If I do, I will call you back."

I began to ransack my library and finally found an article on sound in the *Encyclopedia Americana* containing information on bat squeaks. I called Sprague and read it off to him. "Thanks, Isaac," he said, "that's just what I wanted."

After he hung up, I continued to read the article, starting from the beginning. It was clear, concise, and well written, and that made me uneasy. I don't like to see other writers doing a good job; I don't like the competition. So I looked at the end of the article to see what scoundrel had written it. And there in clear print was the name—Isaac Asimov.

•574

Stephen Leacock was a humorist of great renown (he was also a professor of economics at McGill University in Montreal). One time he was giving one of his humorous lectures in a rather small town, and in order to accommodate the large audience that was expected, he was asked to speak in the largest available room—in the town church.

He gave an excellent talk, but it seemed to drop quietly into a deep pool. There was no laughter. He raised a sweat trying to be funnier than he had ever been and yet everyone listened to him with intolerable gravity. By the time the talk was over, he was in a state of worn-out disappointment.

One of the people who had been in the audience said to him, "Mr. Leacock, that was the funniest talk I ever heard. It was all I could do to keep from busting out laughing right here in church."

•575

When Janet and I got together in New York, she was a shy, very gentle and well-behaved woman. However, no one can hang around me for very long and remain shy, for I am as lower class as can possibly be imagined—loud, boisterous, extraverted, and with a scurrilous wit.

Janet very soon got used to me, however, and didn't even seem to mind when I was very affectionate and demonstrative in public.

Once, for instance, when we found ourselves alone for a moment at a party, I decided to improve the moment by embracing her and handing her a loud kiss, which she returned with interest. And while we were lost in this activity, our very good friend Judy-Lynn del Rey came in and said, "Good Lord, they do this sort of thing even when no one is watching."

•576

As I remarked before, women tend to fall in love with movie stars to a far greater extent than men do. One of Janet's many loves was Alan Alda of the "*M*A*S*H*" program.

One day Janet and I attended an awards luncheon over Janet's protests, because I felt I had to and I wanted her company. Once we were seated (right near the head table), I looked to see who was being honored, and there, six feet from us, was Alan Alda. For a few moments, I absolutely lost my voice, but I had to tell her before she discovered it for herself, and I managed, hoarsely.

Janet's eyes widened satisfactorily and I said, "Do you want me to go over and get his autograph?"

"All right," she said, "if you promise not to embarrass me."

"When do I embarrass you?" I demanded, and taking the invitation card, I marched up to the head table.

"Mr. Alda," I said, "I'm Isaac Asimov."

He said, "Why aren't you home writing a book?"

"I would be," I said, "but my wife wants your autograph, because she is full of intense love for you."

From my wife's table came a loud shriek, and Alda grinned, signed, and said, "Poor woman."

Since then, I have always maintained that Alda said "Poor woman" because she was one of many thousands who loved him hopelessly. Janet, on the other hand, insists he said "Poor woman" because he was sorry for her being married to such a monster. We'll never resolve that issue.

•577

Michael Dunn was a dwarf who, when alive, played a number of parts in movies and television, doing so brilliantly. The story (which

I don't necessarily believe) is that at a party once he spied the statuesque and unbelievably gorgeous Sophia Loren.

Dunn nudged his agent. "You know Sophia Loren. Introduce me."

The agent said uneasily (for he knew Dunn), "Do you promise to behave yourself?"

"Absolutely. Cross my heart."

So the introduction was carried through. Dunn looked up, up, up at the beautiful Sophia and all his good resolutions vanished like snow in August. "Boy," he said, "would I love to fuck you."

Sophia Loren looked down, down, down at him and said coolly, "Well, if you do—and if I ever find out you did—"

This reminds me of my absolutely favorite Harlan Ellison story. People in the field are afraid to tell it out loud, but I will do so. Harlan and I are such good friends that I know he won't kill me, especially when I tell you that I'm sure the story is quite fictional. Of course, he may maim me a bit.

The thing is that Harlan is short and in the days before he married his present fifth wife (who is his own size and with whom he is happy at last) he could not resist going about with giant showgirl types, all of them topping him by two or three feet.

•578

The story goes, then, that Harlan approached one of these giraffelike women, fixed her with his glittering eye, and said, "What would you say to a little fuck?"

And she looked down at him and said, "I would say, 'Hello, little fuck.'"

•579

Mrs. Ginsberg was on a safari in darkest Africa once when a terrible misfortune befell her. A large gorilla suddenly appeared out of the jungle, snatched her up, and before anyone could do anything carried her off to some isolated spot. They tried to find her and failed, and had to leave her to her fate.

She spent seventeen days with the gorilla, satisfying his lusts, and just managing to live on what she could find in the way of nuts and fruits, for his diet of leaves was insufficient. Then, once, when his attention was distracted, she managed to crawl away and make her way through the trees to a native village. There they cared for her, calling the local government officials. Doctors arrived and she was eventually trucked to an airport and flown home to the United States.

Friends came to visit her at the hospital to sympathize with her in her ordeal.

"You must be in a terrible state after being with the gorilla all that time, poor dear," they said.

"I am," said Mrs. Ginsberg. "He doesn't call. He doesn't write—"

My favorite character in early American history was Benjamin Franklin. Somehow, I see a similarity between us. He began poor and became rich through his own talent and efforts, he achieved a reputation as a sage in his old age, he retained an eye for the young ladies, he had a keen sense of humor and laughed at his own jokes, and so on.

One of my favorite pictures of all time is *1776*, in which Franklin plays a large role, along with the loquacious John Adams.

•580

The funniest line in the picture, at least to me, is when Franklin takes leave of Adams at one point. He is clearly intending to keep an assignation with a young woman and he apparently feels a little guilty at abandoning Adams. So he says, "I'd ask you to come along, John, but talking makes her nervous."

•581

During the Revolutionary War, Ben Franklin served in France as a representative of the colonies. There he impressed all the aristocrats with his artfully simple ways and won over all the ladies with his charm. Since it was only the French alliance that allowed us to win our independence, Franklin was worth an army to us.

After the war was won, Franklin came home and Thomas Jefferson became American minister to France. Jefferson was asked by the French foreign minister if he had come to replace Franklin.

And Jefferson answered, quite truthfully, "I merely come to succeed him. No one can replace him."

•582

The most notorious judge in English history was George Jeffreys, who presided over the trial of those involved in a rebellion against James II. He browbeat the defendants unmercifully before sending them to be hanged or into slavery. That was in 1685, and his court was called the "Bloody Assizes." It gives one great comfort to know that James II was driven from the throne in 1688 and that Jeffreys then got his comeuppance, dying in prison in 1689.

During the trial of one defendant, Jeffreys pointed his cane at him and said, "There is a rogue at the end of this cane."

And the defendant answered bravely, "At which end, my lord?"

•583

There is a quality of boredom that is exquisitely painful.

Carl Sagan, another astronomer, and I were once forced, for reasons I no longer remember, to spend some time with a trustee of Boston University who was one of the worst bores I ever encountered. Conversation began in the normal manner, but, as one might surely suspect, the two of us were quickly crushed under the weight of the trustee's foolish chatter, and we fell into silence. That does not bother a bore, who carries on all by himself.

When it was all over and the trustee had gone, Carl said to me in a rage, "What an incredible bore that man was. It was only politeness that kept me from saying something I wouldn't have wanted to say to a person."

"Don't worry, Carl," I said. "I was watching your face and you didn't have to say anything at all. Your face said it for you, if he had only had the brains to understand a look of anguished fury."

•584

A man, walking along the street, saw a well-known bore of his acquaintance coming his way. He gritted his teeth and hastened his steps.

The bore, however, gripped his elbow and said, "You seem to be in a hurry. What's going on, old man?"

Breaking free, the man said, "I am," and did so.

•585

Samuel Johnson prepared the first important dictionary of the English language. Two genteel ladies, on meeting him, saw fit to compliment him on his labors.

"Oh, Dr. Johnson, we are so glad that you did not include, in your dictionary, any scurrilous terms."

And Johnson said, "You mean you looked for them?"

•586

I have always admired Samuel Johnson's answer when someone pointed out an error in his dictionary and asked him how he came to make it.

"Ignorance," he answered. "Simple ignorance, sir."

•587

I keep that in mind, for I have written over a thousand essays on science in my time and occasionally I get a letter pointing out a mistake. Sometimes the person finding the mistake seems quite offended by it and demands to know how I could possibly have made it.

To these letters my answer always is, "I write so quickly, and revise so little, that sometimes things get away from me."

It's true enough.

I regard people who introduce me before I give a talk with the deepest of suspicion. What I would like best of all is not to be introduced at all. I want simply to come out, say, "I am Isaac Asimov," and begin talking.

Here is an example, however, of a ruinous introduction:

•588

I was all set to give a talk and, as it happened, I had recently been interviewed on the very subject I was going to talk about and my comments were written up in a newspaper. The man who introduced me had seen that newspaper and it fell into his stupid head to read it. He read it all from beginning to end.

I sat there, stunned, turned to the gentleman on my left, and said, "He's reading my speech."

The gentleman said, "What are you going to do?"

I said, "Make up another one."

And I did, in the few minutes before I had to go on stage, but I certainly didn't need the strain.

•589

How irritating it is to have someone hide behind an utterly inappropriate catchline.

I was giving a talk at a school on Long Island once and I was being slowly driven to distraction because the preliminaries (a dinner at the president's house) were so prolonged that it was clear we were going to be late. I kept checking my watch and finally I could stand it no longer. Politeness or no politeness, I said, "We must leave, even if we haven't had dessert yet. We are going to be fifteen minutes late."

Whereupon the president said fatuously, "What difference does it make? They can't start till we get there."

"The difference is," I said in a cold fury, "that the audience will grow impatient, and when I come to address them, they will be cold."

They did grow impatient, they were indeed cold, and the talk was a failure.

•590

It is possible for an introducer to say something I will laugh at and then (as in the case of critics) I may forgive the entire group, at least temporarily.

There is the story of the man who was toastmaster at a function. He said, "The purpose of a toastmaster is to be so dull that all the speakers will sparkle by comparison. However, as I look down the list of speakers, I don't know if I can manage to be dull enough."

•591

A young man, obviously of the upper class, was standing just outside the door of one of New York's finest hotels, idly puffing at a cigarette, when he was approached by a man who was just as obviously of the laboring class.

The laborer said to the young man, "Hey, I'll bet your father is rich."

"Very rich," said the upper-class fellow agreeably.

"And all your life, you've always had everything you want."

"Just about."

"And you've never done a single day's work in your life."

"I'm afraid that's so."

The laborer thought it over and said, "Well, you haven't missed a thing."

•592

Mrs. Moskowitz had a chance to see President Kennedy pass by in a motorcade. She took her young daughter, Rosie, and held her up so that she might see.

"That's President Kennedy, Rosie. He's the first Catholic president we've ever had."

And Rosie said in surprise, "All the others were Jews?"

•593

Nikita Khrushchev, during his stint as ruler of Russia, was most famous for a speech he made in which he detailed and disavowed all the cruel and dictatorial acts of Josef Stalin. At a certain gathering, someone yelled out, "If Stalin was such a villain, why didn't you stop him?"

Khrushchev frowned and said harshly, "Who said that?"

A dead silence fell on the group. No one dared stir.

Whereupon Khrushchev said mildly, "Now you know why I didn't stop him."

•594

Back in 1963, I was one of a small group of experts who wrote columns for the *World Book Science Year*. I dealt with the year's advance in science and, among the others, Red Smith dealt with the year's advance in sports.

At one point, Red said to me, "When you read my report on sports, Isaac, do you understand it?"

"Of course," I said.

"Well, I don't understand your report on science and it bothers me."

"It shouldn't, Red," I said. "If you don't understand me, the fault is mine, not yours."

•595

On another occasion, when all of us (except me) had been drinking, Red Smith overdid it a little and when it came time to go back to our hotels, it seemed that he might not be able to make it under his own steam. As he and I were at the same hotel, I was asked to take him in tow and see that he got safely home.

I had never before been responsible for guiding the steps of a slightly inebriated gentleman, but I didn't see my way clear to refusing and, let me tell you, it wasn't easy, for Red's feet did not seem to want to go in the correct direction.

As I managed to baby him along, I thought of the movie clichés I had seen. Perhaps you know what I mean. A kind gentleman gets his drunken friend home; the wife opens the door in a fury and says to the kind gentleman, "So you're the one who got my poor husband drunk," and then assaults him.

I didn't want to be assaulted and, as we were going up the elevator, I was desperate for a way out.

Therefore, when I came to Red's door and knocked and Mrs. Smith opened the door and stared at me in surprise, I quickly manhandled Red into a chair and said, "Thank you, Red, I could never have made it here without your help," and left in a hurry.

•596

The greatest sportswriter was, perhaps, John Kieran, who, to my regret, I never met, though I heard him regularly on the *Information Please* radio program.

Kieran was, at one time, asked to give a talk at a school because the football coach had thought that would be a good idea and would interest the students. The headmaster, a snob of the first water, was more than a little offended at having to introduce a sportswriter and did so in a condescending, if not an offensive, manner.

Kieran, a far greater scholar than the headmaster, responded by giving his talk—in Latin.

•597

The man at the bar was all smiles. "I just managed to beat my wife in tennis," he announced proudly. "I've been trying to do it for years, and now I have."

"How did you do that?" said a crony skeptically. "Wasn't she well?"

"Perfectly well," came the indignant response. "Except for being eight months pregnant."

•598

The sour-faced conductor was chary with his praise and the orchestra knew that it would take an earthquake to force a kind word out of him.

Nevertheless, at one time, everyone played so smoothly and followed the baton so efficiently that the conductor was forced to say, "Good," at the conclusion.

With that, the orchestra burst into applause, and the conductor, eyes narrowed and mouth grim, said, "Not that good."

•599

A musician was asked to come to a society function and perform and was asked his fee.

"Five thousand dollars, madam," he said.

"Very well," said the hostess, "but it must be understood that you will not mingle with the guests."

"In that case, madam, I can shave the fee to three thousand."

•600

I have mentioned Gladstone and his piety before. That piety did not sit well with everyone.

One parliamentarian said, "The irritating thing about Gladstone is that despite all his moralizing, he always has an ace up his sleeve."

"Yes," said another, "but the real irritation arises out of the fact that Gladstone insists that God has put it there."

•601

The effete Mr. Anderson had a habit of coming to the office anywhere from half an hour to an hour late, and the boss was getting to feel a bit ferocious about it.

"Anderson," he said, "I am tired of your coming in late every morning."

"Why?" said Anderson in surprise. "I make up for it by leaving early every afternoon, don't I?"

•602

It is always hard for a skeptic to believe that those who claim to believe the unbelievable really do so. In ancient Rome, for instance, there were augurs who investigated the entrails of sacrificed beasts, or watched the flight of birds, or studied other trivial and unimportant events, and from them purported to foretell the future.

Cato the Censor, that hard-bitten Roman skeptic, used to say, "I am amazed that one augur can pass another without grinning."

•603

Mr. Johnson, in the comparatively early days of automobiling, was faced with a blown-out tire on a lonely stretch of road, but he had a spare and it was just a matter of getting the ruined tire off and the spare tire on.

Unfortunately, however, the ruined tire would not come off. The lugs had all been removed and it should simply have slid off, but it didn't. For some reason, the wheel stuck, and Johnson sweated and strained without result.

He then did what any man would do. He rose into an erect posture and let loose a stream of profanity that did the situation no good but at least offered a vent for his feelings. He did not notice as he indulged in his tirade that a minister was passing in a horse and buggy.

The minister stopped his buggy and said in tones of deep disapproval, "My good man, there is no need to imperil your soul by blaspheming in that shocking manner. If you are having, as I see, trouble getting the tire off, why not pray to the Good Lord for help?"

Johnson, flushed, stared at the interfering minister, then at the tire, and decided he had nothing to lose. He raised his arms high and said, "Lord, please pay attention to the plea of a miserable sinner. It is important to me to change the tire and yet the old one will not come off. Is there anything, Lord, you can do to help?"

And as he said that, the offending tire, of its own accord, slid off the axle.

And the minister, a look of intense astonishment on his face, said, "Well, I'll be damned."

•604

Liberace, the pianist, had a way of getting back at his critics (of whom there were many). He would say, "When critics say bad things about me, I'm so hurt that I cry all the way to the bank."

•605

I once worked out my own version of that. When someone pointed out a bad review of one of my books and asked me if I minded, I answered, "Minded? Of course I minded. I cried so hard I couldn't see well enough to fill out my deposit blanks at the bank."

•606

For a time I did some work for a firm that was located in Fort Worth, Texas. I had heard that there was one of these friendly neighborhood feuds between Fort Worth and Dallas, which were very close to each other. So I said to my Fort Worth friend, "How do you feel about Dallas?"

"Dallas?" he said. "Where's that?"

•607

Teaching at Boston University is an exercise in humility. After all, you are in the same town as M.I.T. and Harvard.

I was once introducing a professor from Harvard who was going to give us a talk. Everyone knew he was from Harvard. I said, "I would like to introduce Professor So-and-so who teaches in that place just across the river. Now, what's the name?" And I snapped my fingers a few times in a vain effort to remember, while the audience roared.

•608

The best tale of Harvard's snobbishness is in connection with its president Abbott Lawrence Lowell. A gentleman came to see him and was told haughtily by the secretary, "I'm sorry, but the president is in Washington at the moment, conferring with Mr. Coolidge."

•609

As everyone knows, there is a small quatrain making fun of the snobbishness of the Bostonian aristocracy. It goes:

Here's to good old Boston,
The home of the bean and the cod,
Where the Lowells speak only to Cabots,
And the Cabots speak only to God.

There is an apparently true story of a small shop owner in Boston named Kabatinsky. He felt he could do better with a more American-sounding name, so he applied to the courts to change his name to Cabot.

The Cabot family immediately interposed, asking that the change not be made. However, the judge ruled that if there was no attempt at fraud—if Kabatinsky, for instance, did not state or imply that he was a member of the aristocratic Cabot family—then he could be called by any name he chose. Kabatinsky became Cabot and someone wrote:

Here's to good old Boston,
The home of the bean and the cod,
Where the Lowells have no one to speak to
For the Cabots speak Yiddish, by God.

•610

There's a story about Thurgood Marshall, the first black member of the Supreme Court, that I hope is true.

He was mowing the lawn at his posh residence in a Washington suburb when a car stopped in the street. The woman driving the car noted a black man mowing a lawn and called out, "How much do you charge for mowing a lawn, my good man?"

Marshall hesitated, and the woman said, "Well, what does the lady of the house pay you?"

And Marshall said, "She doesn't pay me anything, ma'am. She just lets me sleep with her every night."

•611

Golda Meir, the prime minister of Israel in the early seventies, had as her foreign minister Abba Eban, who spoke perfect English (better than mine, by far). At the time, President Nixon's secretary of state was Henry Kissinger, a German-born American who spoke English that was far worse than mine.

One time, Nixon said to Meir, "We both have Jewish foreign secretaries, Madame Meir."

"Yes," said Meir, "but mine speaks English."

•612

Two men were sitting in a carriage in the old days, watching a malefactor being brought out to hang.

One of the onlookers was moved to moralize. He said, "Ah, my dear Fortescue, if we all had our desserts, where would we be?"

"I suspect," said Fortescue, "that I would suddenly be alone in the carriage."

•613

A lawyer had died in poverty (if such a thing is possible) and his friends were taking up a collection to pay for his funeral.

One person, approached for a five-dollar donation, asked suspiciously what it was for. "Well," he was told, "Willard Johnson died and we're taking up a collection to help defray the costs of the funeral."

"Is that so? This Johnson was a lawyer, wasn't he?"

"Yes."

"In that case, here's fifty dollars. Go bury ten of them."

•614

When I was teaching, I loved giving the lectures, but I hated marking papers. I was always afraid I would have to fail someone. The head of my department, when I told him of my worries, was quite unsympathetic. He said that failing people was my job—if they deserved it.

Of course, if the student made it easy, that was different.

A student, despairing of a certain question, stared at his blank examination booklet and finally wrote, "God knows the answer to this question."

It came back with the notation: "God gets an A; you get an F."

•615

I gave my lectures in front of a large blackboard that ran the full width of the room, and an ample width it was. And since I was lecturing on biochemistry, there was plenty of occasion to write chemical formulas on it, so that I went from side to side writing my formulas and got into the habit of walking back and forth as I talked.

Finally the students sent a deputation to speak to me.

"Dr. Asimov," they said, "we wonder if you could refrain from walking up and down as you talk. We follow you and it makes us a little seasick."

I took umbrage. I said, "Come, come, who tells you to follow me as I walk? Just keep your eyes on your notebooks and listen to me and take notes."

There was a short pause and then one of the students, taking his life in his hands, said, "Well, I tried not looking, Dr. Asimov, and just listening to you, and I still got seasick."

Naturally, I burst out laughing and thereafter tried to mend my ways.

•616

I cut my own throat with a lecture at the medical school one day. It was customary for the students to applaud each professor in each course on the occasion of his last lecture. It was usually a very perfunctory bit of applause that no one really meant, for few professors lecture at a truly professional level.

Our department got a new head at the time when I was fighting the administration for survival, and it was important to me to try (if I could) to get the new head on my side. It turned out that he was a rather poor lecturer and, having made that very clear to the class, he then, on the occasion when it was my turn to lecture, came down to hear me.

It occurred to me that if I gave a lecture that was poorer than his, he would perhaps be willing to side with me, but I was damned if I was going to do that. Whatever it cost me, I was determined to show him what a professional lecturer could do, and I gave a talk on hemoglobin that was absolutely the best scientific lecture I ever gave—full of verve and humor.

The class reacted precisely as I expected them to—and more—for against all custom they applauded me for a speech that was not the last of the semester and applauded me lengthily and with enthusiasm.

And the head of the department became my enemy and did all he could to help the administration fire me.

Do I regret that? Not on your life. If I had to do it all over again, that's still exactly what I'd do.

•617

There's a story that was told me by someone who swore it was true. Two faculty members at the medical school were talking in the hall when the sound of distant laughter rang out.

"What's that?" said one of the professors.

"Probably Asimov lecturing," said the other. And it was.

•618

There's a story that someone visiting at Picasso's home remarked that there were no Picassos on the wall.

"Don't you like Picasso paintings?" asked the visitor roguishly.

"Of course I do," said Picasso. "I just can't afford them."

That reminds me that I do not have a high opinion of art critics. Right now, Van Gogh paintings are sold for fabulous sums. One went for $40 million. All right, perhaps the painting was worth $40 million (if you had the money), but in that case why wasn't Van Gogh able to sell any of his paintings while he was alive? Was there no art critic who would look at a Van Gogh and say to himself, "There's a painting worth millions. I think I'll offer him ten bucks for it"?

There wasn't.

•619

John Ruskin, a famous British art critic, was a savage critic, but he always insisted that his criticisms were not meant personally and that he would remain perfectly friendly with the artist after he had ripped him up.

The artists he ripped up did not feel like that at all. One of them wrote to him, "Next time I meet you, I intend to knock you down, but that criticism of your behavior will not be meant personally and should not interfere with our friendship."

•620

When I'm turned down by someone, I usually take it to heart, and if that someone changes his mind later on, I tend to be rather haughty about it. For that reason, I am very pleased with this story about George Bernard Shaw.

In Shaw's early days, one of his plays was turned down by a certain producer. After Shaw became famous, the producer wrote him offering to do the play. Shaw replied: "Better never than late."

All my life I have dreamed of being cross-examined by a hostile lawyer and of making a fool of him. It has never happened because I have stayed out of the courtroom. However, if I really had a chance to face a hostile lawyer, I would certainly try not to be a wiseguy because I've been told a million times that that is the surest way of earning the hostility of a judge and a jury. On the other hand, I have the horrible feeling that I will not be able to resist—that I'll say something witty before I have a chance to stop myself—and that my case will go right down the drain. So I think I had best continue to stay out of courtrooms. On the other hand, there is this story:

•621

A witness, small, uncertain, and nervous, was being cross-examined.

The lawyer thundered, "Have you ever been married?"

"Yes, sir," said the witness in a low voice. "Once."

"Whom did you marry?"

"Well, a woman."

The lawyer said angrily, "Of course you married a woman. Did you ever hear of anyone marrying a man?"

And the witness said meekly, "My sister did."

•622

The defendant was on the stand. He was accused of having punched the plaintiff and having inflicted grievous bodily injury on him. His defense was that the blow was more a love tap than anything else and did no harm at all to the plaintiff.

The lawyer had badgered the defendant unmercifully and judged that, by this time, the defendant was full of hatred, defiance, and anger. So the lawyer said, "All right, suppose you hit me and show me how you hit the plaintiff."

He was quite sure the defendant would not be able to control himself and he was right. The defendant drew back his fist and slammed the lawyer with a blow that sent him reeling backward the length of the courthouse and had him unconscious for a few minutes.

When the lawyer was brought back to his senses, the defendant turned to the judge and said, "Your honor, I hit the plaintiff exactly one-fiftieth that hard."

•623

Socrates was wandering about an Athenian bazaar, closely studying all the rich and flashy items that were for sale there.

A friend, well aware of Socrates' abstemious life-style, said to him in wonder, "Why is it, O Socrates, that you are so interested in this merchandise?"

"Because," said Socrates, "I am struck dumb with amazement to see what a wide variety of things there are that I don't need and can do without."

•624

The great French satirist Voltaire was once asked to give an encomium to someone who had recently died. Since Voltaire was a great enemy of that person, he refused.

The person asking him, however, said, "M. Voltaire, do not carry your enmity beyond the grave. Surely it will not hurt you to say something kind about a man who has died."

So Voltaire agreed, and his encomium went like this: "It is a great grief to me that Monsieur So-and-so has died. He was a loving husband and father, a devoted friend to all, a credit to the nation, and a man of great piety—that is, provided he is really dead."

•625

One of Victoria's grandsons, a little strapped for cash, wrote a letter to his formidable grandmother asking for help. Being Victoria, she refused and wrote a chilly answer recommending to him the habits of frugality, abstemiousness, thrift, and diligence. The young man promptly sold the letter for twenty-five pounds.

•626

The Congress of Vienna settled the map of Europe after the Napoleonic wars, and was attended by all the European nations, even the defeated French. The Duke of Wellington, conqueror of Napoleon at the Battle of Waterloo, was there as a delegate.

Some French officers, unwilling to greet the conqueror, turned their backs on him in disdain.

Wellington shrugged and said, "It does not matter. I have seen their backs before."

•627

When I was in the process of being fired at the medical school, the director of the institution said to me (among many other insulting things): "This school has no money to give to a science writer."

So I was fired and went on with my work and grew rich and famous, and the time eventually came (as I knew it would) when the school came to me and asked for a donation. With what pleasure I said, "This science writer has no money to give to the school."

But that was just to be a wiseguy. I gave them money.

•628

Joseph Wheeler had been a Confederate general in the Civil War. However, after the war was over, he made his peace with the United States and, in fact, was a major general in the Spanish-American War. Still, old habits die hard, and when the Spaniards were driven from their entrenchments at one point, old Wheeler waved his hat and yelled, "After the damned Yankees, men."

•629

James McNeill Whistler, the artist, noted with nervousness a well-known bore approaching him. The bore said, "Mr. Whistler, I passed your house last night—"

"That was very kind of you," said Whistler, who then bowed and left.

•630

Some Greek statements have great significance in English.

Thus, the Argonauts had returned from their successful and adventurous voyage in search of the Golden Fleece. One of them had had a good yield of grapes from plantings he had made before he had left. Wine had been formed and he had a cup of it which he was about to raise to his lips and drink. He called in a soothsayer who had predicted before he had left that he would not live to drink of the wine of the plantings he had made.

"How say you, soothsayer?" said the hero. "Do I not drink the wine you said I would not drink?"

The soothsayer said something (in Greek, of course) and just at that moment, word came that a wild boar was ravaging the estate. The Argonaut put down the cup without drinking, rushed out to hunt down the boar, and was killed in doing so.

What the soothsayer had said in Greek is the saying best known in English as, "There's many a slip 'twixt the cup and the lip."

•631

The Athenian orator Demosthenes had spent years inveighing against the plots of Philip of Macedon and warning Athens that if it remained quiescent, Philip would seize the rule of all of Greece.

Eventually, Athens and Thebes formed an alliance and decided to oppose Philip in war. They met at the Battle of Chaeronea, which ended as a great victory for Philip. In the heat of the battle, Demosthenes, who was fighting in the ranks, threw away his shield and ran away.

When others mocked him for having done so, he said something which in English is best known as, "He who fights and runs away, lives to fight another day."

•632

The reverse of the Demosthenes story is that of the Athenian soldier who was lame. There was laughter over the manner in which he hobbled, until he said firmly, "I am not here to run. I am here to fight."

•633

The Athenians, facing a battle and quite uncertain as to their ability to win it, consulted the oracle at Delphi. The oracle advised them to apply to the Spartans (the military leaders of Greece) for a single soldier.

It didn't seem to the Athenians that one soldier would make a difference, but you didn't argue with the oracle. They applied to Sparta.

Sparta was unwilling to do anything to help a competing city, but again, you didn't argue with the oracle, so they gave the Athenians one of their regimental musicians, who was lame and was no fighter.

Came the day of the battle and the Spartan musician played such stirring music that the Athenians, shouting with enthusiasm, charged the foe and won the battle.

•634

An irascible gentleman tasted his beverage in the restaurant and called over the nearest waiter with a howl.

"Take this slop away," he said furiously, "and bring me something else."

The waiter, who had not served him, said, "Yes, sir, but is it tea or coffee you want?"

"I don't care," said the diner. "If this is coffee, bring me tea. If it's tea, bring me coffee."

•635

Twice recently I have been disappointed at a restaurant beyond endurance. When I lived in Boston, Austin Olney of Houghton Mifflin and I would eat lunch now and then at Locke-Ober's, Boston's most Brahminesque restaurant. I invariably ordered fried tripe with mustard sauce, a delicacy I could never get at any other restaurant, and one that other people watched me eat with the utmost astonishment.

But then I moved back to New York in 1970 and it was many years before I had a chance to revisit Locke-Ober's. Eventually I came to Boston to give a talk and I realized my hotel was within walking distance of Locke-Ober's.

"Let's go," I said to my dear wife, Janet.

We went and they handed me the same old menu I remembered from decades before and there was the tripe. "Have anything you want, Janet," I told her, and to the waiter I said, "And bring me tripe and mustard sauce."

"Oh, we haven't made that for years," he said.

I said indignantly, "It's right here on the menu."

"You can't go by the menu," said the scoundrel, leaving me in a state of furious frustration.

Then, too, there is a restaurant in New York called the Pamplona, which has the best roast duck anyone has ever tasted. Once a year I would go there when I was attending a Gilbert & Sullivan show in the vicinity and I would order the duck and be in heaven.

But then the Pamplona moved and I was very nervous about

that. We walked in and I said to the headwaiter, "Do you have the same chef you had in the other place?"

"Yes, sir," he said. "Our staff is unchanged."

"Do you have the same menu?"

"Yes, sir."

So I sat down, spread out my napkin, and held out my hand for the menu. It was indeed the same as before. The only difference was there was no duck. Everything else was there.

Poor Janet had a hard job controlling my unhappiness. I was convinced I was the victim of a foul conspiracy.

•636

It's all a matter of what you're used to. A farmer slept all night peacefully, even though at 3:07 every morning a train passed and sent out the wild wail of a siren.

Then one night for some reason the train did not pass, and at 3:07 the farmer sat up, wild-eyed, in the dark silence and said, "What was that?"

•637

I find that not at all hard to believe. I can sleep peacefully amid the city traffic because I've been doing it all my life. In fact, when I was between the ages of eight and thirteen, I lived on a trolley line and all night long the trolley cars would go clanking up and down the tracks and clanging their bells, and it was like a lullaby to me.

Then, when I was in my late thirties, I moved to a Boston suburb and every morning in the summer, at dawn, as early as 4 A.M. sometimes, the damn birds would wake up and start chattering in the trees and sleep became impossible. How I longed for my old trolley cars.

•638

A gentleman, much the worse for drink, staggered along the sidewalk and came up against a tree. He felt the bark a bit, then moved away, but, in his staggering, struck the tree again. This happened four or five times, and the drunk lifted his voice and cried out, "I am lost—lost in an impenetrable forest."

•639

A gentleman on a train, who suffered from absentmindedness, carefully searched through his pockets while the conductor waited patiently. Finally he said, "This is terrible. I know I had a ticket, but for the life of me I can't remember what I did with it."

The conductor said, "All is not lost, sir. You can pay me directly. Then when you find the ticket you can return it and get your money back."

"But that's not the point," said the man in agony. "I don't remember where it is I'm going."

•640

A businessman was thinking once of marrying a young woman of astonishingly effective good looks. However, being canny and practical, he realized that looks in themselves were sometimes deceiving. He had never actually taken her to bed and he was not sure that she would pass muster.

So he sent his business manager to see her. The business manager said, "My employer, Mr. Harrison, is considering asking you to marry him. As a businessman, however, he does not wish to go into anything entirely blind. May we make an arrangement whereby he can try out a sample of your work in bed?"

The young lady said, "It is against my own business principles to give free samples. However, please tell Mr. Harrison that I can supply him with any number of satisfactory references."

•641

Talleyrand, the wily French diplomat, was told once that his co-worker, the completely unprincipled Fouche, had an utter contempt for human nature.

"Naturally," said Talleyrand. "He judges by the sample he knows best—himself."

•642

President Harry S Truman was an earthy gentleman who, in discussing agricultural practices, was constantly speaking of how one handled the manure, how one spread the manure here and there, how one had to have a supply of well-rotted manure, and so on.

One of the listeners, rendered uneasy by all this, whispered to Truman's wife, Bess, that she ought to persuade the president to say *fertilizer.*

And Bess whispered back, "You should only know how much trouble I have had getting him to say *manure.*"

•643

A man was shipwrecked and was cast up alone on a desolate shore. He lay there for a while, wondering how he would survive, wondering what he would eat, where he would find shelter, how long it would be before he was found. He was facing, in short, the possibility of being a new Robinson Crusoe.

He staggered off into the forest and had not been going long when he heard a distant voice crying out, "All right, you son of a bitch, if you've got an ace up your sleeve, I'll cut your heart out and make you eat it."

The shipwrecked victim fell to his knees and, raising his weeping eyes to heaven, said, "Oh, thank God, I'm in a Christian country."

•644

A notorious bore, at his club, said to a fellow member with an air of deep indignation, "I was told that a member of this club has said that he would pay me fifty dollars if I were to resign. What do you think of that?"

"Don't do it," said his friend warmly. "Hold out for a hundred. You'll get it."

•645

A bore who was bending the ear of the Greek philosopher Aristotle finally got a dim notion that he might be overdoing his chatter, so he said, "I hope I am not boring you."

To which Aristotle replied, "No, you're not, for I'm not listening."

•646

Talleyrand, having been victimized by a bore, was asked by a friend, "Did you find her a little tiresome?"

"Not at all," said Talleyrand. "I found her a great deal tiresome."

•647

A man went into a bakery and said, "I'd like to order a birthday cake. Chocolate, lots of frosting, and in the shape of an *A*."

"An *A*?"

"Yes, the birthday boy's name starts with *A*. And I've got to have it by Friday."

"You'll have it by Wednesday evening."

In came the man on Wednesday evening and was shown the cake. He said, "I didn't mean a capital *A*. I meant a small *a*. Very graceful. I can't use this one."

"But I can't sell so specialized a cake."

"Make another one. I'll pay for both. And I must have it by Friday."

"Very well, sir," said the baker.

In came the customer on Friday, and here was the cake, in a beautiful small *a*.

"Ah," said the customer. "Just what I want." And he paid.

The baker said, "Do you want me to send it to an appropriate address or will you take it with you?"

The customer shook his head. "I'm the birthday boy," he said, "and I'll eat it here."

•648

At the zoo, a curious woman said to one of those who tended the animals, "How do you tell a male hippopotamus from a female hippopotamus?"

The keeper said, "We don't really have to, ma'am. The hippopotamuses figure it out for themselves."

•649

A man was telling of his encounter with a bear. "It was a tremendous brute and in a very ugly mood, too. I ran like blazes and so did he, and he was gaining on me. Up ahead, though, there was a tree with a good stout branch stuck out horizontally about twenty feet above the ground. If I could get onto it, I might outwait the bear and be safe. I had no time to climb the tree, I had to jump the twenty feet. The hot breath of the bear nerved me on, so I jumped—and missed the branch."

"Good Lord," said a listener. "What did you do then?"

"Oh, it was all right. I caught that branch on the way down."

•650

Old Mr. Anderson was ninety-seven years old and was finally dying. The minister, sitting by his bedside, asked him to forgive all his enemies now that he was about to meet his maker.

Anderson thought a moment, then said in his weak, dying voice, "I suppose I might just as well forgive them. I outlived all those sons of bitches."

•651

When Frederick II of Prussia was dying, he also was asked to forgive his enemies. He agreed, but directed they not be told till he was safely dead.

•652

I have a very short list of enemies, mostly people who have given my books bad reviews.

Martin Harry Greenberg and I have produced over a hundred anthologies, mostly science fiction. At one time, Marty sent me a story for possible inclusion in an anthology, but it was written by someone whom, he knew, I had on my short list.

He said, "What do we do with this story?"

I read the story and wrote back, "Put it in. I'm not in the business of rejecting a good story just because it was written by a bastard."

And in it went.

•653

I was once part of a panel that discussed the space effort. I was the only one who was not actually part of some space organization, though I assure you I was reasonably familiar with the subject. Afterward, newspapermen climbed onto the platform to ask us questions. Everyone was asked questions except me. I wasn't considered important enough.

Finally one newspaperman said, "For identification purposes, gentlemen, which of you have Ph.D.s?"

I waited to let the other experts speak first and not one of them budged, so I finally raised my hand and said, "I have a Ph.D. I'm the science fiction writer." (It was a good moment.)

•654

A certain person was told that a man he thought was his friend had slandered him unmercifully. The man shrugged his shoulders and said, "It's probably my fault. I must have unwittingly done him a good turn."

•655

The usual expression one hears in this connection is: "No good deed goes unpunished."

•656

There are places in the world where there are hot springs and cold springs reasonably side by side. In such places, it is possible to wash clothes in the hot spring and then rinse them in the cold.

A tourist, watching the procedure, said to one of the natives, "How bountiful of nature to supply these springs."

"Not so bountiful," said the native. "You'll notice there's no soap."

I'm not sure if this is one of Aesop's fables, but I'm very fond of it:

•657

A dog was once chasing a rabbit and, after a long and arduous run, the rabbit managed to escape.

The dog was laughed at afterward for having failed to catch the rabbit, but he only said, "I was running for my dinner; the rabbit was running for his life."

•658

A businessman said to his son, "In the first place, my son, honesty is the best policy. However, if you study the law carefully, you'll be astonished at some of the things that are considered honest."

•659

President Lincoln once spoke mercifully of the Confederates to a visitor.

The visitor, full of patriotism, objected. He said harshly, "We must destroy the Confederates. They are our enemies."

And Lincoln said mildly, "And do we not destroy our enemies when we make them our friends?"

•660

A certain man found himself in a serious state of depression, and since he was in Vienna at the time, he thought he would see a young doctor named Sigmund Freud concerning whom people were saying good things.

He obtained an appointment and explained his problem. Freud listened patiently and said, "My friend, this is not something that can be alleviated in a short conversation or even in a few days. You will have to undergo a long course of treatment, if you find someone who is capable of giving it to you. Meanwhile, however, the great clown Grimaldi is in town. I have seen him and I assure you that no one can watch him without laughing uproariously. Why do you not go to see Grimaldi and get at least a few hours surcease?"

"That is impossible, Dr. Freud."

"How so?"

"Because I am the great clown Grimaldi."

I was in the hospital for a couple of months once and I was visited by any number of doctors, residents, interns, and so on. In every case, I would sit up in my bed of pain and tell them jokes and they always left laughing. Invariably, I told them the joke about the great clown Grimaldi. They laughed, but, as far as I could tell, not one of them ever saw the applicability of the joke to myself.

•661

Mr. Moskowitz went to the dentist, who gave him a thorough examination and said, "I am sorry, Mr. Moskowitz, but I'm afraid you need a great deal of work and it will cost you seven thousand dollars."

Moskowitz made a long face. "Who has seven thousand dollars, Doctor?"

"If you don't have the work done, you will lose your teeth before long and you will need dentures. That's expensive, too, and no fun."

"What do I do?" said Moskowitz in despair.

"Well, there's one thing. There's a young dentist in the vicinity who's been in practice only a couple of years. I believe he charges lower prices. Why don't you try him?"

Moskowitz did so. The young dentist examined him thoroughly and said, "I am sorry, Mr. Moskowitz, but I'm afraid you need a great deal of work and it will cost you thirty-five hundred."

Moskowitz said, "I'm willing, but I have a question. Another dentist wanted to charge seven thousand. If you charge only thirty-five hundred, can I be sure you will do a good job?"

The dentist said, "Two years ago, I did this same job for Mr. Cohen. I'll give you his phone number. Call him up and ask him how it went; then, if you wish, come back."

"Thank you," said Moskowitz, and that night he called Mr. Cohen and put the problem to him.

Mr. Cohen said, "Mr. Moskowitz, as it happens, I have a hobby. Every morning, rain or shine, cold or warm, I go down to Jones Beach at the crack of dawn. I take off all my clothes and go wading in the water. There is no one there to disturb me and I find it very refreshing."

Moskowitz said, "I am delighted that you have so interesting a hobby, Mr. Cohen, but it's the teeth I am asking about."

Cohen said coldly, "If you don't mind, Mr. Moskowitz, I must tell this my own way, or I shall simply shut up and say nothing."

Moskowitz sighed. "Go ahead. Talk."

"Just the other day," said Mr. Cohen, "after I had disported myself in the surf and was emerging on the shore in my customary state of nudity, I observed coming toward me a beautiful young woman who apparently had the same hobby I had. At least, she had removed all her clothes and was carrying them under her arm. She seemed not in the least disturbed about that or about my own state of nudity and, as she approached closer and closer, I'm afraid my body responded as you would expect and I displayed unmistakable signs of sexual excitement. This did not bother her either and she came close enough so that our bodies touched. And Mr. Moskowitz, for the first time in two years, my teeth stopped hurting."

Austin Olney once brought me into the boardroom at Houghton Mifflin, where various officials of the firm were meeting, and introduced me. Having done so, he whispered to me, "Tell them a funny story."

Now, there are no people who are more WASPish than those people at the good old Boston firm of Houghton Mifflin, but I felt they had been talking dull junk for hours and were in the mood for nonsense, so I told them the previous joke at full length and in my thickest Yiddish accent. The look of anxiety on Austin's face became extreme.

But they responded with loud laughter and the relief on Austin's face was pitiful to see.

•662

My periodontist, Joel Kleiman, is a wiseguy. At least he's always trying to get to me, perhaps because I usually enter his office with a loud, "Is the butcher in?"

At any rate, while working on my teeth and costing me the usual quart of blood, he said, "Actually, they're in pretty good shape," a compliment he rarely pays me.

I said, "I attribute that to excellent periodontal care."

"I'll buy that," said my periodontist fatuously.

"Of course," I added through my blood, "I sometimes come here."

•663

Once, Joel Kleiman sent me to my regular dentist, Neil Zane, to have some drillings done. Zane capped two teeth and sent me a bill for $1,000.

The next time I saw Joel, I said, "You sent me to Zane and it cost me a thousand dollars. I'll get you for that."

"You already have," said Joel. "You're back, aren't you?"

•664

More recently, Joel told me I would have to see Zane because a bridge in my mouth was coming loose and was probably riddled with decay in the neighboring teeth.

I said philosophically, "Well, that bridge has been in my mouth for forty years and has never given me trouble. I suppose I can't complain."

And Joel laughed fiendishly and said, "You'll complain all right when you get the bill." (You can bet I did.)

•665

At Sunday school, little Jimmie was asked, "Who was the first man?"

"George Washington," said Jimmie.

"No, Jimmie," said the teacher. "It was Adam."

"Oh, well," said Jimmie, "if you mean foreigners."

•666

The teacher, in the civics class she was teaching, stressed that America was a land of immigrants and expatiated on the many different strands of culture that wove together to make American society. She then asked each student to write an essay on foreigners.

Johnny's essay, in full, was, "All foreigners are bastards."

The teacher, stricken, gave another lecture, stressing French cooking, Italian music, British parliamentary government, Russian novels, African rhythms, and so on, doing her best to explain to the class that every culture had its excellences. She then asked for another essay on foreigners.

And Johnny's essay, in full, was, "All foreigners are cunning bastards."

•667

In the bad old days when anti-Semitism could be safely expressed by anyone, a man on a train looked with contempt at the person who had taken the seat next to him. He said, "You're a Jew, aren't you?"

His new companion nodded. "Yes, I am."

"I am proud to say," said the man, "that in the little village in Maine where I come from, there is not a single Jew."

"That," said the Jew, "is why it stays a little village."

•668

A young would-be writer once wrote the eminently successful writer Alexandre Dumas and offered to collaborate with him.

Dumas, offended, replied, "Would you yoke a horse with an ass?"

And the young man wrote back, "Don't call me a horse."

•669

Would-be writers sometimes have peculiar ideas about the value of their thoughts. Once I received a letter from a young man who said, "I have a brilliant idea for a science fiction story. If I give it to you, will you agree to write the story and give me half the proceeds?"

I wrote back, "I have a better notion. Let me give you a brilliant idea. You write the story and give me half the proceeds."

I never heard from him again, to my disappointment.

•670

Annoyed by all the people who offered me ideas and were willing to let me do all the work, I said to my editor, John W. Campbell, "Why do they all think that an idea is so important?"

And Campbell replied, "Has it ever occurred to you, Isaac, that the idea they offer to send you is the only idea they have ever had or are ever likely to have? Naturally, they overestimate its value."

•671

When I was quite young, a person sent me his manuscript and asked for a critique. Since I was quite young, I knew no better than to accede to his request. I went over it carefully and wrote him a long letter, pointing out his mistakes and infelicities.

I got no answer, and I realized that when a young man wants his manuscript critiqued, he means he wants it praised. I have never again critiqued a manuscript.

•672

Beatrice Lillie was approached by a woman at a party—a woman between whom and Bea there existed little camaraderie.

The woman said, "Don't tell me those pearls are real, Bea?"

"They are, indeed," said Bea.

"The only way to tell is to bite them," said the woman. "Do you mind if I test them that way?"

"It won't do any good," said Bea haughtily. "You can't test genuine pearls with false teeth."

•673

An Englishman said to an American, with hauteur, "How unpleasant it must be for you Americans to be governed by people you wouldn't dream of inviting to dinner."

And the American replied, "No more unpleasant than for you Englishmen to be governed by people who wouldn't dream of inviting you to dinner."

•674

A certain rich man was asked repeatedly for a contribution to a worthy cause, but he always refused to give a penny.

One day the solicitor said, "I have just seen a painting of you hanging in the hall of the Chamber of Commerce."

The rich man said sarcastically, "Did you ask it for a contribution?"

"Oh, no," said the solicitor. "I knew it would be of no use. It was a very good likeness."

•675

A certain rich man was a very slow person with a nickel and was therefore unpopular with all and sundry. Eventually he died and at the funeral the minister asked if any attendee would care to say a kind word in memory of the departed. There was a dead silence, but finally one man arose in his seat and said, "Well, there's this. Sometimes he was not quite as miserly as he was most times."

•676

A certain rich man had decided to build a nice convenient summer place in Maine. For the purpose, he hired one of New York's most successful architects to prepare the blueprints. He then took it to the local builder in Maine and said, "I want you to build a house precisely according to these blueprints."

The builder looked over the blueprints and laughed. "Sir," he said, "you don't want a house like this."

"Yes, I do," said the rich man.

"But the architect made a ludicrous mistake."

"No, he did not. I insist you follow his directions exactly."

The builder said, "Very well, but when the house is finished, you'll find it has two bathrooms."

•677

A farmer caught his hired hand out late at night, courting a young woman. Being a genial person, the farmer didn't object. All he said was, "Why do you need a lantern, Zeke? When I courted my wife, I didn't waste money on a lantern."

"Yes," said Zeke. "We can all see that."

•678

I was once invited to speak at Smith College, the famous women's college in Massachusetts. I hesitated, for the fee they offered was not high enough, but they said, "You may stay the night in one of the women's dormitories, Dr. Asimov."

Well, I couldn't resist that, so I agreed to go, trying to repress my glee.

They put me in a women's dormitory—in a special room, with a door that opened out to the street, and with no other door, either.

•679

I did eat breakfast at the women's dormitory, however, surrounded by hundreds upon hundreds of young women.

One of the young women at the table with me told me she was getting married in a short while and would move out of the dormitory.

I said, "Why? If I were in a women's dormitory, I would never leave it."

"Yes, you would," said the young woman positively. "You think that, because you're a man, you could stand it, but why don't you listen to all the soprano twittering? I'm leaving so I can hear a baritone voice now and then."

Whereupon I listened to what was going on about me and paled. She was perfectly right. I couldn't have endured a women's dormitory for long unless all the women agreed to maintain silence.

•680

I was scheduled to give a talk at Swarthmore College on March 21, 1958. I was to talk at the morning convocation at 8 A.M. and the president of Swarthmore told me, when I arrived the day before, that attendance at the convocation was compulsory and the students resented that.

"Some of the students," he said, "express their resentment by ostentatiously reading a newspaper during the speaker's lecture. If they do that, please realize it is not a personal reflection on you."

"That's all right," I said, with my usual self-assurance. "I defy any student to read a newspaper while I am speaking."

However, that night, Philadelphia and its suburbs had the worst slush storm in a hundred years. The slush stood three feet high at least, and of course it was very much like wading through freezing water. I realized that a whole group of resentful students would have to come out in the slush, wading through it in hip boots, if they had any, and they were going to resent the situation so badly that I would get nothing out of them but glowering hatred.

What was I to do? I rose to give my speech and said, "Students, we meet here today on the spring solstice. This is the day when the sun crosses the equatorial line and brings with it all the joys of spring, all the pleasant mild breezes, all the songs of birds, and the wafting perfume of flowers, all the new birth of life. This is the day on which the memory of winter dies, on which the evils of snow and slush are gone—"

By that time, the students were all laughing, and I grinned and gave my speech. No one read a newspaper.

•681

I was once slated to give a speech at Harvard University. I always refused to travel to New England in the winter months, but this speech was to be given on April 7, and that seemed safe.

318

The day before, I went to Fitchburg to give a talk, and on the morning of the seventh it was only necessary to drive the forty miles from Fitchburg to Cambridge. The forecast was for snow, however, so I woke my dear wife, Janet, good and early and said, "Let's beat the snow to Cambridge."

We managed to go twenty miles before the snow began, but once it did begin, it quickly turned out to be the worst spring blizzard New England had had in a hundred years. It took us four hours of very dangerous and difficult driving to make that last twenty miles into Cambridge.

When finally, worn out and exhausted, we were in our hotel, I called up Harvard to see if perhaps the talk had been canceled because of the weather.

I was told haughtily, "Harvard never cancels a function, whatever the weather."

So that evening, my good friend the astronomer Fred Whipple kindly drove me to the meeting place in a car that closely resembled a snow-removal vehicle.

As I walked into the auditorium, the students who were waiting for me, and who obviously thought I had driven that day all the way from New York to Boston, rose and gave me a prolonged standing ovation.

I didn't have the heart to tell them I had only had twenty miles of bad driving, not two hundred.

•682

There is the story of the elderly politician who was slated to give a Thanksgiving day talk.

He rose and said, "You have all been giving your attention to turkey stuffed with sage; now please listen to a sage stuffed with turkey."

•683

Here's the story of the worst speaking engagement I have ever endured. I was asked to speak at the Masonic Temple in Boston. When I entered I was overwhelmed by the rococoness of it all, and I couldn't help but feel it would be unusual to give a talk in such surroundings.

However, they led me down into the basement, where I was to speak in a cellar room with whitewashed walls and people sitting at trestles. This cooled my enthusiasm considerably.

Worse was to follow. We were to have a Chinese meal. Now, the Masonic Temple was located at the edge of Boston's Chinatown, one of the best (from the standpoint of dining) in the nation. You would think that a meal would have been ordered from there. However, those who were running the show, apparently out of a desire to save money, ordered their meal from some dive in the suburban city of Malden.

You can guess what would happen. Traffic was heavy and the meal was delayed.

After I had been sitting there rather impatiently (I like to eat heartily before I speak), the man who was to introduce me came over and asked if I would give my talk now.

"Of course not," I said with some heat. "I haven't eaten yet, and neither has anyone else. If I give my talk to a hungry audience, you can bet I will not be well received. Besides that, the food will arrive in the middle of my talk and if anyone had been paying attention earlier, they would certainly stop at that point."

Having listened to me say that, the introducer stood up and introduced me and I had no alternative but to speak. The audience was indeed cold, and I was fuming, and midway in my talk the food arrived, so I quickly put a period to what I was saying and sat down, still fuming.

And the Chinese meal was easily the worst I had ever tried to eat. One of the dishes was so rancid that it was absolutely inedible.

•684

A young girl was once closely inspecting a British nobleman who was visiting her father.

The nobleman, rendered uneasy by the solemn stare, said, "Yes, little girl, what is it?"

She said, "I never saw an English lord before."

The nobleman smiled. "And are you satisfied now?"

"Not really," said the girl. "I'm rather disappointed."

•685

A woman noted for her nonstop habit of conversation was once referred to by someone as being "outspoken."

"Indeed?" said Dorothy Parker. "By whom?"

•686

I know two women, each of whom can talk rapidly and interminably. I have often wanted to conduct the experiment of locking them in a room together and waiting to see which one survives the experience.

•687

Each of these two women knows she speaks a great deal. I said to one of them, "How can you possibly ever have sex, if you never stop talking?"

She said, "Oh, I stop for orgasms."

And I said, "Briefly, I bet."

•688

At the Gilbert & Sullivan Society, there was once a tall and very shapely woman. She used to sing contralto in the choruses and one day I heard her say, "I'm having trouble with contralto. I may have to slide down a notch and sing tenor."

At which I said, woebegone, "Don't do that. I've always thought of you as quintessentially feminine."

And she answered, "But most tenors are."

•689

Robert Benchley was at a party where they were playing a game called "epitaphs." Each person was supposed to write an epitaph he would like to see placed on his gravestone. One woman, noted for her promiscuity, couldn't think of one. Benchley, smiling gently, said, "Let me help you." And on her slip of paper he wrote, "At last, I sleep alone."

•690

When I used to come into New York once a month and stay at my mother-in-law's place, I was driven mad by the fact that I routinely woke at 5 A.M. and no one else woke before 9 and there was nothing I could do, for I could not disturb the sleepers. In fact, my brother-in-law, John, frequently slept till noon.

I mentioned this to my mother-in-law and said, "Isn't there some way John can wake up earlier?"

But my mother-in-law, who adored her son to the point of infantilization, said huffily, "My Sonny must have his twelve hours of sleep every night."

•691

Mark Twain felt little pride of ancestry. He used to say, "My grandfather was cut down in the prime of life, and my grandmother always used to say that if he had been cut down fifteen minutes sooner, he might have been resuscitated."

•692

I know nothing about my own ancestry. In listening to other Jews, however, I find that each of them was descended from very learned men, remarkable for their wisdom for miles around. Whenever I hear that, I marvel at the total failure of heredity.

•693

It was raining heavily and a belated traveler found himself walking at night along a country road. He noticed a farmhouse in the distance and sloshed toward it. He banged at the door for quite a while before a hard-bitten farmer stuck his head out of an upstairs window and shouted, "What do you want?"

"I want to spend the night here," shouted the traveler.

"Go right ahead, if you can find a dry spot in the mud."

•694

I was once asked on a television talk show what I would do if someone gave me a billion dollars.

I didn't even have to think. I said, "I'd march over to the nearest office of the Internal Revenue Service with it. I would place it on the counter and I would say, 'I have a billion dollars. It is yours. I give it to you freely. Now never let me, or my children, hear from you again for the rest of our lives.'"

•695

A teacher of the freshman class in composition at a certain New England college once sent me a paper written by one of her students and asked me if I recognized it.

I certainly did. It was an outright copy of my story "Galley Slave," a long and complex robot story. It had taken me twenty years to hone my writing ability to the point where I could write that story, and some stupid college freshman thought he could get away with pretending he had written it himself.

Of course, I wrote to the teacher and told him it was a case of plagiarism, by a fool who didn't even have the ingenuity to change the names of the characters.

•696

Some people live in a world populated only by themselves.

For the last fourteen years I have had a quite successful magazine, *Isaac Asimov's Science Fiction Magazine,* and we get letters—some of them quite unreasonable.

One young man, in a white-hot fury over the fact that we insisted that each submission be accompanied by a stamped self-addressed envelope in case of rejection, wrote, "Surely, I'm worth a lousy twenty-five-cent stamp if you don't like my story."

I wrote to him and said, "We are forced to reject about a thousand stories every month. Each one of those thousand people is individually worth a lousy twenty-five-cent stamp. All of them put together, however, are not worth two hundred and fifty dollars in stamps. Don't you think it's easier for each one of them to supply us with twenty-five cents rather than for us to pay two hundred and fifty dollars?"

We never got an answer.

Many people object to form rejections. They want a careful analysis of what is wrong with the story. I have to answer and say:

1) There's no way we can carefully analyze what is wrong with each of a thousand stories every month.

2) The proper rejection in almost every case is, "This story stinks to high heaven," but we feel a form rejection is more kindly.

We don't get answers to these letters either.

•697

There is the case of the contributor who wrote an angry letter to an editor in which he said, "When I sent you a story, I pasted pages 17 and 18 together. It was returned with the pages still pasted. That is evidence that you didn't read the whole story, yet you rejected it. How do you explain that?"

The answer was, "Dear Sir: When I eat an egg, I don't have to eat all of it to know it's bad."

•698

I have never been accused of plagiarism myself, for which I am heartily glad, for no author can be sure of escaping such an accusation from the numerous crackpots who inhabit our world.

The nearest I came to it was in 1989, when a story of mine, *The Ugly Little Boy,* was published by Tor Books.

A young woman wrote me a white-hot letter pointing out that in 1988 she had written a story that was rejected by publishers, and it was quite apparent to her that she was rejected only because she was an unknown, and that the publishers had then given me the plot so that I could write the story. She had not read my story, but, from the publisher's blurb, she knew it concerned a little boy and so did hers (and so did Charles Dickens's *Oliver Twist,* but she didn't mention that.) How did I explain that? she demanded.

I wrote back and told her that if she had actually looked at the story instead of just reading a publisher's blurb, she would have noticed that it was a reprint and that it had originally been published in 1958, not only long before she had written her story, but, in all probability, before she was born.

I addressed her, very politely, as "Dear Crazy Lady." Perhaps that was why she never answered. But she never sued, either.

•699

I've gone on sea cruises in my time and every single time there is a lifeboat drill. It's an important exercise, but it's dull, and sometimes I try to get a little excitement into it.

At one time, as we lined up, the ship's officers cried out, "All right, you know the rules. Women and children in front. They get into the lifeboats first."

Whereupon I called out, "Women, children, and geniuses!"

I got a titter in response, but a young man at my right—one who was clearly of no attainments whatever—cried out, "*Young* geniuses," and the laughter swelled at my expense.

•700

On another occasion, when the cry went out, "Women and children in front," I called out, "Is there any women's-libber in the crowd who would like to step back with the men?"

I felt that there would be a few brave souls who would do so, since there was a vanishingly small chance that the ship would ever be likely to sink.

However, all I got was a chorus of boos. Apparently women's lib sentiment vanished like snow in the glance of the Lord when it was necessary to accept masculine risks as well as masculine prerogatives.

•701

A preacher was well into the second hour of an extraordinarily dull sermon when a young man, unable to bear a moment more of it, rose to leave.

The preacher shouted at him, "Young man, would you rather stay here and listen to the word of God, or would you rather leave and go to hell?"

The young man turned around and said, "That's not much of a choice, is it?"

I had a garage mechanic once who had a habit of telling me jokes when I came in to have my car looked to. They were generally poor jokes, but I was always careful to laugh heartily, for he had my car by the throat. One time, however, he told me the following story.

•702

"Doc [which is what he called me], a deaf and dumb guy went into a hardware store to ask for some nails. He put two fingers together on the counter and made hammering motions with the other hand. The clerk brought him a hammer. He shook his head and pointed to the two fingers he was hammering. The clerk brought him nails. He picked out the sizes he wanted, paid for them and left. Well, Doc, the next guy who came in was a blind man. He wanted scissors. How do you suppose he asked for them?"

Indulgently, I lifted my right hand and made scissoring motions with the first two fingers. Whereupon my garage mechanic laughed raucously and said, "Why, you dumb jerk, he used his voice and said, 'May I buy a pair of scissors?'"

In a way, that is the most unusual joke I know. For one thing, I have repeated it innumerable times in the course of lectures to large audiences. When I get to the part where I make scissoring motions with my fingers, the audience is always perfectly quiet. Not a whisper. Not a snicker. Then, when I come out with the punch line, the whole place rocks with laughter. It has never, never failed. And I always end by saying, when the laughter dies down, "Caught you all, didn't I?"

For another thing, I incorporated the joke into a small essay I wrote which began, "What is intelligence, anyway?"

For some reason, people have asked to reprint that essay dozens of times and each time I charge them fifty bucks for it. I sometimes wonder what my old garage mechanic would say if he knew that that joke he told me has netted me very nearly a thousand dollars so far.

• 703

The teacher asked the student, "Why did the Puritans come to America?"

The answer was, "So they could worship God in their own way, and force everyone else to do it their way also."

• 704

Personally, I think it's the great god Hypocrisy that rules the human race.

I heard a speech recently in which the speaker explained that when the United States nuclear-bombed Hiroshima and Nagasaki, those acts ended the war and saved countless lives, which made it quite obvious that using the nuclear bomb was right.

I raised my hand and said, "Suppose the Japanese had discovered the nuclear bomb first and had bombed New York and Washington. Would not that have ended the war and saved countless lives? And would that be right?"

The speaker hesitated a moment, then said, "It depends on which side you're on."

"Exactly," I said. "So don't be so sure of what is right and what is wrong."

• 705

The artist James McNeill Whistler had a dog, so the story goes, to which he was much attached. When the dog developed a sore throat, no ordinary vet would do, and Whistler called in London's greatest throat specialist.

The specialist, not expecting to be asked to treat a dog, hesitated, then did what he could and charged a large fee.

The next day, the specialist sent for Whistler in a great hurry. Whistler, thinking there was news of the dog, rushed over in mad haste. The specialist said calmly, "Mr. Whistler, I have called you in to ask you to paint my door."

•706

A doctor was called by a man who said, "Doctor, you must come quickly. My wife is clearly suffering from appendicitis."

The doctor said, "Impossible. I took out your wife's appendix three years ago, and I never heard of any woman growing a second appendix."

"Yes," said the man, "but have you ever heard of a man marrying a second wife?"

•707

A movie actress found herself forced to take a New York subway. She had to be directed to the proper platform. She had to have it explained to her that you do not buy a ticket but only a token. She had to be shown the use of a turnstile, and finally she got onto a subway train.

Heaving a sigh, she said in a loud voice, "This is the first time I've ever been on one of these subways."

Whereupon a steady rider looked at her with disfavor and said haughtily, "We ain't never missed you, lady."

•708

When Mark Twain was erroneously reported to have died, he announced that "the report of my death is greatly exaggerated." He then went on to protest to a particular newspaper for carrying the news of his death. The editor scratched his head and said, "How about placing your name in the births column tomorrow and giving you a fresh start?"

•709

A gentleman of no great religious feeling was dying, and it seemed to the minister that it was not too late to rouse some spark of spirituality within him.

He said, "Mr. Johnson, do you know who it was who died to save you?"

And Johnson replied in a weak voice, "Is this a time to ask me riddles?"

•710

The greatest of all escape artists was Harry Houdini. Nothing would hold him. He escaped from chained and locked chests, from straight-jackets in the air and under water, and so on. But as it does to all men, death came to Harry Houdini, and the pallbearers lifted his coffin onto their shoulders.

And one of them stage-whispered to another, "What if he managed to get out?"

•711

A hunter announced that he had been tracking a grizzly bear.

"Did you get it?" asked a friend.

"I'm afraid not."

"Lost the track?"

"I never lose a track. The trouble was the track was becoming too fresh, so I said, the hell with it."

•712

Office seekers are the bane of any elected official. Presidents have been assassinated by disappointed office seekers, and others must have wished they would be, so they could be put out of their misery.

Nor does an office seeker resist playing the ghoul. Someone on the governor's staff had died and before the day was out an office seeker asked the governor if he might not replace the dead man.

"Certainly," said the governor, "if it's all right with the undertaker."

•713

Napoleon was quite aware that he came of a Corsican provincial family. When his brothers, sisters, and assorted relatives scrambled for high positions, Napoleon, with a strong sense of family, tried to satisfy them all. He couldn't resist saying, however, "They all want to share in the patrimony of the king, our father."

•714

Charles II, a jovial, witty fellow, was quite popular with the people. He had no legitimate children, however, so that the heir presumptive was his brother James, a narrow-minded and unlikable convert to Catholicism.

Charles II had a habit of walking about with no concern for security and James protested that doing so was dangerous.

"Nonsense," said Charles. "No one is going to assassinate me in order to make you king."

•715

There is a story that Mussolini was once stranded in a small town in Italy when his car broke down. To pass the time, he visited a local movie house. Came the newsreel, and, of course, his own face flashed on the screen.

Everyone in the movie house stood up, but Mussolini, feeling tired and feeling no compulsion to stand in his own honor, remained seated. Whereupon the man next to him whispered, "I feel exactly as you do, but take my advice and stand up. It's safer."

•716

Xerxes, the Persian monarch, was about to invade Greece with overwhelming forces, chiefly to visit punishment on Athens, which had defeated the army of his father, Darius. Xerxes attempted to isolate Athens by winning over all the other Greek cities. One he could not win over was Sparta.

To the Persian emissaries, Sparta said, "You know not what you ask. Since Persians have never known anything but slavery, you think it a small thing to ask us to submit. But we have known freedom, and we will never cease to fight for it."

•717

A businessman, renowned for his crooked dealings, was denounced for them by an important pillar of the community.

"I'm sorry," said the businessman tartly, "but I must live."

"Why?" came the instant retort.

•718

A certain tradesman would often say that he never asked any gentleman to pay his account.

Said a friend, "But that is terrible. There must be many a gentleman who casually forgets he owes you money."

"True," said the tradesman, "but after a certain length of time, I conclude he is no gentleman, and I send the bailiffs after him."

•719

It is very traditional in the world of jokedom to suppose that in the backwoods there are people who manufacture liquor in homemade stills and who don't bother paying taxes on it. Naturally, tax collectors ("revenooers") are supposedly forever seeking out the stills, either to make the distillers pay or to destroy the equipment and, again traditionally, they are met with gunfire.

A revenue agent asked a young man in the backwoods where his father was.

"Up at the still," came the answer.

"And your mother?"

"Also up at the still."

"I'll give you a dollar if you show me the way there."

"Sure. Let me have the dollar, please."

"I'll pay you when I come back."

"Mister," said the boy, "you're not coming back."

•720

A tradesman asked a customer to pay his long-overdue bill. The customer replied negligently that it would not be convenient for him to do so at the moment.

"If you don't pay me," said the tradesman, "I will tell all your other creditors that you did."

•721

A rich miser was asked by a rabbi for a donation to the local synagogue and was refused.

The rabbi sighed and said, "Come to the window, Mr. Abrahams. Look out and tell me what you see."

The miser looked and said, "People. What else?"

"Now come to this mirror, and look in, and tell me what you see."

"Myself. What else?"

"There you are. The window is glass, the mirror is glass, but the mirror has a thin layer of silver on it. As soon as a little silver is added, you no longer see other people, you only see yourself."

The miser gave a donation.

•722

A man received a notice of a tax violation. It said on it SECOND NOTICE and detailed various forms of punishment to which he was liable.

The man rushed to the local tax office and paid up, saying indignantly, "I never got a first notice."

"We know," said the man behind the desk. "Sending out a second notice gets more rapid results."

•723

I often get communications from the Internal Revenue Service, which I pay no attention to. I simply send them to my accountant and he takes care of it. If there's something I must do, he sends me something, all filled out properly. I merely sign it, write a check (if necessary), and send it off.

What bothers me is that when I do get a communication from the tax people, I can never understand it. I try to make sense out of it and fail. What language they use I don't know, but it isn't English.

One night I couldn't sleep because I constructed a fantasy in which I was being cross-examined by a hostile lawyer.

"Why did you not pay up at once, Dr. Asimov?"

"Because I did not understand the communications, sir, so I sent it to my accountant."

"Did your accountant understand it?"

"He said he did."

"Now, isn't it true that you are more educated than your accountant?"

"I believe I am, sir."

"And more intelligent?

"Possibly, sir."

"Then how is it he could understand the communication and you could not?"

"Well," I said, "he tells me he has the help of a fat book called *Webster's Unabridged Dictionary of Confusion and Incoherence* and that helps him."

In my fantasy, everyone breaks into laughter, including the judge, and the lawyer stands there, an utter fool. In real life, however, I would probably be thrown in jail if I tried to pull a trick like that.

•724

There is a story that, after World War I, when the Germans asked for armistice terms, the French general Ferdinand Foch picked up a piece of paper and read the terms.

The Germans were horrified. They said, "These are terms which no civilized nation would impose on another."

"Of course not," said Foch. "What I am reading to you are the surrender terms forced on the French city of Lille when it surrendered to the Germans."

As a matter of fact, although the Germans wept bitterly over the terms of the Treaty of Versailles and never stopped being sorry for themselves, the Treaty of Brest-Litovsk, which the Germans imposed on the Russians in the spring of 1918, was much harsher, but that didn't seem to bother the Germans.

•725

My brother, Stan, once lost his temper with me (very briefly) and said, "Isaac, you are hard-working, industrious, full of integrity, efficient, and entirely self-absorbed. You have all the unlovable virtues."

•726

General Grant is supposed to have spoken with contempt about a fellow officer. Another officer demurred, pointing out that the officer in question had fought in ten campaigns.

Grant said, "So has that mule yonder, but he's still a jackass."

•727

What a general usually wants is reinforcement. What a general usually doesn't want is interference by politicians. Stonewall Jackson is supposed to have sent the following telegram to the War Office in Richmond: "Send me more men and fewer questions."

•728

General William Tecumseh Sherman had a terrible temper and on one occasion he got into a bitter argument with another officer. The second officer went to see Lincoln in order to complain. Sherman, he said, had threatened to have him shot.

Lincoln thought about it for a moment and said, "The best thing you can do, Colonel, is stay away from the general. If he is threatening to shoot you, he'll probably end up doing it."

•729

A sentry was bitten by a valuable dog and promptly shot him. The owner of the dog sued the sentry.

The cross-examining lawyer said, "Why didn't you hit the dog with the butt end of your rifle?"

The sentry said, "Why didn't the dog bite me with his tail?" and won the case.

•730

A woman appeared before a judge in a traffic violation case, and it turned out she was a schoolteacher.

The judge smiled broadly. "Madam," he said, "I have been sitting here for years waiting for a schoolteacher to stand before me. Now, you sit down at that table and write, 'I must not pass through a red light' five hundred times."

•731

A judge said to the defendant before him, "Have you ever been sentenced to a stay in prison?"

"No," said the defendant, tears running down his cheeks. "Never!"

"Well, don't cry," said the judge. "You will be so sentenced now."

•732

The trial suffered from a hung jury and day after day passed without a settlement.

"Well," said the court officer with resignation, "is it twelve dinners again tonight?"

Said the foreman, "I think you had better bring eleven dinners and a bale of hay."

•733

I received a review of a book of mine which was not only unfavorable but absolutely wrong. I fumed and went to the Dutch Treat Club, clearly furious. A friend said to me, "What's wrong, Isaac?"

I said, "I just received a review of a book of mine which just plain gravels me."

My friend said, "Here! I have a card. I want you to have it. Every time you get a bad review, just pull it out and read it."

I have kept that card ever since and here is what it says:

"Your frank criticism has been greatly appreciated. Fuck you very much."

•734

There is a famous story about the Texas Rangers.

A riot was threatening in town and the mayor called on the rangers for help. The next day, a single ranger came ambling into town.

The mayor said, "Did your people send only one ranger?"

"Yes," said the ranger. "You're only threatened with one riot, aren't you?"

•735

A man walked into a bank and said to the bank manager, "I would like to speak to Mr. Reginald Jones, who, I understand, is a tried and trusted employee of yours."

The banker said, "He was certainly trusted. And he will be tried, as soon as we can catch him."

•736

I was hospitalized a few years back and was forced to cancel several speeches I was scheduled to make. I strongly recommended that my good friend the science fiction writer Ben Bova give them in my place. I had heard him speak and he was good.

Ben was kind enough to oblige and did an excellent job. You can imagine, though, my feelings when I got a phone call from the man who was in charge of the first talk and who told me that Ben insisted the check for it be sent to me.

"What?" I said. "No such thing. You send me such a check and I will tear it up at once. It has to go to him."

Ben came to see me some time later and I said to him angrily, "How dare you activate my Jewish guilt, Ben, when I'm lying here on a bed of pain, by asking them to send me the check?"

"What about my Italian guilt?" asked Ben.

"What Italian guilt?"

"Italian guilt arises when you profit by the misfortunes of another."

I said, "What are you talking about, Ben? The Mafia—"

And Ben said, "If you *cause* the misfortune, of course, things are different."

•737

While in the hospital, my dear wife, Janet, brought me the manuscript of my autobiography. It was a long one and was eventually published in two volumes running to 1,500 pages.

Ben Bova came to visit and found me poring over the stack of manuscript. "What's that?" he asked.

"My autobiography," I said.

"A-ha," he said. "Now you'll have a chance to make yourself out to be a hero."

"On the contrary," I said austerely, "I'm putting in every dumb thing I ever did."

And he said, "No wonder, then, there are so many pages."

•738

Being a celebrity has its conveniences now and then.

I was waiting at the corner for a taxi on a blustery day and there were none. I was in a reasonable hurry, and I was cold and uncomfortable and I must have looked woebegone.

A taxi skidded to a halt in front of me. The front window cranked down and the driver called out, "I'd love to pick you up, Dr. Asimov, because I'm a fan of yours, but I already have a fare."

"I understand," I said. "Thank you anyway." And I motioned him on.

But now the back window cranked down and the fare shouted, "I'm a fan of yours, too, Dr. Asimov. Get in."

So I got in and was driven to my destination—but I insisted on paying the fare. Noblesse oblige.

•739

I was meeting someone inside a certain building facing Central Park. Night had fallen, and the streets were absolutely empty. The only living things I could see were three hulking teenagers on the steps of the building. I was going to have to pass them in order to get inside and it seemed to me I was prime bait for a mugging.

I quailed and my steps faltered, but I had this appointment and I didn't like to play the role of coward, so I gathered my courage in both hands and began to walk up the stairs.

One of the hulking teenagers who had kept his eye on me in the dim light that emanated from the building said, "Aren't you Isaac Asimov?"

I stopped short. "Yes, I am."

"I like your books," he said.

So I shook hands all around. They weren't the least bit threatening. Fine, upstanding youths, I decided.

•740

At a small science fiction convention I was once accosted by a young writer and the following conversation took place.

WRITER: Dr. Asimov, I've been trying to write for a number of years and I've managed to sell a couple of items.

ASIMOV: Congratulations. I'm happy to hear it. Keep it up.

WRITER: I've used you as my model. I've read a lot about you and I thought I would try to write the way you do. Easily. Prolifically. All that sort of stuff.

ASIMOV (cautiously): And have you managed?

WRITER (frowning): No, I haven't. I have to keep thinking about what I write, and more thinking. And rewriting. And starting over.

And getting stuck for periods of time.

ASIMOV (uneasily): I'm sorry.

WRITER (perceptibly angrier): I couldn't figure out what was wrong with me. So I talked to other writers, and I found they all have the same trouble. Just like me. There's nothing wrong with me.

ASIMOV (relieved): I'm sure there isn't.

WRITER (pointing his finger in a controlled fury): But I'll tell you what, Dr. Asimov. There is something seriously wrong with *you*.

And he stalked off.

•741

I never voluntarily talk about the number of my books. However, I am sometimes nudged into it against my will.

I was at a luncheon once and someone made reference to the fact that I was a writer. The person on my left, who had never heard of me, obviously, asked who my publisher was.

I said, "Well, I have several, but Doubleday is my most important one. They have done three-eighths of my books."

Whereupon he turned up his nose and said in a very nasty way, "I suppose you're trying to make yourself sound better than you are. I guess that you've written eight books and Doubleday has published three."

"Not exactly," I said, "you guess wrong. I have written, so far, two hundred books and Doubleday has published seventy-five."

And everyone grinned, including me. It was a pleasure.

•742

My dear wife, Janet, and I have a small ritual that consists of tracking each other. We rarely separate, but when we do, we have to say where we're going and when we'll be back and we have to call each other once we get there so we'll know we're safe, and call again if we're unexpectedly delayed, and so on.

So one evening, Janet went off to her psychiatric institute with the understanding that she would be home between 9 and 9:15 P.M.

The trouble was that I got busily involved at my word processor and when I looked at my watch it was 10 P.M. and, unfortunately, it was Monday and, instead of having my mind click, "Where's Janet?" it clicked, "Whoops, time for the *Newhart* show." So I turned it on and at 10:05 Janet came home, having been unavoidably detained.

She was convinced I would be half dead with worry and there I was, watching television, and I waved at her, unconcerned.

She said rather sharply, "Weren't you worried?"

I knew better than to admit I had lost track of the time. I said indignantly, "Of course I was worried. Fearfully worried."

"And what were you going to do about it?" she wanted to know.

"I was going to run down to the institute and find you and take you home."

She said, "When were you going to do that?"

And I said, pointing to the TV, "Just as soon as *Newhart* was finished."

Fortunately, Janet has a sense of humor and laughed.

•743

My dear wife, Janet, is incredibly solicitous over my well-being. She sees to it that I bundle up, that I wear rubber boots when it rains, that I have my umbrella, and so on. I hate it—as all husbands do.

In fact, I complain a great deal about the matter, and I can be very eloquent about it, too, but do I get sympathy? I do not.

To all my complaints, my friends and acquaintances look at me coldly and say, "But that's because she *loves* you."

You have no idea how irritating that is.

One time I was in a limousine, being ferried to a talk. The driver was an Oriental who drove with perfect accuracy and who was clearly intelligent, but who had only a sketchy command of English. Being aware of this, he took the trouble to practice his English on me and I answered carefully and with good enunciation so that he might learn.

At one point, he looked at the smiling sunshine, felt the mild breeze, enjoyed the surrounding greenery, and said, "It—is—vair—byoot'ful—day."

At this my sense of grievance rose high and I said, "Yes, it is. So why did my wife make me take an umbrella?" And I raised the offending instrument and waved it.

Whereupon the driver, choosing his words carefully, said, "But—your—wife—she *lahv* you."

I sat back defeated. It was a cross-cultural conspiracy.

Janet and I met on May 1, 1959, and fell in love at once. Unfortunately, there was nothing I could do about it. I was married. It was an unhappy marriage, but I was married. And I had two small children.

So we could only correspond and yearn for each other, until my marriage broke up. Since then, we have lived together, gotten married, and the point is that for thirty-two years now we have stayed deeply in love.

I'm afraid that my life has just about run its course and I don't really expect to live much longer. However, our love remains and I have no complaints.

In my life, I have had Janet and I have had my daughter, Robyn, and my son, David; I have had a large number of good friends; I have had my writing and the fame and fortune it has brought me; and no matter what happens to me now, it's been a good life, and I am satisfied with it.

So please don't worry about me, or feel bad. Instead I only hope that this book has brought you a few laughs.

INDEX